S0-BUD-431

HARVARD
BUSINESS SCHOOL
Executive Education

Lynn S. Paine

Capitalism at Risk

Capitalism at Risk

How Business Can Lead

Joseph L. Bower
Herman B. Leonard
Lynn S. Paine

Harvard Business Review Press

Boston, Massachusetts

HBR Press Quantity Sales Discounts

Harvard Business Review Press titles are available at significant quantity discounts when purchased in bulk for client gifts, sales promotions, and premiums. Special editions, including books with corporate logos, customized covers, and letters from the company or CEO printed in the front matter, as well as excerpts of existing books, can also be created in large quantities for special needs.

For details and discount information for both print and
ebook formats, contact booksales@harvardbusiness.org,
tel. 800-988-0886, or www.hbr.org/bulksales.

Copyright 2020 Joseph L. Bower, Herman B. Leonard, Lynn S. Paine

All rights reserved

Printed in the United States of America

10 9 8 7 6 5 4 3 2 1

No part of this publication may be reproduced, stored in or introduced into a retrieval system, or transmitted, in any form, or by any means (electronic, mechanical, photocopying, recording, or otherwise), without the prior permission of the publisher. Requests for permission should be directed to permissions@harvardbusiness.org, or mailed to Permissions, Harvard Business School Publishing, 60 Harvard Way, Boston, Massachusetts 02163.

The web addresses referenced in this book were live and correct at the time of the book's publication but may be subject to change.

Library of Congress Cataloging-in-Publication Data

Names: Bower, Joseph L., author. | Leonard, Herman B., author. | Paine,
    Lynn Sharp, author.
Title: Capitalism at risk : how business can lead / Joseph L. Bower, Herman
    B. Leonard, Lynn S. Paine.
Description: Boston, MA : Harvard Business Review Press, [2020] | Includes index.
Identifiers: LCCN 2020004738 | ISBN 9781633698253 (hardcover) |
ISBN 9781633698260 (ebook)
Subjects: LCSH: Capitalism. | Business planning. | Globalization. | Risk. |
    Financial institutions—Effect of technological innovations on.
Classification: LCC HB501 .B73768 2020 | DDC 330.12/2—dc23
LC record available at https://lccn.loc.gov/2020004738

ISBN: 978-1-63369-825-3

eISBN: 978-1-63369-826-0

The paper used in this publication meets the requirements of the American National Standard for Permanence of Paper for Publications and Documents in Libraries and Archives Z39.48-1992.

Contents

Preface to the Expanded Edition

When we wrote the first edition of this book over ten years ago, we were interested in fueling a public conversation about how business could address what we and others then saw as potential threats to market capitalism. We hoped that calling attention to these problems would spur leaders in business and government in the United States and abroad to take action. Since that time, the problems we wrote about have worsened, new ones have emerged, and efforts to address them have fallen far short of what's needed. Today, the very foundations of the global market system are under threat by an array of demographic, environmental, political, economic, social, and technological forces around the world.

In this new, expanded edition, we review these developments and share insights from the work we have done over the past decade to better understand what companies and business leaders can do to address these problems and put the market system on a more sustainable trajectory. We write with the hope that readers will share our sense of urgency and that more entrepreneurs and other business leaders will step up to the challenge before it is too late. The private sector has enormous potential to drive positive change—if its leaders commit to doing so—and leadership by business is crucial for solving the problems at hand. We urge business leaders everywhere to seize this opportunity to rebuild public confidence in capitalism and its ability to function in a way that generates inclusive and sustainable prosperity.

The problems we wrote about in the first edition were defined initially through a series of conversations with business leaders from different parts of the world. In 2007 and early 2008, in preparation for the Harvard Business School's centennial celebration, we held a series of forums with business leaders in Europe, Asia, Latin America, and North America to learn what issues were on their minds and how their concerns might inform our research and teaching over the next decades. The World Bank had recently published projections for the global economy out to 2030, and we were particularly interested in these leaders' reactions to those projections and, more generally, in their own views on the future of the global market economy. How did they see it developing? What problems did they anticipate? What opportunities lay ahead?

It was a time of great optimism and limitless possibility—just before the financial crisis—and we expected the group as a whole to foresee a continuation of global growth and rising standards of living. We also expected them to deliver a (relatively) clean bill of health for a system that had lifted 450 million people out of poverty in the previous two decades—an achievement that many economists attributed to the spread of markets and open trade across the globe.

What we actually heard was different. Many of the participants, while applauding the achievements of markets and open trade, shared what they perceived to be looming problems that needed to be addressed for global growth to continue and for the market system to maintain its political and social legitimacy. They cautioned that continued progress was far from assured, and some worried that failure to address these problems would give rise to forces that could undermine or even destroy the system. That is why we called this book *Capitalism at Risk*.

As described in chapter 3, the business leaders identified several core problem areas and one overarching concern. The ten core areas are as follows:

- The financial system
- The state of trade

- Inequality and populism

- Migration

- Environmental degradation

- Failure of the rule of law

- The state of public health and general education

- The rise of state capitalism

- Radical movements, terrorism, and war

- Pandemics and disease

The eleventh, and overarching, concern was the inadequacy of existing institutions of governance—corporate, national, and international—to deal with the other ten issues. Our leaders feared that without improvements in governance and management at all important levels of society, the ten underlying problems would only get worse. They worried that those worsening problems would, in turn, lead to economic stagnation, social unrest, political upheaval, natural collapse, military conflict, or other outcomes that would fatally weaken the market system and the social and political conditions necessary to sustain it. This dynamic is shown in figure 4-8. Because of the serious and far-reaching consequences of neglecting these eleven problems, we called them *threats* or *potential disruptors*.

As the participants in our forums discussed these disruptors and the interrelationships among them, we noted a recurring reaction. As one of the leaders put it, "We've thought about every one of these problems before—but we never thought about *all* of them *on the same day* before . . . and when you do that, you see not only that they are interconnected, but that they are reinforcing one another."

We argued, as did many participants, that business needed to take a leadership role in addressing the threats both because governments alone could or would not solve them and because business had distinctive skills and capabilities that could help. We argued further that companies could do so in ways that made strategic sense and could enhance their own growth and future profitability.

In this revised edition, we develop this argument further and offer additional examples of private-sector leadership. Like the earlier examples, the new ones describe companies that are introducing new business models, driving industry collaboration, and mobilizing cross-sector coalitions to help mitigate various problems or otherwise strengthen the market system.

Our vision of business leadership has challenged received wisdom and conventional economic thinking about the role of business, and in the previous edition of the book and this one, we have addressed what we know to be the standard objections. We hope that the line of thinking we put forth here will draw more business leaders into the debate and encourage them to take up the challenge of transitioning to a more sustainable form of capitalism.

Capitalism at Even Greater Risk

Over the past decade, we have continued to study the issues identified in our earlier work and to write case studies about business leaders' and companies' efforts to address them. Despite some noteworthy examples, however, these efforts in the aggregate have fallen dramatically short of what's needed to right the system. The language of sustainability has become widespread, but the activities undertaken in its name have been modest at best. While the CEOs of leading institutional investors such as BlackRock and Vanguard have called on companies to pay more attention to the macrochallenges facing society, capital-market pressures to produce predictable quarterly returns have kept many boards and management teams focused on short-term financial results, crowding out discussion and planning for larger, longer-term issues.

At the same time, the global financial crisis of 2008–2010 and the struggles of nations, companies, and individuals to survive and recover from it served jointly as a distraction from—and sometimes as an excuse to avoid addressing—longer-term, deeper-seated threats. In a time of great economic, social, and political stress, voters in many democracies have responded by turning inward and away from broad problems whose causes and consequences cannot be dealt with in their own nations and regions.

At least partly as a consequence, many of the core problems identified in our earlier work remain unchanged or have worsened in the last decade. The wealth gap continues to widen in many countries, and advances in technology are threatening greater numbers of middle-skilled jobs. Carbon emissions are on the rise, and the world is falling further behind on meeting the climate goals set by the Paris Agreement.[1] To be sure, bright spots and improvements can be seen in some areas and in some geographic locations. The financial system appears by some measures to be stronger than it was during the recovery from the financial crisis and its immediate aftermath, though threats to stability remain.[2] And a number of developing countries have seen improvements in living standards and education. In some countries, wealth inequality has declined. But on the whole, the picture is no better than it was ten years ago, and in many ways, it is worse.

Indeed, to our original list of eleven threats, we now must add a twelfth: the cluster of problems associated with advances in digital technology—problems such as cyberattacks; the spread of misinformation through social media; and the displacement of workers through automation, robotics, and new uses of artificial intelligence.

The digital revolution had barely begun when we held our initial business leader forums. Cloud computing for business was a new idea, *big data* was a new term, the iPhone had just been released, and social media had not yet taken off. Facebook and Twitter were in their infancy, and entrepreneurs were just beginning to see the potential of social media for marketing and political communication. Since then, digital business has become ubiquitous and digital technologies have insinuated themselves into every aspect of life. Many of today's largest companies were born digital, and all businesses everywhere—whatever their size—rely to some degree on the internet and digital technologies. The use of social media has soared. Facebook alone had nearly 2.5 billion users worldwide in the third quarter of 2019.[3] Increases in computing power, an explosion in the quantities of available data, and the emergence of advanced algorithms have fueled the spread of deep-learning technology for a limitless set of applications for everything from facial recognition and fraud detection to diagnosing disease, predicting consumer behavior, and driving autonomous cars.

This transformation has brought enormous wealth and benefits to society, but it has also produced a new set of problems. The past few years have shown that social media are at least as good (and arguably far better) at spreading false information as they are at spreading the accurate variety, thanks to the anonymity enjoyed by users, the absence of any systematic form of editorial accountability, and a patchwork of ineffective governance and regulation. This state of affairs has allowed social media to be used to propagate all manner of false, misleading, inflammatory, and otherwise distorted information in ways that breed divisiveness and distrust and undermine the functioning of markets and democratic processes. Both of these core institutions depend on the wide availability and free flow of accurate and truthful information for their effectiveness and for their legitimacy. The enormous increase in corporate power enabled by massive amounts of data, high-powered computing, and artificial intelligence is also altering the nature of competition and the balance of power between companies and consumers in ways that challenge the basic premises of market capitalism.

Digitalization has spawned a number of unfamiliar threats. The adoption of digital technologies has made many businesses more efficient, but it has also made them more vulnerable to data breaches, network intrusions, and other forms of cyberattack. Malicious actors have embraced the new technologies no less than their targets have, and cyberattacks have increased steadily in both number and sophistication in recent years. The WannaCry ransomware attack of 2017 was unprecedented in scale, affecting computer systems in 150 countries, including those of the National Health Service in England and Scotland, as well as those of companies such as Renault, FedEx, Telefónica, and many others.[4] Although many organizations successfully repelled the attack with little damage, others experienced serious business disruptions and had to undertake costly remedial work.

As hacking tools and techniques become ever more sophisticated and more widely accessible, the threat of large-scale theft and destruction to companies, governments, and critical systems mounts. In 2010, attacks by nation-states and state-affiliated actors barely registered, but by 2018, they accounted for an estimated 23 percent of breaches.[5] Advances in technology have also given democracy's opponents new tools of influence and attack. The past few years have seen an escalation in the level and scope of data- and social-media-driven efforts to undermine electoral processes in numerous democratic nations.[6] Working for state and nonstate actors, the now-defunct political consulting firm Cambridge Analytica reportedly used a combination of hacking, data misappropriation, data profiling, and social media in its attempts to influence voters in as many as sixty-eight countries.[7] It is not hard to imagine how an orchestrated cyberattack on critical infrastructure, major financial institutions, and key government agencies, perhaps coupled with a social media disinformation campaign, could do serious damage to the global market system. Indeed, the U.S. government's Financial Stability Oversight Council counts cyberattacks as among the key risks to the financial system's stability.[8]

In a sense, issues like cybercrime and social media disinformation campaigns can be seen as internet-related versions of other problems in the original list of eleven disruptors, such as weaknesses in the rule of law. We think it useful to call out these problems separately because they have emerged so recently and are so widespread. Whatever their benefits—and we are not questioning those—advances in technology have also had negative effects that will need to be reckoned with. If these effects—the growth of massive data centers with increasing needs for energy, the displacement of jobs and workers by automation, the propagation of false and misleading information, to name the most salient—are not well managed, they will only exacerbate preexisting problems.

Experts in artificial intelligence themselves worry about the effects of automation and artificial-intelligence applications on income inequality, for example. Nearly half the experts responding to a Pew Research Center survey in 2014 anticipated that these technologies would displace more jobs than they created.[9] Almost surely, the jobs they displace will tend to be lower-skill, production-oriented tasks, while the jobs they create will often require higher-level skills—so that the people displaced will be in a poor position to apply for the new jobs that do arise. McKinsey Global Institute estimates that by 2030, up to 375 million workers worldwide may need to move out of their current occupational categories to find work.[10] To the extent that this displacement develops, it will certainly increase income inequality.

The leaders we spoke with before the financial crisis worried that failure to address growing inequality, environmental degradation, financial system dysfunction, and the other problems they identified would strengthen social and political forces hostile to the global market system. Their worries now appear to have been prophetic.

The failure to deal with the problems identified in the book ten years ago has fed into a worldwide backlash against globalization and the free-market ideology that underpins it. The past decade has seen the rise of nationalist, populist, and antiglobalist forces in countries across the world: Donald Trump in the United States, Jair Bolsanaro in Brazil, Boris Johnson and Brexit in the United Kingdom, Matteo Salvini in Italy, the Yellow Vests (*les Gilets jaunes*) in France, Viktor Orbán in Hungary, and Rodrigo Duterte in the Philippines, to name a few of the most visible. The particular grievances fueling these movements vary from country to country, though anti-immigrant sentiment, identity politics, and felt inequity are common themes.

Whatever the specifics, the retreat from open borders and free trade is widespread, as is the embrace of authoritarian leaders who openly disdain international institutions. Many of these leaders brazenly flout the rule of law, use public office for private gain, walk away from what they regard as inconvenient agreements on a whim, and scorn scientific inquiry and even basic facts. Such behaviors directly contradict the norms needed for a free-market economy to function effectively and, by encouraging others to follow suit, undermine the requisite conditions for market capitalism.

Today, in early 2020, the prospect of continuing trade tensions between the United States and China looms large, and business leaders across the world predict further declines both in global trade and in their home country conditions.[11] Worries about geopolitical instability are also running high, with potential conflicts over immigration, nuclear capabilities, trade, and natural disasters brewing at flash points across the world. The forces of fragmentation are making it harder still to deal with problems that cannot be confined within national borders such as climate change, cybercrime, contagious disease, and social-media-fueled disinformation campaigns. In early 2020, a coronavirus (COVID-19) pandemic that appears to have originated in Wuhan, China, became a global crisis threatening the health of populations as well as the economies of many nations, and social-media-amplified misinformation made it more difficult to manage from the outset.[12] Once hailed as a channel for enabling a global citizenry to hold its leaders accountable, the internet has become just the opposite—a channel for leaders to divide and manipulate the citizenry. Even the internet is being fragmented into distinct territories, with Chinese, European, and American areas defined by firewalls and differing regulatory regimes.

Growing Concerns About Capitalism's Future

Since the first edition of *Capitalism at Risk* was published, books and commentaries on the failings of capitalism have proliferated, especially in the past few years as the financial crisis has receded and other problems have become more salient. Many of these accounts were written not by anticapitalists wanting to destroy and replace the system but by authors who, like us, believe that market capitalism offers the best hope for global prosperity. They too are deeply worried that capitalism cannot survive if its foundations are not shored up and its flaws not attended to. The titles of these books, articles, blogs, and podcasts are telling. Here is a sample:[13]

- "Why and How Capitalism Needs to Be Reformed," by Ray Dalio, investor and manager of the world's largest hedge fund, 2019

- *People, Power, and Profits: Progressive Capitalism for an Age of Discontent*, by Joseph Stiglitz, economist, Nobel laureate, and professor at Columbia University, 2019

- *The Future of Capitalism: Facing the New Anxieties*, by Paul Collier, development economist and professor at Oxford University, 2018

- *Can American Capitalism Survive?*, by Steven Pearlstein, business and economics writer and columnist for the *Washington Post*, 2018

- "The Crisis of Democratic Capitalism," by Martin Wolf, chief economics commentator for the *Financial Times*, 2018

- *Capitalists, Arise!: End Economic Inequality, Grow the Middle Class, Heal the Nation*, by Peter Georgescu, chairman emeritus and former CEO of Young & Rubicam, with David Dorsey, business writer, 2017

- *Saving Capitalism: For the Many, Not the Few*, by Robert Reich, former U.S. labor secretary and professor at the University of California at Berkeley, 2015

Although these writers offer somewhat different diagnoses, they all treat rising inequality as the central problem and, together, offer a rich menu of proposals for change. Most of the proposals are directed to agencies of government, and most find solutions in law or public policy initiatives. They call, variously, on lawmakers, regulators, or policy makers—as the case may be—to strengthen antitrust enforcement, enact a more comprehensive safety net, or adopt a more progressive tax system. Others propose better coordination between monetary and fiscal policy or more investment in education, infrastructure, and basic research. Still others want lawmakers to provide tax incentives for corporate profit-sharing or to require companies to disclose their purpose or social and environmental impacts in their regulatory filings. The list goes on.

With a few exceptions, very little is said about what the private sector can do to address rising inequality or help effect a more equitable allocation of wealth and opportunity (other than, presumably, to follow the proposed new laws and regulations if they are enacted). A notable exception is Georgescu and Dorsey, who, in their *Capitalists, Arise!*, urge business leaders to invest more in their employees.

A New Role for Business

As is evident from the original edition of this book, we share with these authors a belief that the growing gulf between the haves and have-nots is a threat to capitalism and that corrective action is urgently needed. We also agree on the importance of changes in policy and regulation. But as we look at the current situation, we see a need for action on multiple fronts—recall the twelve threats—and by actors at multiple levels: individual, company, and industry, as well as government. Getting capitalism onto a more sustainable trajectory is simply not possible without the active involvement of—and, indeed, leadership from—the private sector.

Whatever policy changes may be enacted, this effort will take imagination, investment, and a willingness to innovate on the part of businesses in every domain of the economy. Companies will need to embrace new approaches to governance, step up investments in research and development (R&D), adopt new valuation techniques, develop new capabilities, and experiment with new technologies, strategies, and business models—all of which are, by their very nature, risky. They will also need to become more thoughtful about the positions they take on matters of regulation and public policy. Without leadership by executives and investors who believe in the need for change and are willing to act on that conviction, little progress can be made—even if, as seems unlikely in the current moment, a political consensus could be achieved to adopt some of the policy prescriptions mentioned above.

To be sure, business has limitations and individual companies can do only so much. As we discuss at length in the book, business leaders' expertise may not match the problem at hand and they may lack the political legitimacy required to take certain actions. But there are many things companies *can* do—on their own or in collaboration with others—to help mitigate the disruptors and facilitate the shift to a more sustainable economic order. Even when legitimacy is an issue, it may be addressable through engagement and collaboration with governments, nonprofits, foundations, and other civic organizations.

Too little attention has been paid to the role of the private sector in the public discourse on reforming capitalism. Judging from the business response to date, many business leaders themselves have not yet grasped the significance of the threats and the implications for their companies and industries. The new statement on corporate purpose by the Business Roundtable, an association of U.S. CEOs, suggests that awareness is growing. Signed by 181 CEOs of leading U.S. companies and issued in August 2019, the statement and its preamble explicitly rejected the group's 1997 embrace of shareholder primacy—the view that maximizing returns to shareholders is the principal objective of a corporation—in favor of a commitment to lead for the benefit of all stakeholders. Whether the statement is a harbinger of change in how companies allocate resources or just a PR gesture is hard to say, but commentary by some of the signers suggests that its practical effect is likely to be minimal. In any case, pushback from investor groups may limit its impact.

Despite such signs of growing awareness, which we discuss in Part Three, a real sense of urgency is lacking, and there is a large gap between rhetoric and reality. Troubled or not by the evidence of looming problems, and lofty statements aside, too many boards, managers, and investors are continuing to operate on a business-as-usual basis.

A Renewed and More Urgent Call to Action

We have updated *Capitalism at Risk* in the hope of galvanizing more business leaders to take these problems seriously. In this new and expanded version, we have added three new chapters. In chapter 9, we expand on the eleven threats discussed in earlier chapters and show how the threats interact with one another and with the new forces of digital disruption to create even more complex and unwieldy problems. In chapter 10, we reiterate with heightened urgency our call for businesses to take a more active role in addressing the disruptors. We provide additional examples of companies that are implementing innovative strategies to do just that. In chapter 11, we summarize some of the lessons learned from early corporate efforts to mitigate the forces of disruption.

We reiterate even more strongly our overarching conclusion: Government alone cannot solve these problems. Business must step up to the challenge. Business leaders (individually and collectively) are in a better position to find practical solutions to the challenges they will face in their respective companies and industries than we are as academics. One of the great virtues of the market capitalist system is its encouragement of ingenuity and imagination and its ability to muster resources behind better answers. Business leaders—perhaps organized to enhance their collective capacity—are the most likely source of new ideas and approaches once they see the situation with the urgency we believe is appropriate to it. But we try to point in directions that are most likely to be productive, including the possibility of mounting a coordinated effort to show that capitalism can function in a way that preserves its own foundations and produces inclusive prosperity.

The earlier parts of the book are unchanged. Part One looks at threats to the global market system that were emerging even before the financial collapse of 2008. In chapter 1, we explain the origins of our project, define market capitalism, and describe the business leader forums that we held in 2007 and 2008, just before the financial crisis, to gather their views on the global market system's future.

In chapters 2 and 3, we examine the prospects for the global economy as seen through two complementary sets of lenses. Chapter 2 relies mainly on aggregate data, drawing heavily from the World Bank's economic projections at the time of our business leader forums. Chapter 3 fills out the picture through the experiences and perspectives of the business leaders who participated in our forums. Together these two chapters lay out the eleven threats that emerged from our study.

Chapter 4 introduces a framework for understanding market capitalism as a system embedded within a larger political and social ecosystem and for revealing how the threats relate to one another and to the system as a whole. The framework focuses on the free-market capitalist system's necessary antecedents, or preconditions; its internal operating rules; its possible consequences both positive and negative; potential internal and external disruptors; and the feedback loops that reinforce or undermine how the market system functions. In its graphic form, the framework makes abundantly clear that the eleven threats should not be viewed in isolation and shows how they can evolve from mere problems to disruptors of the entire system if they are not effectively managed. Conversely, the framework also helps show what it takes for the system to function in a way that is effective and sustainable.

The chapters in Part Two examine the role of business in mitigating the threats and improving the system. In chapter 5, we discuss four possible responses by business and argue that companies can and should take a leadership role rather than, as conventional economic theory teaches, sitting on the sidelines and waiting for governments to act. Chapter 6 presents examples of companies that have made businesses out of tackling various disruptors. Chapter 7 explores the possibility of a more constructive relationship between business and government and offers examples of companies collaborating with industry or multisector groups to this end. Chapter 8 discusses some of the standard objections to our proposal that business should involve itself in what are conventionally defined as public-goods problems outside the private sector's purview.

———————

Back in 2008, the world's socioeconomic, geopolitical, and environmental situation was alarming. Today it is even more so. Some might say the situation is dire. Through this new, expanded edition, we hope to inspire more business leaders to take the disruptive problems seriously and to bring their own and their companies' considerable talents and expertise to bear on solving them.

Capitalism triumphed in the Cold War because it promised a better life for the great majority of people around the world, and the improving conditions for many millions seemed to affirm its claim. But dramatically unequal access to capitalism's benefits and mounting evidence of its collateral damage have cast doubt on that promise and provided grist for ideological naysayers to challenge its fundamental soundness as a basis for economic organization.

We believe that time to deliver on the core promise of free-market capitalism is running out. If market capitalism cannot be made to work for almost everyone, then it will eventually not be allowed to work at all. It will lose its legitimacy and collapse from within or fall prey to hostile forces from without.

Preface and Acknowledgments
to the First Edition

This book had its beginnings nearly five years ago, when preparations began for the celebration of the hundredth birthday of Harvard Business School. Dean Jay Light convened various groups of faculty to develop plans appropriate to the occasion. A major gathering of distinguished alumni and business leaders would mark the occasion with presentations and debate. As we took in the discussion, we realized that while the idea of a business school was quite ordinary in 2007, Harvard's decision to set up a business school in 1908 was anything but. The founding of Harvard Business School was a forward-thinking and somewhat radical idea. Was there an equivalent idea today?

Steeped as we are in the case-method approach to the development of new ideas, we thought it might be helpful to talk to business leaders to see what challenges they thought were at the top of an agenda that should concern an institution like ours, blessed with a great faculty and resources. So that is what we did. We identified leaders in various parts of the world, and then cajoled them into meeting with us to build an agenda that HBS should consider. We presented our findings from that research first to our faculty and then to the large group that assembled for the Centennial Business Summit in October 2008.

As we listened to business leaders in various regions, we discovered that they were actually concerned with the future of market capitalism as we knew it. They worried that rising income inequality, migration, and climate change have the potential to seriously undermine global capitalism. This seemed somewhat alarmist at the time. Unfortunately, by the autumn of 2008, the future of global capitalism had become the broad topic discussed by the Centennial Business Summit, and very timely at that.

After the summit, we stepped back to consider what we had heard. Many voices in the press and in public forums were criticizing business and calling for a stronger role for government, but our findings seemed to lead in a different direction. It was not that government couldn't play a valuable role; it could. Indeed, it had to. But many of the business leaders who participated in our project pointed squarely to the limitations of governments—especially the democratically elected governments that characterized the nations of the economically developed world. Our colleagues at HBS had also urged us to consider how entrepreneurs would think about the difficult challenges taxing the system. And as we worked with business leaders and studied how companies were addressing these problems, we learned that some companies were helping by the very way they did business. They were bringing tens of millions of impoverished people into the market economy. They were working with governments to manage migration. And they were finding ways to conserve energy and reduce their carbon footprint while increasing sales and profits.

This finding intrigued us. If some companies could actually lead in the resolution of major problems that threatened the capitalist market system, more companies could and should. Being academics—and not politicians—that observation led us to write this book.

We could not have done this work without remarkable help from many people. To begin, Dean Jay Light and Senior Associate Dean Srikant Datar wholeheartedly endorsed our proposal to take off around the world to ask business leaders what they thought were important problems that needed to be addressed. We are grateful for the resources that Deans Light and Datar provided, both in the work leading up to the 2008 business summit and thereafter and for support for the writing of this book. We greatly appreciate the support and encouragement we received from our colleague Warren McFarlan, who chaired the summit. We are also grateful to our faculty colleagues who were particularly helpful to us as we formed our ideas. David Moss was part of our team when we ran a series of regional forums for business leaders, and Bill Sahlman cogently called our attention to the way entrepreneurs viewed the questions we were asking. The business leaders who attended the forums enriched our understanding and provided many of the core ideas that inform this book. We are indebted to Bertrand Collomb, Victor Fung, Jorge Paolo Lemann, and Jamie Dimon, who respectively were the cohosts of the regional forums. They helped in the critical job of convening really thoughtful groups of leaders. The leaders of the HBS regional research centers provided vital support in the logistics of the forums: Vincent Dessain, Michael Shih-ta Chen, and Gustavo Herrero. Sonja Ellingson Hout organized and conducted the video interviews that were so important to the data gathering for this book and produced the video shown at the business summit. We think of her as an invisible coauthor. Stefany Shaheen provided excellent research assistance in the early phases of our work, and Colette Ciregna, Marais Canali Young, and Maura Mack were indefatigable in arranging the endless logistics of the regional forums.

Once the book was in draft, Lara Adamsons worked tirelessly with us in reviewing issues large and small. This would literally have been a different book without her careful help. We drew on extensive help from Chris Allen, Jeff Cronin, and David Lane for assembling exhibits and checking facts. Paul Montie turned our rudimentary graphics into the splendid presentation of our model in chapter 4. Kathy Farren and Lauren Pyle helped prepare and keep track of endless drafts and revisions. Melinda Merino at Harvard Business Review Press provided wonderful help in framing the book and then in guiding us to completion. We are grateful to Rod Hills and two anonymous reviewers who provided invaluable comments on an earlier draft of the manuscript.

As with all such ventures, we have been helped by many. We are grateful to them for all the good aspects of this book. For its flaws, we take full responsibility.

Part One

The Future of Market Capitalism

Introduction

S FACULTY at Harvard Business School, we serve in an organization devoted to improving the leadership of business enterprise. Our school's mission is "to develop leaders who make a positive difference in the world." We do that with research that builds and communicates concepts useful to the managements of firms, by training the MBAs who go on to careers as business leaders, and by providing midcareer development programs for the top executives of companies.

In all this work, the faculty share a common, underlying set of beliefs that motivate our diverse approaches to our mission. Managers make their contribution to our society by guiding the organizations that provide goods and services to customers. For this contribution to be sustainable, the organizations must operate at a profit in the face of competition and a changing environment within the constraints of relevant laws and societal norms. Competitive markets—the invisible hand—insure that when firms behave this way, they are doing the best they can for society. That is the glory of the capitalist market system.

In that context, this book sets forth a radical proposition. We believe that the role of business needs to change. The capitalist market system has generated enormous wealth in recent decades, but if the system continues to operate more or less as it has been operating, then it is vulnerable to breaking down in serious ways. As we will discuss, plausible forecasts point to challenges on multiple fronts. To stanch these potentially disruptive forces and ensure that the system continues to function in an effective manner, we believe business must stop seeing itself as merely a self-regarding participant in a system that is largely "given"—or shaped and maintained by others—and start seeing itself as a leader in protecting and improving the system that gives it life.

We will argue that business must begin taking a more active role in assuring the market system's ongoing health and sustainability. Much as we might wish to believe that the system will take care of itself through the magic of the invisible hand, we cannot in good conscience claim that narrow self-interest and competitive forces alone will ensure the system's performance for society. But, unlike many writing in the aftermath of the financial crisis, we do not see government as the system's savior, either. Good government is crucial, to be sure. But government, we will argue, needs the support and engagement of business to function effectively.

In the chapters that follow, we will share the research and reasoning behind our view and spell out the practical implications for companies and their leaders. We will offer concrete examples of what we have in mind when we call for business to take a leadership role in protecting and improving the system. We believe that today's global enterprises—large and small, but especially large—are uniquely positioned to help address many of the most pressing challenges. Some of these challenges may lie beyond the current capabilities of most companies, but we are confident that with suitable leadership, they can acquire new knowledge and bring their talent and resources to bear on developing and implementing innovative solutions.

A Centennial Project

This book is the result of a project we launched as part of Harvard Business School's centennial celebration. Initially, we viewed the approach of its hundredth birthday as a time to reflect on what the school had accomplished since its founding in 1908 as a training ground for managers of the railroads and other large industrial concerns that had arisen in the late nineteenth century. As envisioned by the university's president and the prominent alumni who had urged the school's creation, the school would prepare young men (young women were not mentioned) for a wholly new role in U.S. society—that of the professional manager. After a bumpy start and some trying periods, the school evolved as a source of training, research, and communication that eventually catalyzed the widespread growth of business schools across the United States and then, after World War II, around the globe.

Reflecting on the school's past, we very quickly realized that in terms of the original vision, the school had far outstripped the imagination of its founders. By the fall of 2008, Harvard Business School had conferred the MBA degree on nearly fifty-six thousand aspirants, both male and female, including many who have gone on to head prominent companies in the United States and elsewhere around the world—as well as an array of government agencies, nonprofit organizations, and even countries. Whether or not management could be called a profession, knowledge had accumulated and pedagogy had progressed so that graduates came to their calling far better equipped to fill roles as general managers of companies and other organizations. One striking example lay in the contrast between the success rate of entrepreneurs with MBA training and those without. A study of ventures started by HBS MBAs found that they had a 50 percent chance of success, compared with the average of 10 percent.[1] Moreover, although Harvard's approach to teaching and research was unique in its commitment to case teaching and field research, many other business schools were developing capable graduates as well.

We concluded that an inquiry into what was on the minds of outstanding alumni would be more useful—and more interesting—than a self-congratulatory reflection on the past. As these leaders looked at the world around them and then ahead, what challenges did they see facing business that ought to provide the agenda for our school? In effect, if we were building a new school today, what areas would require attention? While that question is often asked by faculties when they are engaged in strategic planning, the answers they give typically reflect a subtle reframing of the question. They study what problems they should address, *given the skill set of their faculty*. We wanted to ask a different question: What did the best business leaders around the world think was important, and how did they view the health of the global market system? And since we were fortunate enough to be based at Harvard Business School, we had access to some of the very best business leaders and the resources to go talk to them. So we did.

We are longtime colleagues in the general management area at Harvard Business School, but we brought very different perspectives to this project. Joseph Bower and Herman "Dutch" Leonard are trained as economists; Lynn Paine's formal training is in law and moral philosophy. Although we are all students of leadership, we have pursued this topic from different angles: Joe's research has focused on corporate strategy and resource allocation; Dutch's on business-government relations and corporate citizenship; and Lynn's on ethics, culture, and corporate governance. In addition to teaching in the school's educational programs, where we have interacted with thousands of MBA students and executives from all parts of the world, we have all worked as consultants to companies and served on corporate boards. Despite our diverse backgrounds, we all came to the project with a belief that as faculty members, we needed to lift our sights and take a dispassionate look at the future of the market capitalist system that has been the source of prosperity and wealth for so many during Harvard Business School's first century.

In this spirit, we organized a series of forums in Europe, East Asia, Latin America, and the United States. We called on close business friends to recommend invitees, and in each region, we had a cohost who helped encourage participation. In the end, forty-six leaders took part in the meetings. Mostly CEOs (some had retired and taken other roles), the participants included Bertrand Collomb, longtime chairman of Lafarge; Sir David Scholey, CEO of S.G. Warburg and later vice chairman of UBS; Nancy Barry, CEO of Enterprise Solutions to Poverty; Victor Fung, chairman of Li & Fung; Ana Maria Diniz, president of Sykue Byoenergia; Jaime A. Zobel de Ayala, chairman of Ayala Corporation; Jorge Paulo Lemann, founder of Garantia and AmBev; Elaine Chao, U.S. Secretary of Labor; Carlos Cáceres, president of Instituto Libertad y Desarrollo, Chile; Jamie Dimon, chairman and CEO of JPMorgan Chase & Co.; and Jeff Immelt, chairman and CEO of General Electric. The full list of participants is provided in the appendix. Two other executives provided their views outside the forums proper.

The sample was certainly not random, and we did not even touch some important parts of the world, such as the countries of the former Soviet Union and Africa. What's more, we were speaking with what some might call a biased sample, the winners in the past pattern of global progress. We did this, however, for a reason. We were asking a very specific question: If we stipulate that the system of market capitalism has been the source of remarkable economic growth, what problems might undermine that growth in the future? What aspects of the system at the level of firms, industries, nations, or multilateral institutions might cause serious difficulties? The people we were asking understood the system well and were viewing it from perspectives as varied as New York, Caracas, Turin, and Brunei. Each individual had decades of experience with global markets as well as considerable interaction with government leaders. They understood what they needed in order to function.

A Working Definition of Market Capitalism

Before describing the forums, we should perhaps say something about our definition of market capitalism, since it is the future of that system that we are examining. (We will take up this topic at length in chapter 4.) In general, we have in mind an economic system characterized by these key features:

- Private ownership of personal and enterprise assets

- Adequate provision of physical security for life and property

- The sanctity of private contracts

- A banking system that provides a sound currency

- Prices set by independent enterprise

- Free trade among nations

As will become clear in chapter 4, we also include important facilitating conditions such as:

- An educated population

- Good public health

- An effective legal system

- Effective and accountable government

Different countries have developed a variety of arrangements for providing these elements. The United States, for example, takes a highly decentralized approach, relying heavily on the fifty states to make laws and provide services to the populace. Moreover, the U.S. Constitution provides for a unique degree of individual liberty. This approach has led historically to the delegation of schooling to the states, but also to political suspicion of centralized economic intervention, for example, in resistance to the creation of a national bank. From Andrew Jackson's presidency in the early nineteenth century to today, there has been fierce political resistance to both central direction and strict regulation of the banking system. At the same time, the United States has a long tradition of federal support for enterprise, going back more than two hundred years. "No taxation without representation" was as much a reaction to the British unwillingness to support American land speculators against the French in the Ohio territories and beyond as it was a reaction to taxes on tea.[2]

In contrast, France, Germany, and Japan all have strong central governments that are deeply involved not only in education and health but also in banking and industrial policy. Furthermore, ownership of enterprise is more complicated, given the importance of large complexes of enterprise with interlocking holdings. Through their various holdings and other relationships, companies such as Banque Nationale de Paris, Allianz, and Mitsubishi have had outsized influence in the management of their economies. How that influence is used, however, is considerably constrained by a communitarian ideology that many in the United States would find . . . well, *foreign*.

When we consider the so-called BRIC countries—Brazil, Russia, India, and China—the picture gets even more complicated. In these nations, state ownership of enterprise remains an active element of national economic strategy rather than a vestige of past arrangements. China has identified a group of national champions such as CNOOC, Ltd., and Haier; these companies look like independent enterprises but are partially owned by elements of the state and have the full backing of the state as long as their objectives align with those of the nation. Other companies, such as Baosteel, China National Building Materials, and China Mobile, are wholly owned by the state but have subsidiaries that are partly owned by the shareholding public. Brazil and India provide different versions of a mixed approach to ownership and regulation. Finally, Russian heavy industry is either privately owned by politically subservient oligarchs or, like Gazprom, state owned. Just as the United States controls where its high-tech firms sell their advanced technology products, Russia controls the terms on which Gazprom sells gas.

As these examples suggest, drawing sharp boundaries around what is—and is not—market capitalism in practice is not a straightforward exercise. Key elements are present to a greater or lesser degree in different countries, and some observers would argue that the rules of market capitalism are themselves in flux. Some countries are clearly outliers, embracing some features of the market system but rejecting others and at times behaving in ways that challenge the system. But even countries strongly committed to market capitalism will override market principles from time to time. National economic arrangements are inevitably embedded in a national political system that modifies those arrangements to reflect what its political leaders consider necessary for political stability. For example, George W. Bush's administration—ideologically committed to free markets—imposed new barriers to trade with Canadian lumber producers and supported old barriers against Pakistani textiles in order to maintain political majorities in the United States, despite strong ideological and foreign-policy reasons to do neither.

When we talked with business leaders about the future of market capitalism, we did not get very specific about definitions. There seems to be a widespread consensus that independently managed enterprises that set their own goals, policies, and programs so that they choose which products to produce, when and where to sell them and at what prices, in the context of a stable but decentralized banking system and a trading system with open borders lie at the heart of market capitalism. The market determines success or failure.

As noted, however, the consensus definition leaves much room for interpretation and variation in political and economic arrangements. Today's debate centers on the "Chinese system" versus the "U.S. system." But in the 1980s, many people were enamored of the Japanese system ("Japan Inc.") or the German system ("Germany AG"), both of which involved significant government involvement in the economy. Of course, in keeping with the practice of intervening when useful for domestic political purposes, the U.S. government is also deeply involved with the economy through fiscal and trade policy (e.g., the housing interest deduction and the protection of industrial agriculture) and government-funded research by agencies such as the National Institutes of Health and DARPA (the Defense Advanced Research Projects Agency, an arm of the Defense Department). A prototypical example is DARPA's development of the ARPAnet, the precursor to the internet. And it was a Republican president who built the national highway system in the 1950s and promoted the study of national goals.

Since we wanted to learn from business leaders with diverse perspectives and experiences, we approached our forums with an open definition of a market capitalist system and a broad view of the territory we were examining.

Regional Forums with Business Leaders

The meetings started with a working dinner and lasted through lunch the next day—and so involved about eight hours of discussions. The sessions were off the record, but we asked individuals to take part in one-on-one, on-the-record interviews in which they offered their views. To provide focus for the discussion, we gave participants a briefing book consisting of exhibits and very brief explanatory text that we drew from a then just-published World Bank study that provided a scenario for the world economy in 2030.

The study, which is referenced heavily in chapter 2, provides a carefully worked-out set of projections of what the world will look like if events proceed in the same general fashion as the last several decades. It is not a straight extrapolation, but the many models used to develop the projections assume no major war, no serious pandemic, no breakdown of the financial system, and no environmental disaster of global magnitude. The study presents a fine-grained scenario that permits the exploration of growth rates and income distribution in many countries, as well as patterns of trade and migration. Environmental factors such as climate change and water usage are also discussed.

The briefing book served as the "case" for our discussion. Just as our going to business leaders to learn their views reflected a Harvard

Business School approach to identifying research issues, so too was the use of a common set of data as a basis for discussion. Far from biasing the discussion toward one set of conclusions, the data freed members of the group to take what they could agree were almost certainly the kinds of problems that lay ahead as a starting point for a debate about causes and solutions. We present a summary of this data in chapter 2 so that as we share the views of our forum participants with you, you will know precisely the set of projections from which they were working.

We opened the forum discussion by reviewing the remarkable economic progress of the last half century and outlining the core themes of the World Bank's projections. We then asked the participants what if anything in the projections concerned them. Many were already familiar with the data from the studies their companies had made in planning their growth and long-term development. For example, at GE, Jeff Immelt has turned the focus of that huge organization to the opportunities posed by infrastructure growth in emerging markets and by the need for more efficient management of energy production and consumption. At Lafarge, Bertrand Collomb had led a steady expansion of the company's facilities in developing markets. And Victor Fung has presided over the building of the world's largest network of textile and apparel suppliers and consumers. From his base in Brazil, Jorge Paolo Lemann has built the world's largest beer company. For these leaders, the questions we were addressing were fundamental to the progress of their companies. The executives had not always looked at these issues in the way that we were doing collectively; nor did they all agree on what the implications of the questions might be, but this was their world and they took it very seriously.

The problems that the leaders identified at the evening session provided the agenda for the morning discussions. We asked them to tell us why the problems were important, what the consequences might be if the problems continued to develop as forecast, and what they thought should be done about them by individual firms, by business leaders, by industry (or other business) associations, and by government.

Perhaps surprisingly, we found that many of these business leaders were concerned about the very same issues that agitate critics of globalization—but for different reasons. As we describe in chapter 3, where we quote extensively from their comments, many are concerned that rising incomes are often associated with growing inequality and that global growth is contributing to environmental degradation and climate change. They worry about the destabilizing impact of millions of people migrating from poor countries to rich ones and about the rise of protectionism in many nations. They are troubled by the lack of transparency and by the fragility of the global financial system. And many question society's ability to address these and other first-order problems, citing weaknesses in governance at the level of firms, industries, nations, and international institutions.

The difference between our business leaders and the critics of globalization is that our leaders see a healthy system of market capitalism not as the problem but as the solution to these ills. Indeed, some leaders see remedying these problems as business opportunities. Still, as we probed for what could be done to mitigate these disruptive forces and ensure the health of the system, we uncovered a range of views and some substantial disagreements. In particular, our discussions revealed deep philosophical disagreements about the appropriate role of business in this effort. We address these differences at length in the second part of the book as these discussions have led us to conclude that the business community and Harvard Business School have a good deal of work to do.

The Chapters Ahead

As a first step, we decided to write this book to share what we had heard from business leaders around the world and to offer our own perspective on the role of business in ensuring the market system's health. Some readers will, no doubt, find our perspective problematic and fault us for not offering a fully worked out vision of how this perspective will ultimately play out in practice. But we think a discussion of the role of business is sorely needed now. We offer our views in the hope of loosening the ideological straitjackets that all too often impede fresh thinking and authentic debate about this critical issue. The remainder of the book unfolds as follows.

We begin in chapter 2 as we began our forums, by setting the context for our inquiry. We review the remarkable economic progress of the last half century and describe key elements of the world economy in 2030 as forecast by the World Bank.

In chapter 3, we present what we learned from our discussions and lay out ten potential *disruptors*—ten forces that could severely disrupt the market system's functioning in the decades ahead. We quote extensively from participants in our business leader forums and draw on data from the World Bank and other sources to argue that the global market system is vulnerable to serious breakdown if it continues to operate more or less as it has in the past.

Chapter 4 builds a framework showing how these disruptive forces are related to one another and to the market system as a whole. We argue that the market system is itself a subsystem of a much larger sociopolitical ecosystem that supports and legitimizes it—and that the market system's effective functioning and sustainability depend on the health of this larger ecosystem. We conclude that insufficient attention is being paid to mitigating the potential disruptors and maintaining the health of this larger ecosystem. But we are then left with a question: Who is responsible for looking after the system as a whole?

Chapter 5 considers what role business, in particular, should play in combating potential disruptors and ensuring the system's health. We examine four views that emerged in our forums: business as bystander, business as activist, business as innovator, and business as usual. We then propose a fifth view—business as leader—that builds on what we heard. We argue that companies can and must do more to advance the healthy functioning of the system both as innovators developing new business models and strategies, and as activists for good government and more effective institutions.

In chapter 6, we elaborate the argument that individual companies can make a difference by developing innovative strategies and business models. We offer four detailed examples of companies that are pursuing the types of innovations we have in mind and distill some general observations on the leadership capabilities needed to drive these efforts. Our examples illustrate four generic approaches to helping sustain the system: amplifying its positive consequences, mitigating its negative consequences, counteracting exogenous threats, and strengthening its necessary antecedents and preconditions.

Chapter 7 examines business-led innovations in the broader institutional environment and explores the possibility of a more constructive relationship between business and government. We offer some historical examples—both negative and positive—to illustrate how business can help strengthen the market system by mobilizing others and engaging across sectors at the community, national, and international levels. Drawing from these examples, we discuss the challenges presented by this idea and outline the changes in thinking and other skills required for business to take on a larger role in this arena.

We conclude, in chapter 8, by reviewing the central argument of the book—that business must take a more active role in sustaining the system—and considering some of the new leadership and organizational capabilities that may be required to play this role effectively. We then offer a set of questions that companies and their leaders can ask to inspire practical ways to implement the book's core idea and better align their strategies and activities with the needs of a sustainable market system. We conclude with further illustrations of what companies can do to tackle the pressing problems and challenges facing the system today.

In developing our argument, we often quote the business leaders who participated in our forums. As noted earlier, these meetings were off the record, but some participants provided us with one-on-one interviews that they gave us permission to quote. Most comments are cited anonymously with reference to the forum from which they came (to provide regional context). While we were writing, we were mindful of a comment made during the U.S. forum in New York by Elaine Chao, an HBS alumna and U.S. Secretary of Labor at the time of our discussions:

> I think Harvard Business School, being the beacon of capitalism or the beacon of free enterprise, really needs to look forward to the next one hundred years and talk about its role in our society, and its value to the world community again, because we are now part of a globalized world economy. There are many detractors to the free-enterprise system who believe that captains of industry are selfish and that they only hew to the interests of the shareholders.

With this book, we invite you to join the discussion that began in our business leader forums and that led to our proposal for rethinking the role of business. Whether or not you agree with our analysis and conclusions, we hope you will find the ideas in this book provocative. We hope they will help you sharpen your own views on the role of business in maintaining and improving the market system's performance for society.

Even more important, we hope the book will inspire fresh thinking and experimentation with innovative business models, new organizational forms, new institutional arrangements, and other new approaches to collaboration within business and across sectors. We are optimistic that the challenges we have outlined can be addressed—if only we tap into the creative energy and entrepreneurial drive that have brought society this far. Of course, we recognize that entrepreneurs around the world are already working to develop new products and technologies to address the cost of food, the waste of energy, and the threat of disease. We applaud these efforts with enthusiasm. But our argument is different. We think a comparable level of energy and creativity should be brought to the strategies and institutions that drive the larger system— and to addressing the challenges to the very core of that system.

To give you a more concrete idea of where this book is headed, we conclude this chapter with a brief case study:[3]

In underserved, overexploited rural India, the Indian conglomerate ITC identified an opportunity to transform the lives of many rural Indians while at the same time solving some of its own problems. Continually plagued by an inefficient supply chain in rural agriculture, ITC implemented what it called the "e-Choupal" initiative in 2000. (*Choupal* is Hindi for community meeting place.) Under the initiative, ITC set up Internet kiosks in villages where small farmers could get direct access to information about the weather, crop prices, productivity improvements, and markets and learn about the prices ITC was offering for their produce. By establishing a direct and transparent channel between the farmer and ITC, e-Choupal significantly reduced the role of the traditional middlemen, or *mandi*, in getting farmers' produce to market. The result: a higher return and greater access to markets for farmers and a more efficient and higher quality agrarian supply chain for ITC (as well as new and better-paying jobs for some former *mandi*). By January 2007, ITC's e-Choupal system was facilitating the purchase of agricultural commodities from some 4 million farmers in nearly forty thousand villages.

Although e-Choupal was conceived as ITC's answer to its supply chain woes, the company was quick to realize that it had discovered the delicate balance between achieving corporate profitability and making a social contribution. Aware of the multitude of challenges faced by impoverished rural Indians, ITC extended its e-Choupal framework to deliver other core services such as access to health care, education, and information. ITC saw the opportunity to coordinate with other companies, including fast-moving consumer goods companies and finance companies, to deliver to Indian farmers products and services that had previously commanded huge premiums or were simply unavailable—from motor bikes to health insurance. With the addition of these new sales and distribution capabilities, e-Choupal was evolving into a platform for community development, helping reduce poverty and chipping away at rural isolation while improving the efficiency and functioning of ITC's own procurement and distribution systems.

In 2010, ITC announced plans for a new version of e-Choupal to be launched in 2012. Designed to offer personalized crop management services, the new version was expected to extend ITC's reach from four million to twenty million rural farmers, thus strengthening the company's competitive position relative to the many imitators that had entered the field and bringing millions more into the modern agricultural system.

In this case, the company was able to open up the large market comprising India's huge population of rural farmers only after constructing many aspects of a modern market system. ITC drew on its resources and distinctive capabilities as one of India's major conglomerates to provide the necessary information, distribution, and financing. With those essentials in place, the company could provide other products and services, thus bringing a previously marginalized and exploited population into the market system as active and vital participants.

This example may seem idiosyncratic or its lessons particular to India or to agribusiness, and it might therefore be tempting to narrow it down and interpret it (or dismiss it) as a mere single instance. But we think this example holds greater possibilities—possibilities we will see repeatedly in this book. The e-Choupal example shows a business:

- Thinking differently and more comprehensively about the larger environment in which it operates

- Consciously and intentionally intervening to improve a broader system of which it understands itself to be a part

- Operating and cooperating with a wider and different range of partners than it would have been likely to engage with in the past

- Operating in a way that takes advantage of its unique ability, as a private company, to be undistracted and undeterred by potential political ramifications that might have stymied a government agency trying to undertake similar actions

- Using its planning and resource-allocation mechanisms to rapidly scale a project that was proving to be beneficial and successful

We have found that forward-looking companies across the spectrum are thinking creatively and learning how to address what have hitherto been regarded as problems for governments and nongovernmental organizations (NGOs) by developing strategies that enhance the prospects for sustaining the market system and often generate financial benefits for the company at the same time. For us, what is important about the e-Choupal example and others like it is that in the face of major challenges to the functioning of the market system, business took on a new stance. In this case, it was principally one business, and the company had at least some short-term financial incentives to take a new position as a market facilitator. In other cases, an individual business leader, a group of leaders, or a network of businesses might redefine its position as a player in the market system. And these actors might do so without a well-developed prospect of immediate financial returns but with the recognition that it is in their self-interest to be part of a well-functioning system.

The most promising examples show business leaders taking a system perspective to their entrepreneurship and creatively redesigning the role that business plays in maintaining and enhancing the wider system in which it operates and on which it depends. This book is grounded in the belief that such creative redefinitions and entry into new roles are both *necessary* and *possible*.

A Projection of
Global Prospects

T HE IDEA that the market system may be in trouble has
become quite popular since the financial crisis of 2008. The
meltdown of the financial system has spawned an outpouring
of articles, books, and conferences calling for a new view of capitalism. In many cases, that "new" view centers on an expanded role for
governments. The business leaders with whom we spoke were also
very concerned, but not because of 2008. Theirs was a precrisis view,
but they were already worried about the very forces that were leading up to the financial meltdown and, more generally, about how the
global system might evolve over the coming two or three decades. In
this chapter, we consider what the world might look like if the market system continues to function more or less as it has functioned in
the recent past.

We start by recognizing that the last half of the twentieth century
was a period of unprecedented prosperity across a very significant part
of the globe. Nations with vast populations that had been bypassed by
economic development in the first half of the twentieth century, such
as China and India, began to see rapid economic growth as the century neared its end. While citizens of the Organisation for Economic
Co-operation and Development (OECD)[1] nations became wealthy by
historical standards, the income per capita of most developing nations

also improved.[2] Between 1975 and 2002, more than 97 percent of the world's countries experienced increased wealth, and almost half saw annual increases in real GDP of more than 3 percent.[3]

It is hard to exaggerate the progress made. The Organization of the Petroleum Exporting Countries (OPEC)–led rise in oil prices that began in 1973 imposed a huge tax on the world economy and slowed growth. But by 1982, with the absorption of the tax in the West and the opening of China, growth rates in mature economies steadied and, in developing nations, began to rise. Although some groups clearly benefited from this growth more than others, wide swaths of the global population experienced unprecedented improvements in their standard of living. By the World Bank's reckoning, global income has doubled since 1980, and more than 450 million have been lifted out of extreme poverty since 1990.[4]

This progress can be attributed to several major forces, but most observers would probably begin with the internationalist perspective guiding those in charge of rebuilding after World War II. Former colonies became nations, and nations chose to organize their relationships among themselves through a series of agreements and institutions that were historically unprecedented. Faced with the appalling destruction of the war, the leaders of major nations sought to create organizations that would prevent a recurrence. The United Nations, the Bretton Woods accords, the International Monetary Fund, the World Bank, and, later, the European Economic Community (EC) (followed by the European Union [EU]) were designed to enshrine human rights, democracy, stable currencies, and open markets as principles to guide the development of national policies.

Partly because of the political and economic challenge posed by the Soviet Union, the victors in the war chose to rebuild their enemies rather than plunder them so that their former foes might resist communism through economic strength. Wherever they could, the United States and its allies supported the development of market-based economies. Countries invested in education and a skilled workforce. One result was that thirty years after the war, Germany and Japan had emerged as politically liberal economic powerhouses. The success of their strategies of export-driven growth provided models for a host of other nations ranging from the East Asian "tigers" of the 1980s (Korea, Taiwan, Singapore) to China, India, and Brazil in the 1990s.

The fall of the Berlin Wall in 1989 and the collapse of communism brought many more countries into the market system. The adoption of liberal political regimes and open economies by countries across the world, together with the opening up of the international trading system, gave further impetus to global growth. China, while remaining an authoritarian state, further opened its economy to market principles and became a member of the World Trade Organization. And around the world, formerly insoluble problems suddenly appeared tractable. South Africa abandoned apartheid, and Latin America's nations became more democratic.

These system-level changes were both facilitated and catalyzed by technological and management changes. Faster transport and better communication broke down political and economic barriers and made producing enterprises more efficient. In turn, the new technology was developed and exploited by new management structures. Most major corporations adopted a product divisionalized form that facilitated growth to massive scale. In many countries, the companies worked in concert with government-supported centers of basic research. These arrangements permitted the development of vast global companies based on sourcing in the developing world, very efficient logistics networks for bringing goods to market in a timely fashion, and low-cost finance. At the level of the nation-state, policies were adopted that facilitated the rapid transfer and application of new technology and the relatively free flow of capital. At the international level, tariffs and other barriers to trade were reduced.

In this complex picture, there were many forces at work internationally, nationally, and within companies. But the result has been a period of unprecedented and broadly shared growth driven largely by the widespread adoption of market capitalism to a greater or lesser extent both within and across countries. The important practical question now, however, is whether this system can continue to generate wealth at these same rates in the future. More generally, what are the long-term prospects for the global economy and the market system that drives it?

The Bank Forecast: Our Base Case

One source of insight on this question comes from scenarios developed by the World Bank. As noted in chapter 1, we turned to the Bank's work as background for our forums with executives from Europe, Asia, Latin America, and the United States. At the time of our initial forums, the World Bank had just published an extensive study describing how the global economy and its components might look as far out as the year 2030. The study encompassed two scenarios—a central, or base-case, scenario and a high-growth scenario using assumptions that were more optimistic. Based on economic models developed at the Bank and elsewhere, the scenarios incorporated a number of studies on particular issues such as trends in income distribution, shifts in demography, patterns of migration, and environmental impacts. The result was a rich tapestry of data for understanding what the global economy might look like in 2030.

A brief review of the findings and projections that we used as a catalyst for our discussions may be useful for understanding what we heard from our business leaders. (Their own perspectives on the future of market capitalism will be the subject of chapter 3.) Readers may wonder about the validity of these projections, since they were developed just prior to the financial crisis in 2008. Although the study—the output of a major effort—has not yet been fully redone with input from the financial crisis, some postcrisis analysis conducted by the World Bank indicates that the long-term outlook has changed very little. While the near-term forecasts prepared before the crisis now seem to be somewhat optimistic, the long-term model continues to provide a useful picture of the world we are headed for.

This conclusion may seem counterintuitive, given the sharp economic downturn experienced by many countries in the wake of the crisis. But the slowdown has had some positive consequences for some poorer nations. For example, the decline in economic activity meant that food and fuel prices returned to lower levels. The World Bank's own conclusion is that the "longer-term prospects for developing countries have changed only modestly," because of the countries' long-term supply potential.[5] Indeed, analysts expect developing countries to make up for lost output from the recession by 2015 and, in the wake of the crisis, were projecting GDP per capita in developing countries to grow at 4.6 percent annually between 2010 and 2015.[6] The financial crisis has also reduced some of the gross imbalances in the system overall, with a higher savings rate in the United States moderating its very high negative trade imbalance.

Moreover, the Bank's forecasts do not have to be precise to be informative. Even if they are more optimistic in the short term than forecasts prepared after the crisis, the Bank's projections can provide useful insight into what the world might be like if the global market economy continues to develop in the decades ahead much as it has been developing in the past. Here, then, are some highlights of the World Bank study that we shared with participants in our forums.

More growth is possible—and growth will be faster in developing countries

Looking ahead toward 2030, the Bank's models show the world economy continuing to grow. The projected rate of world growth in per-capita income is somewhere between 2 and 3 percent annually.[7] The higher rate is associated with the high-growth scenario, but even the lower 2 percent exceeds the world's per-capita growth rate between 1980 and 2005 by 0.6 percent.[8] Of course, growth will not be uniform across countries. Collectively, low- and middle-income countries are expected to grow faster—at 3.1 to 4.5 percent—than high-income countries. In some developing regions, such as China, growth rates are projected to be considerably higher—averaging as high as 7 percent annually in the more optimistic scenario.

Developing countries' share of global wealth will increase, and the income gap will narrow

In light of these growth projections, the developing world's share of global wealth is expected to increase to 31 percent in 2030—up from 23 percent in 2005.[9] And the gap between average incomes in the developing world and those in the mature economies will narrow somewhat. The models show average incomes in low- and middle-income countries rising to 23 percent of those in high-income countries—compared with 16 percent in 2005.[10] Although the gap will still be considerable, millions of developing country residents will see significant improvement in their standard of living.

The global middle class will expand, and poverty will be reduced . . .

As incomes in developing countries increase, the global middle class will expand. In low- and middle-income countries, the population earning between $4,000 and $17,000 annually is projected to triple, from 4 percent (400 million) to almost 15 percent (1.2 billion) in 2030 (figure 2-1). Many in the lower-income portions of the population will move from positions outside the modern economy to positions on the lower rungs but still inside. Even the very poor will benefit—the

FIGURE 2-1

Percentage of population earning $4,000–$17,000 (purchasing power parity, per capita)

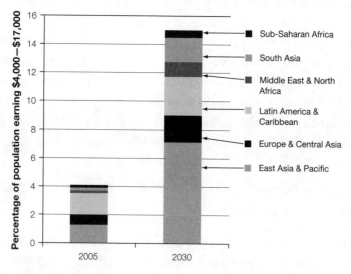

Source: Adapted from Richard Newfarmer et al., *Global Economic Prospects 2007: Managing the Next Wave of Globalization* (Washington, DC: The World Bank, 2007), xvi, fig. 7.

number of people living on less than $2 per day is expected to decrease by some 800 million. An important implication of the World Bank's study, then, is that globalization can benefit the poor.

. . . but growth will be uneven *across* countries, and sub-Saharan Africa may lag considerably

The World Bank's forecasts represent a dramatic improvement in the lives of millions of people, but as the authors of the study emphasize, there are important caveats. Despite the high rate of progress in low- and middle-income countries, incomes in those countries—particularly in sub-Saharan Africa—will still be noticeably lower than those in high-income countries (figure 2-2).

FIGURE 2-2

Per-capita income, 2005–2030, as percentage of per-capita income in high-income countries

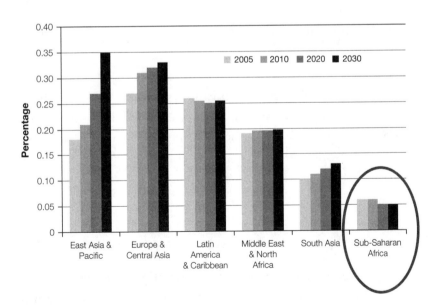

Source: Adapted from Richard Newfarmer et al., *Global Economic Prospects 2007: Managing the Next Wave of Globalization* (Washington, DC: The World Bank, 2007), xvii, fig. 8.

FIGURE 2-3

Population share in bottom decile of global income

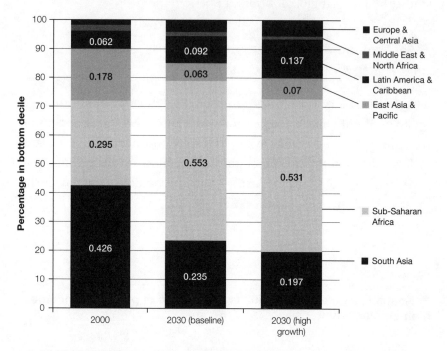

Source: Adapted from Richard Newfarmer et al., *Global Economic Prospects 2007: Managing the Next Wave of Globalization* (Washington, DC: The World Bank, 2007), 78, fig. 3.3.

As in the past, sub-Saharan Africa looks unlikely to keep up with growth elsewhere. Increases in the world population—expected to reach 8 billion by 2030—will be concentrated in developing countries, and the world's poor may well be concentrated in Africa, where more than half the world's poorest 10 percent are expected to reside (figure 2-3).

The benefits of growth will be unevenly spread *within* countries

Even within countries, the benefits of growth will not necessarily be evenly distributed. In the United States, for example, the gap between rich and poor has been increasing (figure 2-4). Even as the country as a whole has grown and the very rich have seen huge increases in their incomes and wealth, the poor have not grown richer for decades. As

FIGURE 2-4

Change in gap between 90th and 10th percentile earners, late 1970s to mid-1990s

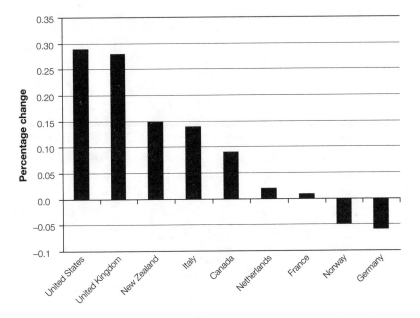

Source: Adapted from Richard Newfarmer et al., *Global Economic Prospects 2007: Managing the Next Wave of Globalization* (Washington, DC: The World Bank, 2007), 106, fig. 4.2, using data from Larry F. Katz and David H. Autor, "Changes in the Wage Structure and Earnings Inequality," in *Handbook of Labor Economics*, vol. 3A, ed. Orley C. Ashenfelter and David Card (Amsterdam: Elsevier, 1999).

figure 2-5 makes clear, the benefits of growth have gone to the top 60 percent and especially to the top 10 percent. Looking ahead and across the world, more than two-thirds of the low- and middle-income countries studied by the World Bank are expected to experience increases in income inequality despite high rates of overall growth.

Demographic changes will be strong drivers of increasing inequality

The reasons for increasing income inequality are complex. Income is the product of a country's workforce size and its productivity, and demographic shifts can have a major impact both on overall totals and on patterns of distribution. In countries where the population is aging,

FIGURE 2-5

U.S. real household income by percentile

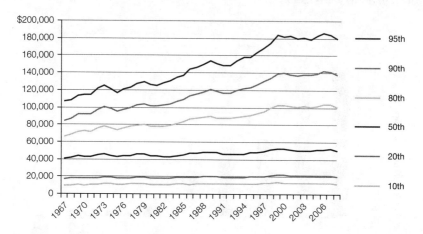

Source: Compiled from data in Carmen DeNavas-Walt, Bernadette D. Proctor, and Jessica C. Smith, "Selected Measures of U.S. Household Income Dispersion: 1967 to 2009," table A-2 in *Income, Poverty, and Health Insurance Coverage in the United States: 2009* (Washington, DC: U.S. Census Bureau, September 2010), 40–43, available at www.census.gov/prod/2010pubs/p60-238.pdf.

the burden of generating income falls on a shrinking portion of the workforce. A dramatic illustration is provided by Japan, where the over-65 population more than doubled and the working-age population shrank by more than 4 percent between 1985 and 2009.[11] By 2030, the number of over-65 citizens per 100 workers in Japan is expected to reach 63, compared with 16 in India.[12] A variant of this phenomenon plagues Africa, where AIDS has attacked the young adult population, leaving the elderly to care for the young.

Growth will worsen income disparities where barriers to mobility are high

Barriers to mobility can also skew the distribution of gains from growth. The Bank's analyses suggest that increasing people's ability to move from one sector of the economy to a better-paying one—from agriculture to manufacturing, for example—has a huge impact on reducing inequality. By the same token, where segments of the population are excluded from access to education or jobs for the educated—by discrimination against class, race, gender, tribe, or religion, for example—inequality actually worsens with growth. In other words, the rich get richer, and the divergence between rich and poor increases, because the rich are capturing the bulk of the gains. Simulations suggest that low mobility increases the Gini coefficient (a widely used measure of income inequality) by nearly ten points—a huge impact.[13] Low mobility also deprives the country of potential contributions to growth from the excluded segments of the population.

The increase in returns to skilled labor will be a major driver of inequality

The main driver of increasing income disparities, however, will be the increasing returns to skilled labor. As the investments and technology necessary for growth heighten the demand for skilled workers, the premium for skilled labor increases and the wage differential between skilled and unskilled workers diverges further. According to the projections shown in figure 2-6, the differential will be highest in regions where the poor are concentrated—in sub-Saharan Africa and South

FIGURE 2-6

Ratio of skilled to unskilled workers by region

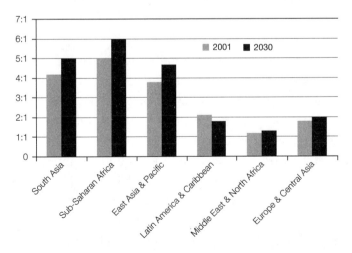

Source: Adapted from Richard Newfarmer et al., *Global Economic Prospects 2007: Managing the Next Wave of Globalization* (Washington, DC: The World Bank, 2007), xviii, fig. 9.

Asia. In these regions, barriers to mobility will mean that unskilled workers are trapped in low-paying, unskilled jobs.

Education will help spread the benefits of growth as long as mobility is high

The Bank's studies indicate that lack of education is the most widely shared attribute of those at the bottom of the income distribution. One implication is that access to education is crucial for managing inequality and spreading the benefits of growth. China's income distribution is changing quickly because as a matter of policy, tens of millions are moving from a relatively basic agricultural existence into urban centers where education permits them to join the market system. At the same time, the spread of modern agribusiness into the agricultural regions improves incomes there. Brazil and India are attempting to encourage the same change.

But education is not a panacea. Where growth is driven by higher productivity and the application of technology, for example, returns to education are high and a high proportion of the benefits from growth accrue to the educated. If education and income are also closely related, the top quintiles of the population benefit, leaving those in the bottom 40 percent behind. The Bank's analysis suggests that this dynamic may be one aspect of the rise in income inequality in the United States and the United Kingdom in recent decades.

Mobility is thus crucial. When there is no mobility, portions of the population can be stuck in low-paying jobs despite the progress of the global system and despite growth in the region or country. Companies may take advantage of the low wages, but the benefits of that economic activity do not go to the workers. Where oligarchs and government officials collude to capture the benefits of growth, economic exploitation of the workforce can continue for quite some time.[14] Only when the system runs into the limits of growth imposed by the uneducated and disenfranchised workforce does change from the top typically occur. The end of apartheid in South Africa, which we discuss in chapter 7, provides an unusual example of such change led in part by business leaders. More usual is the case where things do not change until there is some sort of violent upheaval.

Migration from poor countries to rich countries will increase

When income gaps across nations are significant, one result is migration from poor to rich countries, often with difficult political consequences in the recipient nations and economic and social problems in countries that have suffered the drain. According to World Bank figures, the number of immigrants in high-income countries grew from roughly 40 million in 1975 to more than 110 million in 2005. During this period, immigrants as a percentage of these recipient countries' populations nearly doubled, from around 6 percent to 11.4 percent (figure 2-7).

Authors of the Bank's study expect these trends to continue, despite the projected shrinkage of the wage gap between developing and mature economies and despite the political challenges that immigration poses for recipient nations. As noted earlier, even though incomes in developing countries will converge somewhat with incomes in the richer nations of North America, Western Europe, and Japan, a very

FIGURE 2-7

Immigrants as percentage of host population

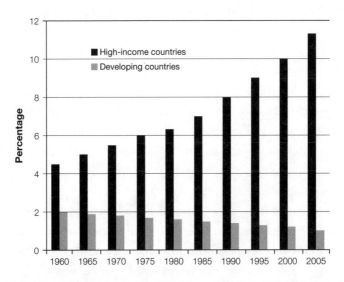

Source: Adapted from Richard Newfarmer et al., *Global Economic Prospects 2007: Managing the Next Wave of Globalization* (Washington, DC: The World Bank, 2007), 32, fig. 2-3.

noticeable gap will remain. If, as some estimate, average income in the rich countries reaches $100,000 in 2050—compared with $30,000 in developing countries—a sizable segment of the developing-country population will earn one-third of what their northern neighbors earn. For many in this lower-income group, migration to a richer country will be a very attractive option. Moreover, because of declining birth rates, high-income countries will increasingly need immigrant workers to supplement their native-born workforce. In the twenty-five countries that were members of the EU at the time of the study, for example, the natural increase in population has declined from 3.5 million a year in 1964 to something near 0.5 million, well less than what is needed to support economic growth. Net in-migration passed natural growth in 1989, reaching 1.5 million in recent years.

The politics of immigration does not always track its economics. A survey of a wide range of studies of the economic impacts of immigration found that there are large differences in economic impact, depending on the country of emigration and the age of the immigrant. The study also noted that the impact of immigration is affected by public-sector expense related to population size, and that the expense is considerably higher in Europe. The authors further observed that lack of access to employment opportunities in Europe compared with the United States has made immigration a greater problem in Europe, but that in any event, the net impact is quite small, whether estimated to be positive (the United States) or negative (Europe).[15] In both the United States and Europe, immigration is important to future economic growth, but most governments have found it nearly impossible to devise policies that successfully manage the reception and productive integration of immigrants into their societies. Although reform of immigration laws remains an unfulfilled objective in the United States, many commentators rate the nation's comparative ability to absorb immigrants successfully as exemplary.

The impacts of migration also vary widely among originating nations. There are countries like the Philippines, where the export of workers and the associated remittances are a critical component of the economy. And there are countries like Uganda, where the emigration of the highly skilled has had a significantly negative effect. The economic, social, and political impacts of immigration are thus quite varied, but immigration is likely to continue to be challenging for both the recipient nations and the originating ones—not to mention the immigrants themselves.

Large pools of unskilled workers in developing countries will be underemployed

Immigration is an important feature of the outlook for 2030, but the number of international migrants is ultimately small relative to the world's total population. Looking at the bigger picture and factoring in the projected demographic shifts, the Bank's models imply that with all the progress that can be anticipated in overall economic growth, there will be vast pools of unskilled labor sitting unemployed or underemployed in less developed countries. That is where almost all the growth in unskilled workers will be. Of the world's 4.1 billion workers in 2030, some 3.5 billion will be unskilled and some 3.3 billion will be located in developing countries (table 2-1).

Greenhouse gas emissions will continue to fuel global climate change

The primary focus of the World Bank study is economic growth and its implications for income distribution, labor issues, and migration

TABLE 2-1

Growth in global labor force

	All workers (millions)			Unskilled workers (millions)			Skilled workers (millions)		
	2001	2030	Annual growth (%)	2001	2030	Annual growth (%)	2001	2030	Annual growth (%)
World	3,077	4,114	1.03	2,674	3,545	0.98	403	598	1.37
High-income countries	481	459	−0.16	327	276	−0.58	154	183	0.60
Developing countries	2,596	3,684	1.21	2,347	**3,269**	1.15	249	415	1.78

Source: Adapted from Richard Newfarmer et al., *Global Economic Prospects 2007: Managing the Next Wave of Globalization* (Washington, DC: The World Bank, 2007), 110, table 4.2.

patterns, but the study also addresses global climate change and a number of other environmental issues that affect—and are affected by—patterns of growth. Drawing on work conducted by the UN's Intergovernmental Panel on Climate Change (IPCC), the World Bank report underscores the role of greenhouse gas emissions in global warming and spells out some of the likely human and environmental consequences of a continuation of carbon emissions at current levels.[16]

Some of the more catastrophic scenarios could affect the development of whole countries. And the brunt of the impact appears likely to fall on low-lying developing countries that are the least able to handle it. The anticipated spread of desertlike conditions in sub-Saharan Africa, for example, will only exacerbate the problems of poverty and income inequality discussed above.

According to papers produced by the IPCC, climate-change impacts considered virtually certain or very likely are increases in the frequency and duration of warm spells and heat waves, as well as heavy precipitation in many locales. The agricultural sector will be one of the hardest hit, with increasing agricultural yields in colder regions, decreasing yields in warmer ones, and damage to crops from soil erosion and water shortages. Other expected consequences include reductions in water available from snow melt, rising sea levels, increased demand for water, and water-quality problems. All of these impacts will be differentiated by region. None of this is any longer a surprise, but the consensus among scientists and disarray among national governments is disturbing.

Of course, the actual extent and impact of climate change over the long term will depend on what is done to mitigate it in the meantime. The IPPC's work on the possibilities of mitigation indicates that there is much room for governments to shape incentives that encourage households and firms to reduce their carbon emissions. Improvements are possible in almost every sector: in the production and use of energy (supply and distribution efficiencies, renewable resources, carbon capture and storage, advanced nuclear power and solar); in transport (more efficient vehicles, shifts from road to rail, second-generation biofuels, more powerful and efficient batteries); in homes and industry (more efficient buildings and factories); in agriculture (improved crop and grazing yields, reduction of methane emissions, and energy efficiency); in forestry; and in waste management. In most of these sectors, the technology to increase energy efficiency and reduce carbon emissions is commercially available today.

Importantly, the IPCC has found that the cost of reducing carbon emissions is low when expressed as a percentage of GDP growth rates. Given the huge long-term costs associated with climate change, the difficulty in reaching agreement among nations is surprising.

A peculiar aspect of climate change is that its manifestations are global and they affect the quality of life without respect to the geographic source of the aggravating influence. In fact, all nations have an interest in cooperating on the amelioration of global climate change. Unfortunately, reaching effective agreements among the major nations has been difficult as long-industrialized nations have demanded from developing nations efforts that are comparable to their own and the developing nations assert the right to catch up with the nations that "caused" the problem over the past decades. Fortunately, important individual nations are moving on their own to reduce carbon emissions. For example, China is now reportedly a leader in the installation of greenhouse gas (GHG) capture technology in new electric power facilities.

Increasing demand will put stress on the availability and quality of freshwater

Water is another challenge in achieving sustainable growth. In many regions, intensifying use of this relatively fixed resource by industrial manufacturing and agriculture is leading to deterioration in the availability and quality of water. Some three-fifths of the world's estimated annual water use can be attributed to agriculture.

Of particular importance is the uneven distribution of freshwater. Research cited in the World Bank study indicates that over 600 million people in developing countries face acute shortages of freshwater today and projects that 2 to 3 billion people around the world may face severe shortages by 2020. In the United States, the city of Denver is expected to experience shortages in 2016, even with conservation efforts, and water is being rationed to California agriculture.[17]

Studies have shown that with appropriate political agreements and proper pricing, water can be used far more effectively. It is uneconomic in the extreme for scarce water from the Rocky Mountains to be used for growing cotton in the U.S. Southwest. In the Middle East, the water from Northeast Turkey and Iraq is adequate to support the region's development if political agreements can be reached.

When the effects of climate change are factored into the water picture, the situation worsens. Forecasts show decreased water resources in many semiarid areas, including the western United States and the Mediterranean basin. And as noted earlier, scientists generally agree that climate change will almost certainly lead to an expansion of the Sahara and the drying out of North Africa.

Other factors will also affect the future of the economy

This summary of the "case" for our business leader forums covers only a few of the key findings from the World Bank's comprehensive analysis of the global economy to 2030. An even more comprehensive analysis would incorporate additional elements and probe the implications of growth for other facets of the economy. The World Bank itself has looked at other factors in other studies.

For instance, in a separate study, the Bank examined the impact of economic growth on the availability and price of resources, especially commodities.[18] The nearly fourfold rise in oil and metal prices since 2000 ended in early 2008, but it provides a good illustration of the uneven impact of market prices on development. Weaker nations, in particular, are vulnerable to the supply-and-demand effects of rapid growth in China and other importing developing nations. When prices of commodities rise, the effect is to aggravate inequalities in income and the quality of life across regions.

Although the collapse of oil and metal prices in early 2008 significantly offset the negative impacts of the financial crisis on importing, developing nations (while hurting the oil exporters), the tensions arising from increasing prices for commodities and other essentials must figure significantly as sources of political instability in any attempt to develop scenarios for long-term economic development. And the prices of oil and other commodities have resumed their climb as the

global economy recovers. The ability to manage the uneven consequences of major shifts in prices, like the ability to manage the uneven
impacts of major environmental shifts, can have a significant impact on
growth.

Reacting to the Forecast:
Hope for the Best, or Assume the Worst?

The picture provided by the World Bank's studies is complex and
decidedly mixed. On the positive side, the forecast of continuing global growth—at rates possibly exceeding those of the past two
decades—is encouraging. As discussed earlier, the middle class in
developing nations will triple and the percentage of people living on
$2 per day or less will decline. More worrisome are projected increases
in income inequality both within and across nations, and the expected
rise in global temperatures due to increasing greenhouse gas emissions. Tensions and conflicts over these issues could easily flare up in
ways that would derail the projected growth scenario.

Even if the picture is a roughly accurate description of how things
are likely to go under a "steady ahead" regime, difficult questions of
interpretation and evaluation remain. The picture itself cannot say
how we should react to it. Nor can it tell us how seriously to take the
potential risks presented. Should we accentuate the positives or focus
on the negatives? Should we hope for the best or assume the worst? Is
the future of market capitalism clear, or are there storm clouds on the
horizon? As we will see in chapter 3, the business leaders with whom
we discussed this forecast were quite concerned.

It is possible that the potential problems, if they arise at all, will be
no worse than the limited shocks of the last half century. The oil crises
of 1973 and 1982, the U.S. rust bowl of the mid-1980s, the Japanese
slowdown of the 1990s, the Asian financial crisis, and the dot-com bust
all influenced the global economy, but, as it turned out, ultimately
nudged it off track only slightly (figure 2-8). If these events and this
period are taken as analogues for interpreting the Bank's projections,
the outlook to 2030, while presenting significant challenges, would
appear to be largely favorable. From the vantage point of 2030 looking

FIGURE 2-8

Ten-year per-capita real GDP growth

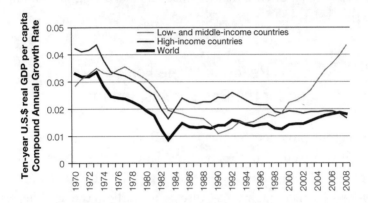

Source: Compiled from data in International Monetary Fund, *World Economic Outlook: Rebalancing Growth* (Washington, DC: IMF, April 2010), data file for fig.1.2 available at www.imf.org/external/pubs/ft/weo/2010/01 /index.htm.

back, the economy's growth over the previous two decades will have closely tracked the Bank's forecasts.

A very different possibility is that the potential problems will fester into major disruptions that seriously undermine the global economy's projected growth. When the World Bank analysts went back to the future and applied today's economic modeling techniques to circumstances as they would have appeared in 1900, the forecasts generated for the early twentieth century looked quite promising. Like the present, that too was a period in which liberal economic thought celebrated the progress of unfettered capitalism. But things didn't work out as projected. Political and economic mismanagement gave the world two great wars and a global business slump of gigantic proportions. As figure 2-9, from the Bank's report, makes clear, geopolitics and the Great Depression upset progress so much that the GDP for France, Germany, Japan, the United Kingdom, and the United States (today's G-5 countries) followed the lower bound of forecasts. By 1949, actual GDP was below the lower bound by an amount equivalent to 13 percent of actual output.[19]

Taking the first half of the twentieth century (rather than the last half) as the analogue for interpreting the World Bank study leads to a considerably less sanguine assessment. The projected income

FIGURE 2-9

G-5 GDP: forecast versus reality, 1900–1949

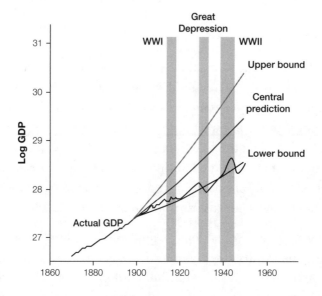

Source: Based on Maddison 2001 and World Bank staff estimates, as reproduced in Richard Newfarmer et al. *Global Economic Prospects 2007: Managing the Next Wave of Globalization* (Washington, DC: The World Bank, 2007), 55, box 2.2.

Note: GDP is expressed as a natural log (mathematical convention used to facilitate comparison of numbers over time) in millions of 1990 international dollars (a hypothetical unit of currency used to facilitate cross-country comparisons).

disparities and resource stresses implicit in the scenario for 2030 are no longer minor blemishes on an otherwise compelling canvas, but are potential sources of tension and rivalry that, under the right circumstances, could erupt into major disruptors of the world economy.

A concrete description of how this gloomy scenario might unfold has been developed by the U.S. National Intelligence Council (NIC). In an exercise quite independent of our study but launched at roughly the same time, the council engaged some two hundred people from forty countries in a scenario-building project. The group imagined the world as it might develop under three scenarios corresponding to whether the forces discussed above evolve in a benign, muddled, or malevolent fashion. The published report *NIC Global Scenarios to 2025* essentially shows that poverty, worsening gaps in income within and between nations and regions, economic migration, the management of energy resources and water, and global climate change can become time bombs if allowed to trigger cycles of mistrust and conflict.[20] Consider this synopsis of the report's "Borrowed Time" scenario as it unfolds through 2025:

From 2009 to 2012

- With a failure of the Doha trade negotiations, protectionist sentiment in the United States and Europe feed off each other as pressure from the great recession eases very slowly and commitments to openness wane. Populist sentiment dominates the U.S. midterm elections, and the new Congress rescinds several trade agreements, including the North American Free Trade Agreement (NAFTA). European anger over faulty medicines from India and China leads to a ban on imported pharmaceuticals.

- Nuclear states put reductions on hold as ambiguity over the Iranian situation leads other nations to accelerate their programs. Saudi Arabia announces a multibillion-dollar assistance package to Pakistan—a deal that is generally believed to be a quid pro quo for nuclear know-how. The United Nations Security Council is unable to agree on sanctions over Iranian and North Korean testing. The multipolar world, in which U.S. leadership is limited, poses growing pains for many nations.

- India and China withdraw from post-Kyoto rounds after it becomes apparent that the United States and Europe will team up and insist on deep emission cuts for all. Emissions from China, now the world's largest carbon dioxide (CO_2) producer, continue to rise. Despite evidence that global warming is accelerating, major nations continue to focus on the weak economy.

- The populations of the poorest nations continue to increase with the rise in fertility rates, despite the AIDS epidemic.

From 2013 to 2021

- Growth in the BRIC countries decelerates sharply as exports weaken. The price of oil crashes after news of the slowdown in

China and India spreads. Russia exerts political influence in the former Soviet Union to influence prices on its imports, while working with Iran to create an organization like OPEC for natural gas.

- The energy crisis precipitates a great power rivalry in the Middle East as weapons are used as currency in the fight for long-term access to energy resources.

- Growing unemployment in Europe and the United States leads to a near cessation of immigration while recent Muslim migrants in Europe are subjected to separation from their communities. Riots erupt in French cities. Al Qaeda in the Islamic Maghreb announces a reverse crusade to retake Spain. A dirty bomb attack occurs in Granada. More terrorist attacks take place in Europe and Russia, with links established to groups of scientists working in Europe and the United States.

- Ten percent of Bangladesh is submerged after a devastating cyclone. The disaster sets off serious border tensions with India as the migration of millions leads to a debate in the United Nations as to whether the displaced people are climate or economic refugees.

- The bioweapon attack and discovery of the network of scientists leads to a decline in scientific cooperation across borders. The internet is monitored closely. Intellectual exchange and cooperation are limited. And research and innovation slow down in a variety of areas.

From 2022 to 2025

- Political problems in China develop, as faulty construction of projects leading to large numbers of deaths is discovered to be the responsibility of certain party officials who have secreted funds in Switzerland. Trials are announced.

- A deepening global recession leads to political change in several nations, each country focusing on its own issues. In Iran, a reform government struggles with the ayatollah. Russia, China, and India develop greater trade with Iran in return for access to Iranian gas fields. Western energy companies stay out.

- Turmoil affects governments in Egypt, France, Italy, and Holland. The scramble for resources between China and India continues, with the primary beneficiaries being corrupt governments in sub-Saharan Africa.

- Territorial conflicts emerge in the Arctic; Chinese and Japanese navies trade shots near the Spratly Islands. Rioters set embassies on fire in Tokyo and Beijing.

Of course, this bleak scenario is only one of many possibilities, but it underscores a crucial point: how companies, governments, and other institutions deal with the issues raised by the World Bank study can have a material impact on the ability of the global market system to function. How business and other leaders view the projected developments—and whether leaders see these developments as positive or as problematic for the future of market capitalism—is thus central to how the forces are likely to play out. In the next chapter, we turn to the views of the business leaders with whom we spoke about these issues. One former CEO's reaction to the World Bank study provides a preview:

> The biggest concern I have over a very long period of time is that, if the World Bank numbers we looked at are anywhere near correct, we're going to have an awful lot of people disenfranchised and not benefitting from the capitalistic system, even though economies in general will be. History tells us that when an awful lot of people are disenfranchised, they have no incentive to play by the rules, and given today's communications availability, weaponry, [and things of this nature], that's an issue we have to really think about, probably over a very long period of time. (U.S. forum)

Threats to the Global Market System

THE MODELING by the World Bank discussed in chapter 2 provides reason for some optimism. The forces *of* market capitalism, and the forces *for* market capitalism, seem to have been gathering strength. Even after the impact of the 2008 financial crisis is considered, long-term prospects show reasonable growth. The global middle class grows, and the gap between the mature, rich nations and the growing, developing nations narrows. But there are also challenges. The benefits of growth will not be evenly spread across countries or within countries, and collateral damage to the environment will be significant. Scarce resources will be consumed, and the world's climate will continue to change.

How should we view these challenges? Can they be dealt with through standard operating procedures, or do they represent potentially major threats to continued global growth or even to market capitalism itself? Are there important challenges ahead that are not addressed in the World Bank study? Many of the concerns raised by the Bank's work seem to arise from the inner workings of capitalism—to be, as it were, potential *threats from within*. What about *threats from without*? Are there forces originating from outside the market system that might undercut its future performance or operate in ways that are antithetical to its continued expansion—or even its very existence?

Consider, for example, breakdowns in the rule of law, the rise of religious fundamentalism, or the spread of illness and disease.

When we put these questions to business leaders from Europe, Asia, Latin America, and the United States, we heard a wide range of opinions expressed from varying perspectives. What they told us, though, might be summed up in a sentence: Market capitalism has proven to be a golden goose providing historically unimaginable economic benefits to many, and if we don't look out, we may kill it. In other words, many saw the challenges to capitalism—both from within and from without—as very serious indeed. Drawing from their own extensive knowledge and experience with businesses across the world, these leaders offered a range of observations on emerging forces and threats that have the potential to disrupt the capitalist system in serious ways.

In this chapter we offer a synthesis and analysis of their observations. In reviewing our transcripts, notes, and recollections from the business leader forums, we have sought to draw out the central themes and organize them into coherent lines of argument and analysis. This exercise led us to ten major lines of argument describing active forces that could significantly disrupt the success of the free-market system. While the lines of argument are not perfectly separable—at the edges, they overlap or reference one another—they are for the most part reasonably distinct. Together they constitute a significant array of forces potentially directed at the heart of capitalism. (In chapter 4, we will consider in more detail how these forces relate to one another systemically.)

Frequently, as our discussions continued, participants turned from a focus on one or several of these ten forces to consider why *existing* institutions are not adequate to the challenge of addressing these matters. Many and perhaps all of the threatening trends and forces the leaders identified are already visible, they noted—so why aren't these problems being resolved by the institutions and processes put in place to establish and protect the free-market exchange of goods, services, and capital?

As a result of these discussions, we formulated an eleventh line of argument, focused on why existing institutions seem inadequate to cope with the ten active disrupting forces we identified. While this eleventh concern does not identify a separate force in itself (but instead explains why the other forces may not be successfully contained), it nonetheless frames a potential need for prescription and intervention in much the same way that the ten active forces do. In the second part of the book, starting with chapter 5, we explore the role that business can play in helping combat the disruptive forces and institutional weaknesses discussed in our forums and summarized below.

The Perceived Threats: The Disruptors

Our synthesis and interpretation of the discussions we heard suggest that the potential disruptors of the global market system can be usefully grouped into these eleven areas: the functioning of the global financial system; barriers to world trade; inequality and consequent populism; migration; environmental degradation; failure of the rule of law; failures of education and public health; state capitalism; radical movements and terrorism; pandemics; and the inadequacy of existing institutions. This is a long list—and the ability of the market capitalist system to prosper depends on positive developments in each of these areas.

As noted, these forces are not independent: a serious breakdown of one will easily destroy the trust necessary for progress on the others. The challenge for governments is daunting. The challenges for businesses with a long-term view may be even larger. But the challenge will be made worse if the participants in the system aggravate the problems that tax the system. In light of the growth of regressive and inward-looking political movements in the United States, there would seem to be a real chance that exactly this sort of aggravation may develop. We consider each of the disruptive forces in turn.

The Financial System

As financial markets currently function, trillions of dollars move around the world daily at very high velocities. New financial products are introduced regularly to permit investors to hedge positions or speculators to make bets on the price movements of these products or the assets to which they are linked. There is nothing inherently dangerous about these flows as long as the assets and liabilities involved are transparent and understood and hence can be reliably valued by those buying and selling them. When instead the underlying claims are obscure or poorly understood—so that they are subject to significant swings in value as new information about them becomes apparent—the risks to the stability of the overall financial system are profound. These risks to "financial" assets can be transmitted to the "real" economy of employment, manufacturing, products, services, and trade—through their effects on banks. When the assets and liabilities that these claims represent show up on the balance sheets of the banks and "nonbanks" (financial organizations that resemble banks in their structure and actions but are not regulated as banks under most current law and practice) that provide credit necessary for the functioning of the real economy, then problems can develop. A decline in the value of those *derivative assets* then affects the ability of the economy to function by undermining the asset side of lenders' balance sheets. If the value of the derivative assets shrinks, the lender's equity also shrinks, reducing its ability to make loans. One result can be a collapse in the availability of normal financing of trade.

The financial crisis of 2008 provides an illustration. That year, the financial system was subjected to extraordinary shocks. In both the United States and Europe, banks and nonbanks grew very large through the use of very high levels of debt, most of which was very short term—often overnight. This leverage permitted firms to earn high profits on trading and on the issuance of derivative securities despite relatively low margins on individual transactions. In the United States, some investment banks operated with debt-to-equity levels of 30 to 1 and with even higher levels between reporting periods. In Europe, leverage at banks reached 100 to 1, as derivatives were used to reframe balance sheets so as to satisfy the requirements of the intergovernmental Basel II accords. Over time, as the market for the derivative products slowed, those products ended up on the balance sheets of their issuers, financed by further debt. Systemic risk grew exponentially. In 2008, the financial products group of AIG eventually issued credit default obligations with a notional value of $1.6 trillion.[1] At its peak, the credit default obligations had a face value of $62.1 billion against no dedicated reserves.[2] When assets underlying these transactions were found flawed, values plummeted and the system froze as banks and nonbanks refrained from lending to each other out of fear of the unknown quality of counterparty balance sheets. The efforts of the United States, the United Kingdom, and other governments to restore confidence to the system were not proven until early 2010. By early 2011, it remained to be seen whether the rebound of the global economy is sustainable. Table 3-1 shows the World Bank's 2010 estimates of the impact of financial collapse on the global economy. While the percentage declines are not huge, the pervasiveness of the slowdown is unprecedented in the postwar period, and the absolute declines devastating.

Another crisis of this sort is the first contingency on our list. Even though a breakdown in the financial system was not the number one threat flagged in our forums, business leaders in all regions worried

TABLE 3-1

The recovering global economy (percentage change from previous year, excluding interest rates and oil prices)

	Percent change, by year[a]			
	2008	2009	2010e	2011f
Real GDP growth[b]				
World[c]	**1.5**	**−2.2**	**3.9**	**3.3**
High income	0.2	−3.4	2.8	2.4
OECD countries	0.1	−3.5	2.7	2.3
Euro area	0.3	−4.1	1.7	1.4
Japan	−1.2	−6.3	4.4	1.8
United States	0	−2.6	2.8	2.8
Non-OECD countries	2.5	−1.8	6.7	4.4
China	9.6	9.1	10	8.7
Russia	5.2	−7.9	3.8	4.2
Brazil	5.1	−0.2	7.6	4.4
India	5.1	7.7	9.5	8.4
Sub-Saharan Africa	5.2	1.7	4.7	5.3
World trade volume	**2.7**	**−11**	**15.7**	**8.3**

a. e = estimate; f = forecast.

b. Aggregate growth rates calculated using constant 2005 dollars GDP weights.

c. Calculated using 2005 purchasing-power-parity weights.

Source: Adapted from the World Bank, http://web.worldbank.org/external/default/main?contentMDK=20675180&menuPK=612509&theSitePK=612501&pagePK=2904583&piPK=2904598 (April 18, 2011).

about the tensions created by the powerful forces in the financial economy and the lack of transparency into those forces. In every meeting, they commented on the increasing complexity of the global financial system and the difficulty of regulating it.

The comments that follow give a sense for the unease expressed at our European forum in Paris in 2007:

> There's been a big development of the financial world, which obviously is benefiting the capitalistic system, but is also developing in its own ways—ways that are not necessarily consistent with what society considers to be good. There is a lot of discussion about private equity and hedge funds. Private equity groups, in many instances, are playing a useful role, but they are shortening the horizon of companies. So how do we make it consistent that we can have this flow of capital going to private equity and that we still have a long-term development of the economy, of innovation, research, et cetera? (Europe forum)

> My only issue is, if we extrapolate the trend, where are we going? And if we extrapolate the trend, what kind of reaction will happen or will not happen? There is a lot of accountability for big industrial companies. But there's absolutely no accountability for financial institutions, and there cannot be any accountability, because it's an international network. (Europe forum)

> Control the financial forces? Nobody understands what they're doing. Derivatives, for example: I've seen a paper by a professor from the University of Texas who describes situations where an investor is using short sales to increase their holdings in a company which they want to take over. So they voted at the shareholders meeting of the target company so as to destroy the value of the target company. It's just an example. So maybe this kind of thing can be checked. But there are so many possibilities, nobody is able, really, to understand what's happening and what [to do] to control it. (Europe forum)

One participant distinguished between private equity's use of debt and the role of large hedge funds, again expressing wariness as to where the markets were headed:

> The private equity firms, I think, are not very far from the sort of institutional transparency we'd seek by the way . . . The second segment, which is quite different, not transparent at all, and from my viewpoint dangerous for the balance of the world system, I would [say is] the hedge funds—they are completely different from the private equity [firms]—and the use by the hedge funds of all the derivative instruments that they can. (Europe forum)

But we heard similar comments elsewhere, for example, at our Asia forum in Hong Kong:

> One question is, can you sustain market capitalism in the face of heterogeneity and beliefs at the national level about [private equity financing]? And then also . . . the things that are necessary for market capitalism—the flows of people, skills, capital, et cetera, and devise a rule structure that we can agree on, when the underlying linchpins of that at the national level are not clear. (Asia forum)

Some of the forum participants viewed the short term with some perspicacity:

> All this is fine if you don't have a very severe economic slowdown. If we have a very severe economic slowdown . . . The problem we will see is that the financing they're getting is then sold together with these collateralized debt deals. The CDOs [collateralized debt obligations] are then all sold to a bunch of investors. At the end of the day, who will be the guys holding these liabilities? We have no idea today. (Europe forum)

While the majority urged the importance of greater transparency in the financial system, some questioned that prescription:

> I tend to believe that the world is becoming more and more transparent. And today, it's more transparent than it was twenty or thirty years ago. I think that what is becoming more and more difficult is regulation. It is much more difficult to regulate in general than it used to be ten, twenty, thirty years ago. (Europe forum)

The State of Trade

A breakdown in trade and the trading system is a second factor that could severely disrupt the growth scenario of chapter 2. As the financial collapse of 2008 demonstrated all too clearly, a breakdown in trade can occur precipitously and with far-reaching effects for the economy and society. The reduction in asset values experienced by industrial companies, consumers, and financial institutions during the meltdown was accompanied by a decline in consumer demand and industrial output everywhere. With finance frozen, world trade slowed dramatically. Figure 3-1 shows the steepness of the declines. Total world trade declined 2.8 percent in 2009, the first decline since World War II.

Threats to trade were on the minds of business leaders even before the crisis:

> There is another threat for the capitalism nowadays, and the threat is the protectionist wave that we have in countries, not only talking about U.S. but also talking about Europe. And I think it's very important to see it as a threat for capitalism, to face this brutal fact, and also to open the discussion not only among governments but also with businesspeople and all the other entities that can contribute with this. (Latin America forum)

FIGURE 3-1

Growth in global trade

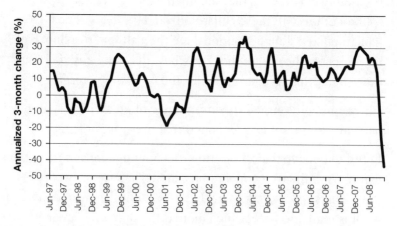

Source: Compiled from data in International Monetary Fund, "World Economic Outlook: An Update of the Key WEO Projections," January 28, 2009, fig. 2.

A glance at history suggests that such concerns about protectionism, which we heard in various parts of the world, are well founded. Observing how nations deal with the unemployment associated with the postcrisis downturn and the attendant political challenge to imports brings to the mind of every economist over the age of fifty memories of Charles Kindleberger's chart of trade implosion during the 1930s (figure 3-2).

As the chart shows, the argument works in both directions. Weaker economies lead to the decline of trade. But the decline of trade also weakens economies. One political consequence of economic decline is political pressure from companies and unions to lessen competition from imports and immigrants. Protectionism sets off reciprocal actions by other countries, slowing agriculture, mining, and manufacturing everywhere. That is the dismal path charted by Kindleberger. And it is a path that worried our leaders:

> There's two types of threats. The first is that you get trade and investment retaliation on the back of growth. And the second is that you actually get people, for their own reasons—good or bad—actually start[ing] to question whether market capitalism is an appropriate model. (Asia forum)

The differences between the declines throughout the 1930s and the progress forecasted by the International Monetary Fund after the recent trade collapse lies in the aggressive fiscal stimulus and the automatic stabilizers put in place by the OECD governments and the similar aggressive moves by China and Latin America. Governments initially acted in parallel rather than together, but in sum, their efforts are expected to have a positive impact, as shown in table 3-1.

Energy trade is a special case. Because energy is so important to modern economies, the state of trade in energy is critical. Imbalances can wreck the prospects of supplier or customer nations and reshape the balance of power among them. The relationship between the availability and the price of fossil fuel has been a major subtheme of recent history. Consider the move of the British into Mesopotamia in the early twentieth century to assure oil for its fleet, the Japanese invasion of Southeast Asia in the late 1930s in response at least in part to the U.S. oil embargo, and OPEC's use of the "oil weapon" in 1973 and 1978 to take advantage of extremely tight supply-demand situations.

FIGURE 3-2

The collapse of world trade, 1929–1933

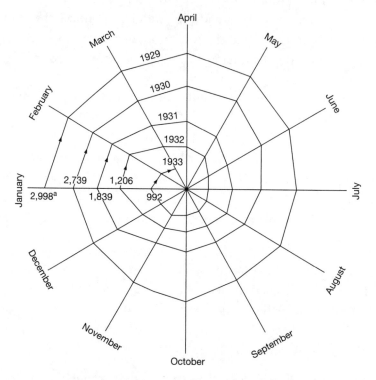

a. Numbers refer to total imports of 75 countries, in millions of dollars.

Source: Charles Kindleberger, *The World in Depression 1929-1939* (Berkeley: University of California Press, 1986 [revised and enlarged edition]), 172.

These actions are just four of the many incidents in which shifts in the energy economy have had dramatic effects on the global economy—and therefore also on global political affairs.

A central aspect of modern economies is their dependence on the widespread availability of relatively inexpensive energy in the form of hydrocarbon fuels. Modern transportation, production, and domestic life—not to mention warfare—require energy, particularly for electrical power and for transportation. A great deal of the economic development of emerging nations is also premised on the availability of hydrocarbon fuels. For example, the remarkable economic growth of China has been associated with a staggering increase in the generation of electricity and the consumption of gasoline (table 3-2). Chinese foreign policy is no less concerned with the availability of fuel than was British policy a century earlier.

The same focus on fuel is apparent in the plans and actions of Russia, Brazil, and India. Indeed, Vladimir Putin's domestic policy and foreign policy seem to be grounded in thinking about Russian hydrocarbon resources that he first developed in his doctoral thesis. Brazil has devoted thirty years to developing its energy policies.

But the pattern of energy development has other effects. Consider, for example, Saudi Arabia, where the social and political tensions produced by the country's post-1973 oil wealth and conspicuous consumption in the context of a fundamentally feudal political structure fueled the rise of jihadi fundamentalism. Regardless of the specifics, wherever governments throughout the world have been weak, tenfold swings in the price of oil have had destabilizing effects on developing nations—whether the nations are producers or consumers of oil.

Because oil prices are a primary driver of food prices, oil shocks have a disproportionate impact on the poor. Table 3-3 shows the effect of rising food prices on consumption by the poor in developing countries between 2006 and 2008.[3]

TABLE 3-2

Consumption of energy and petroleum in China

Year	Energy consumption (million tons of standard coal equivalent)	Percentage of energy imported	Petroleum as percentage of consumption	Imports as percentage of petroleum consumption
2000	1,455	9.8	15.5	43.3
2001	1,504	9.0	15.2	39.8
2002	1,594	9.9	15.5	41.4
2003	1,838	10.9	14.8	48.6
2004	2,135	12.5	14.9	54.5
2005	2,360	11.4	13.8	52.7
2006	2,587	12.1	13.5	55.8
2007	2,805	12.5	13.1	57.7
2008	2,915	12.6	12.8	61.7
2009	3,067			

Source: CEIC China Premium database, www.ceicdata.com.

TABLE 3-3

Food price hikes and consumption

Region	Percent increase in food prices, 2006–2008	Food as percentage of household expenditures
Rural population		
East Asia & Pacific	12.4	71.5
Europe & Central Asia	−0.2	63.4
Latin America & Caribbean	6.9	51.2
Middle East & North Africa	25.9	64.5
South Asia	5	65.3
Sub-Saharan Africa	9.6	68
Developing world	6.7	66.1
Urban population		
East Asia & Pacific	13.8	67.5
Europe & Central Asia	−0.5	57.9
Latin America & Caribbean	1.6	44.1
Middle East & North Africa	12.5	57.1
South Asia	4.8	64.4
Sub-Saharan Africa	4.9	53
Developing world	4.1	60.4

Source: Andrew Burns et al., *Global Economic Prospects 2009: Commodities at the Crossroads* (Washington, DC: The World Bank, 2009), 11.

Oil prices also have major implications for national politics and strategy. In Russia, the rise in the price of oil in the first part of this decade has been linked to the centralization of power in the Russian presidency; the rise has enabled the central government to subsidize an otherwise inefficient economy.[4] Figure 3-3 shows the impact of oil price changes on the Russian economy.[5]

A very different example is provided by Brazil, a country that has adopted a policy of energy independence through development of local renewable fuel, primarily ethanol from sugar cane. While the state oil company Petrobras has enjoyed notable success with its exploration off the Brazilian coast—these finds were fortuitous in that they have accelerated the way to independence—rather than being crucial to its possibility. As a consequence, Brazil has benefited from a considerable ability to pursue national policies independent of the state of global energy.

FIGURE 3-3

Russian oil production and GDP

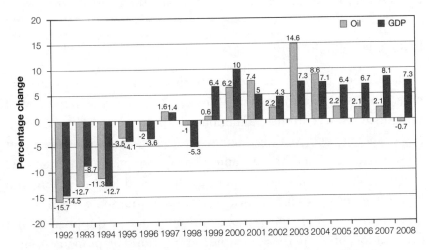

Source: Marshall Goldman, *Petrostate: Putin, Power, and the New Russia* (Oxford: Oxford University Press, 2008).

By way of contrast, China is remarkably dependent on the state of the global energy economy. The legacy of arrangements between the major oil companies of the rich Western nations and the established producer nations has left China scrambling to lock up short- and long-term petroleum reserves for its own use. This has on occasion left it dealing closely with nations, such as Sudan, that China might otherwise want to treat with more distance and has precipitated conflicts with neighboring Vietnam over ownership of offshore fields. The scarcity of oil has also led China to rely heavily on relatively dirty coal-fired power plants—despite a rapidly growing understanding of the second-order costs of pollution—to provide the electricity needed by the nation's growing industries and cities. Only recently has China begun using modern technology for its coal-based power.

The World Bank scenarios discussed in chapter 2 are based on assumptions that the energy economy develops at a pace adequate to support continued economic growth and at prices that do not interfere with growth. As shown by the impact of oil price changes such as those in the 2006–2007 period in both consuming and producing nations, the functioning of the economy is highly sensitive to the state of the energy trade. Breakdowns in that trade or in trade, more generally, could severely disrupt the market system and the Bank's scenarios.

Inequality and Populism

By far the most widely held concern, the one regarded by our business leaders as the most significant challenge, is the tendency of capitalism as it currently functions to produce extreme disparities of income and wealth. Executives from all regions worried that these extremes could breed—and, in some regions, seem now to be breeding—a form of populist politics that could lead to severe and harmful government interventions such as burdensome bureaucratic regulation of market transactions and outcomes, expropriation and confiscation of property, and other abrogations of property rights. Under these conditions, investors would be far less willing to support and sustain capital flows, which would, in turn, lead ultimately away from a sustainable free-market economy. To many observers, vast accumulations of individual wealth and extreme inequalities in income and in value captured from the success of individual firms—and the relatively stagnant inflation-adjusted earnings of low- and middle-income workers in most regions—appear to have fueled populist movements and a political backlash against capitalism (and, not incidentally, capitalists).

A number of elements raised by different observers fit into this general complex. Some leaders pointed to what they regard as excessive compensation earned by CEOs, observing that packages amounting to tens and sometimes hundreds of millions of dollars in a given year strike many people as intrinsically unjustified. Others pointed to the development of enclave communities, where extremely wealthy families live behind armed barricades to insulate themselves and keep themselves secure from a rising tide of violence that includes kidnapping, extortion, and armed robbery. Still other forum participants referred to what they see as a spreading sense among lower-income communities that the success of capitalism and corporations has little to do with them and has done little to lift their standards of living.

The participants in our forums, including this European executive, spoke frequently to this point:

> There are a lot of issues. The first one is the increase of inequality within countries and between different countries. I could say that between different countries, the only countries which do not benefit from globalization and the free-market economy are ones where the political system, governance system, and social system just cannot address the open free-market. (Europe forum)

This comment concisely expresses a key problem: where national governance is weak or corrupt, the benefits of market capitalism are not shared. One of the Asian executives also spoke to this point and spelled out a troubling implication:

> Herein lies a major challenge, because the world has become very much more prosperous as a result of market capitalism. The rich have become richer. The poor in most cases have also become richer. But the gap between the rich and the poor has also grown wider, as the poor have grown richer. Now everyone can see how each other lives, and there is this growing sense of being left out, even as people are getting better off. And I think this poses enormous challenges for business and for market capitalism because you cannot achieve a sense of legitimacy— you cannot have moral credibility—if large numbers of people believe that the system doesn't work for them or is unjust to them. (Asia forum)

One European participant linked inequality to changes in governance:

> It reminds me of [the old idea] that the manager should not earn more than forty times the salary of the lowest-paid income. And in the old days, shareholders delegated operations to the managers. But what we have seen in the last years is an increasing power of the shareholder as such. And they are making managers part of the shareholders community. That's why in the States, the rule of one to forty is now like one to five hundred. And that explains a lot of what is happening in these respects in the company. (Europe forum)

An executive in Asia expressed concerns specifically related to trends in China:

> We really need to focus on the entire distribution of income, most particularly the tails [of the income-distribution curve], for different reasons. On the lower end, I think the alleviation of poverty is absolutely a pressing problem. We need to deal with that. On the high end, I think it's a slightly different issue. As the average goes up but the high end of the tail stretches out, we will have a lot of situations in which we have, shall we say, very conspicuous consumption, very conspicuous discrepancies of income and so on, which actually creates a very bad perception of the idea that the rich are getting richer. So as the market works, not only does the average need to move up over time, we need to think about helping one end of the tail and also thinking about how we, in a sense, think about dealing with the excesses of the top end of the tail. (Asia forum)

Another executive in Asia elaborated further on the need to address the entire distribution rather than just the low-income portion:

> When we talk about disparities, the perception issue comes in, which leads me back to thinking, we've got to manage the full distribution of income. We keep saying that the mean is improving—"You guys should be very happy." We keep saying, "Everybody's better off. Therefore, why are you complaining?" And . . . then we say, "OK, you're complaining because the low end is still very low." Therefore, we did something about the low end. We alleviated, and we pull[ed] a lot of people out of [being] really poor, and that's not enough. We've got to manage the high end. Because as that high end stretches out more and more, the perception issue gets worse and worse. I think capitalism, in order to solve the disparity issue, has to start learning to manage the whole curve. (Asia forum)

The idea that perceptions of inequality would cause political problems was echoed in Europe:

> [We have to understand] the idea that there are some [levels of] wealth which are no longer acceptable to public opinion because they are made on the back of some workers. (Europe forum)

One European framed it as a moral question:

> And on top of this, there is another aspect which is creating a huge problem that, in fact, what was the good of capitalism? Was it the fact that we were building a very large, very well-off, not wealthy but well-off, middle class? We are not doing this anymore. What we are doing, and you can look at numbers, we get the poor less poor, so improving a little bit their life. We improve slightly the middle class. And in some countries, we built the real middle class because they had none. That's India and China. And we get, in all the countries of the world . . . a small group of people who are really making a lot of money. And that is leading to another issue, which is an issue of—I don't know how to call it—is it moral high ground, is it ethics? Is it something which is simply unacceptable to public opinion? (Europe forum)

The situation in Latin America was seen to be worse, because inequality was coupled with persistent poverty:

> Latin America is probably the most unequal region in the world, where you have the top decile making thirty times what the bottom decile is making. And that's the largest gap in the world. But beyond income distribution, you have the issue of poverty. Because there are some countries that actually don't look that bad in the Gini index, or in this measure of top decile versus bottom decile, but that's because they're all poor, and that's obviously something you don't want. So I think mitigating poverty is probably what keeps me awake at night over time. (Latin America forum)

Participants in the U.S. forum in New York also spoke to this issue:

> The issue of income disparity, that's a harder issue for me to think about. I know what we do in the company. I think we consciously try not to exploit. We're very conscious of equity with respect to contribution and performance, and I think most of the people who we're together with today [at the forum] do it the same way in terms of their own practices. On the other hand, it's undeniable that in a country like ours, unfettered capitalist impulse on a global basis does seem to exacerbate the problem and doesn't seem to be addressing it. (U.S. forum)

Another executive at the U.S. forum expressed the point more forcefully:

> [The] biggest threat to market capitalism is that the large corporations in the U.S. and in the emerging markets will not figure out that they need to be part of the solution to poverty. And if we are talking about the rich getting richer and the poor getting poorer, that is a huge threat to capitalism. (U.S. forum)

Not everyone agreed that populism was a threat to social and economic stability. A Latin American executive argued that Brazil's recent stability was due to a large and growing constituency of voting poor—and decidedly not due to traditional business interests that preferred instead cheap money, closed borders, and various forms of favoritism and government protection:

> If you look at what happened in Brazil in nineteen sixty, which was the last free election before the military regime, only twenty percent of the population voted. In this last election, seventy percent of the population voted. And of course, the poor are much more represented today than they were some years ago. And that's what explains Lula's popularity [Luiz Inácio Lula da Silva, then president of Brazil]. If you look at the top ten percent or twenty percent of population, they didn't vote for Lula; Lula was elected by the fifty to sixty percent poorest people. So the poor are getting more represented. But of course, there are still special-interest groups; there are many things. So there is this power play which makes the situation extremely complex and fluid. But it is because of the support of the poor that macroeconomic stability continues in Brazil. That is something that people do not realize. It is the pressure from the poor, not from the businesspeople—they want low interest rates and protection. (Latin America forum)

A related idea—that oligarchic business interests also blocked the opening of trade and modern industries—was provided by a leader from another Latin country:

> And so the question, it seems, then, is, What's the balance of power in the country? So if the power is dominated by old

business, you have no options, right? I mean, then, you're really—you're stuck. And if you can figure out ways to diversify, decentralize, modernize, then you start to have these options to do all the things that you're talking about. (Latin America forum)

Where there was no progress and "old business" used its power to block change, the result was Hugo Chávez or his equivalents. Or the military could exploit the frustration of the poor to capture power. We also heard that multinationals could play a very useful role in preventing such developments if they served to open the country to global trade.

The ideas captured in the quotations immediately above did not emerge in the discussions in Europe, Asia, or the United States. Only in the Latin America forum did we hear about how the close and opaque relations between business communities and government were blocking the progress of market capitalism. The idea that the voting poor could be a force for open markets and macroeconomic stability, as suggested by the interpretation we heard of Brazil's experience, was also particular to the Latin America discussion.

In stark contrast, business leaders in the United States and Europe were concerned that populist pressure would lead governments to pursue policies that would impair trade and destabilize the macroeconomic balance:

> Another factor is, as we've discussed, income distribution. Income inequality can pose a threat to capitalism through voters putting demands on politicians and then politicians changing the rules. So that's another major threat that we face. And then there can also be fear of other countries and economies, and so a move to protectionism, again caused by voters and politicians. So I think those are the primary threats that I would highlight. (U.S. forum)

Migration

As noted in the World Bank's scenarios, an immediate consequence of inequality is massive migration, either internally (from rural areas to cities) or across international boundaries (as experienced by the United States and, to a lesser extent, by Europe). Much more than cross-border flows of capital or trade in goods and services, cross-border movements of people tend to trigger political sensitivities and protectionist sentiments, especially when immigrants and the host country population do not share a common culture.

Anti-immigration sentiment can undercut the capitalist market system by creating social and political instability and, potentially, domestic or international conflict that disrupts investment, trade flows, and the general functioning of the market. As noted, the popular fear is that by increasing the labor pool, immigrants lower the wage rate or displace lower-skilled workers in the host country, or do both. The fear is exploited politically, despite the evidence noted in chapter 2 that the feared effects themselves are not in fact significant in the United States and Europe. Indeed, some participants in our forums expressed concern that migration from Latin America to the United States and from Africa to Europe was politically destabilizing, despite the usefulness of the immigrants to the receiving economies. As a result of such political pressure, businesses in the OECD nations with stagnating populations often lack the workers they need to prosper.

Views on the disruptive threat from migration were strongest in Europe and most positive in Asia:

> There are growing numbers of people in Europe, especially of the Muslim faith, who view themselves as completely disconnected from their host societies. (Europe forum)

> A lot of people are immigrating from one country to others, one region to others. And I think to reach some conclusions about what to do with these flows—what kind of policies to develop in relation to immigration—it's a very important issue that has a lot of repercussions in economic and social [life]. And I think this is an area where the business community and the companies should have a voice. I think that this is also an area where it will be much easier for companies to reach an agreement and to reach a kind of consensus than maybe for governments. (Europe forum)

A leading executive from Asia spoke to the need to solve the problem:

> I think it's up to . . . the developed countries, the multilaterals, and other governing institutions to find efficient ways to move people

in and out. There are examples of this. The shipping industry, for example, of which the Philippines provides a significant percentage of staff globally, [has] a very efficient system of visas, permits, all under global standards where they are required to go back after certain points in time and visit their families, and yet it's smooth enough to get them back onto their jobs in any part of the world because there are rules that govern the way they move. The shipping industry has been very progressive in that sense.

The point I'm making is that the world must find a positive way of integrating people across borders. The service gap is there, the needs for the services are there, and they in turn feed back to their host countries and help bring up standards of living. If we can find a solution, a positive solution, a progressive one to that movement of labor that's accepted around the world and that has global standards to it, then I think we're really helping fulfill a very big need around the world. (Asia forum)

One European leader saw the challenge as linked to domestic fiscal policies:

It's a continental European problem. We have this huge state debt, and a lot of our budget is really being misused to pay back interest on this debt, instead of investing it into education and things that look forward, rather than paying off the past. And we've seen that with missing integration. We have this huge migration, on top of that. So we see disintegration in large markets, like France. We see that in Italy, we see this huge pressure of Africans who just want to make it. And they're coming in boats, ships, on planes, just to get a chance to participate. So education is, I think, one of the most important things that governments should drive, but they won't drive, because they're dealing with legacies of the past rather than investing in the future. (Europe forum)

Environmental Degradation

The ability of the global system to grow can be undermined by any of a number of second-order consequences of the way it currently functions. As discussed earlier, evidence gathered by the United Nations Intergovernmental Panel on Climate Change indicates that emission of greenhouse gases is leading to climate change. Efforts to cap carbon emissions through pricing are moving slowly as developing nations resist making commitments that will slow their growth and as developed nations resist treaties that leave out the world's newest polluters. Meanwhile, scientists generally agree that among other consequences, sea levels will rise at some point—and indeed may already be rising—if nothing is done to reverse the accumulation of greenhouse gases in the atmosphere. Some estimates suggest that damage to low-lying areas such as Bangladesh is already inevitable.

Somewhat similar, though less widely discussed, has been the damage to ocean life as a result of pollution and overfishing. Local interests and inappropriate pricing have led to significant damage to available fish stocks, while local political interests block efforts to reach regional settlements to limit overexploitation and allocate access. The result may ultimately be the destruction of a critical food source. Overfishing ought to be comparatively easy to deal with, given the limited number of nations involved, but several countries, including Spain and France, appear unwilling to confront their commercial fishing constituencies, and so far the challenges of overcoming the tragedy of this commons have not been successfully met. Ocean pollution, too, poses increasingly significant challenges. Large areas of ocean are effectively dead, and the island of plastic debris in the Pacific is estimated at thousands of square miles.[6] If these problems remain unresolved, they could cause local disruptions in the economies dependent on fishing, though they are not likely to cause a dramatic slowing of growth within the next two decades.

Freshwater is a different matter. It is both limited, irregularly distributed, and poorly priced in that it tends to be free where it is in surplus and very expensive where scarce. Where proper pricing schemes are introduced, it is possible to rationalize use within nations, and frame treaties that would have the same rationalizing effect across nations. The Middle East, for example, has been studied carefully. Proper pricing and treaties would permit dramatic improvement in water use across the region. Fortunately, this is an area of policy (one of very few, so far) that has enjoyed any significant level of cooperation among the nations of the Middle East—but in many other areas of the world, the rise of sharp conflicts over freshwater may be only a matter of time. If not resolved through negotiation, conflicts over water could even lead to war.

How climate change, water scarcity, and other environmental issues are dealt with will have important consequences for the economy. In the 1980s, it was widely thought that product quality and product cost existed in an opposite relationship, that one could only be achieved at the expense of the other. Later it was discovered that careful attention to quality could reduce cost. In similar ways, companies are learning that careful attention to water use and waste emission can reduce the cost of production. More perplexing is the emission of greenhouse gases, a consequence of most production and transportation. How governments design their interventions to regulate public goods will have a major effect on the path of global economic growth.

Business leaders in all our forums voiced concern that capitalism as currently operated is producing environmental damage that could impair the system's future functioning in one or two main ways. One is through a political backlash of overregulation that will undercut free capital and goods exchange, disrupt flows of capital, and generally suppress the gains that capitalism might otherwise be able to produce. The more dramatic possibility is that such widespread environmental damage would make natural systems collapse, triggering breakdowns in global agriculture, raising sea levels, flooding heavily populated coastal zones worldwide, and generally leading to economic and political chaos.

The level of concern was not matched by a clear view as to how action should proceed:

> It's a [challenge] very often of problems that have no solution or we do not know the solutions, or there are conflicts of objectives. And the climate change has a little bit of all this. Models of climate change are very sensitive to a small change in the assumptions. And so there is a lot of disagreement. The Chinese and the Indians will tell you, "Well, you created a problem and you [now] want [us to] solve it. Why don't you pay for all the CO_2 that you have created in the last two centuries; and you compensate us for that and [then] we will comply with [an agreement]." It will be very difficult to convince the Europeans [and] Americans who did that. (Europe forum)

How [can we] reconcile, for example, high economic growth with care for the environment—with ensuring that growing affluence doesn't mean a lowering of health standards? (Asia forum)

There's really a consensus among business and individuals that the environmental issue is a top-priority issue in Hong Kong, yes. And I think there is a consensus that we need to clean up the air. (Asia forum)

In Brazil, you know, the picture has been very mixed. On one hand, they continue to burn the Amazon forest, which is very bad. But on the other hand, there are some people who are now impeding progress. For instance, you cannot do any work in infrastructure in Brazil at the moment, because of environmental restrictions. So it's very difficult now to build a dam, or pave a road, or do anything. And I think this is the other excess. So if you are going to look at the environment, I think there are two sides of the coin which you have to look at. (Latin America forum)

Fortunately, nations with strict environmental laws and high carbon taxes are already generating examples of innovation that is eliminating the cost-versus-green trade-off that worried so many in our sessions. Denmark, for example, has reduced greenhouse gas emissions 14 percent while growing its GDP more than 40 percent through a combination of energy taxes, carbon taxes, the cap-and-trade system, strict building codes and labeling systems, subsidies for wind power and biomass fuel, and new "green" technology.[7]

Failure of the Rule of Law

The rule of law was at the center of another set of concerns expressed by our leaders. Many noted that the quality of law and legal institutions varies dramatically around the world. A particular focus of discussion was a perceived rising tide of corruption, extortion, thug-gery, and expropriation that is making it increasingly difficult to operate a capitalist system that respects property rights and upholds contracts through fair and effective enforcement mechanisms. In the absence of an effective rule of law, bribes replace product competition as a means of determining winners, and investment collapses as the ability to enjoy the fruits of economic value creation evaporates in the face of theft and expropriation. These forces are mutually reinforcing. As corruption rises, increasingly only parties involved in corruption can survive.

The need for a stronger rule of law and more effective legal institu-tions was a particularly salient theme in our Latin America forum, but it was voiced by business leaders from other regions as well:

> We have, no doubt, attitudes of and toward government. We are not trusting, and there is a reason why. (Latin America forum)

> Well, what we want is effective governance that has the inter-est of the society at heart, rather than being a looting process in which a few people are able to claim everything. And there are various different governmental schemes that might be able to produce that. I don't think we want to treat good governance as exogenous. It is precisely that we don't regard it as exogenous. We regard it as the outcome of things that smart people in the society do. (Asia forum)

> There is a role for the private sector to monitor how govern-ment goes about spending its money. And I think creating and supporting watchdog organizations that monitor government spending and have a regular report on government spending in depth . . . would be very valuable. Because our governments, I think, get away with a lot of spending that is unaccounted for. And I think that is a very important source of problems. (Latin America forum)

An executive in the Latin America forum linked the problem of corruption to outsized government:

> A worker works eight months of the year to pay taxes. And so if you create this awareness in people, you have a taxpayer's revolt; then you can tackle big government. But big government is just a consequence of huge taxation. You know, it's a vicious circle. They grow, they need more taxes, they charge you more taxes because they can charge you more taxes, they can grow even more. (Latin America forum)

Although our forum discussions focused mainly on the damaging effects of weak and insufficiently developed legal institutions, some of our European business leaders took issue with what they regard as an overly legalistic and litigious environment in the United States:

> The approach to many problems [in the United States] is based on rules—a formal approach that makes the system more expensive and less efficient. (Europe forum)

The State of Public Health and General Education

One of the simplest relationships in economic theory is that among the size of the labor force, its productivity, and the level of output. The product of the first two yields the third. The size of the labor force depends in part on its health, and its productivity depends on its education as well as its health. A high level of public health is thus a centrally important feature of modern societies. Clean water, robust sewage treatment, and adequate medical care are important elements. But so are appropriate diet, exercise, and the avoidance of smoking and other hazardous drugs. The last three elements are proving problematic, as obesity is a growing problem in the lower-income segments of developed countries and the middle class of developing nations. Substance abuse, including tobacco and alcohol, is a second major threat to public health and, by extension, to high levels of productivity.

Growth depends further on education, another vexing challenge. As discussed earlier, the World Bank study makes it clear that education is important to improved income in most countries. But as the Bank's research also shows, national social and governance arrangements in some countries block mobility among the most impoverished so that the potential value of education to the nation is negated. This problem is most often associated with developing countries controlled by oligarchies, but some evidence of the same problem can be found in developed nations. In contemporary Europe, well-educated students graduate with very limited job prospects because a large, unionized, and entitled public-sector workforce blocks employment of the young and imposes on the economy very large costs that limit private employment and economic growth. Unemployment among graduates in countries like Italy and Spain is running over 20 percent.[8] In the United States, a combination of capricious funding by state and local governments and resistance to changes in curriculum, in some cases by teachers' unions, has weakened the quality of education in the public schools. In contrast, Pakistan is typical of the problem in some less developed nations. Large portions of the population have no access to education other than in madrassas that make no effort to provide students with tools such as science and math—tools that are essential in a modern economy. The general level of education may well be associated with the refusal of the country to engage in any sort of land reform.

The perceived failure of public education systems to provide adequate skill development and opportunity for advancement, particularly in low-income communities, was viewed by many business leaders in each region we visited as a matter of great significance. This concern links with the third line of argument outlined above: a poorly functioning public education system might contribute to the increasing disparities in outcomes, with the income growth of skilled workers substantially outpacing the gains experienced by lower-skilled workers. Inadequate public education also contributes to a shortage of the skills necessary to allow robust development of successful competitive businesses and thus may contribute to the differences in economic outcomes across regions.

Many forum participants regarded education as a particularly significant problem in Africa and thought that it might be a significant cause of a continuing lack of economic progress that would leave much of Africa increasingly further below the average standards of living in other regions. On the other hand, their comments also focused on the problems facing their own countries:

> Most Latin countries have inequality as one of the critical issues that is threatening the democracy in the region. Inequality is only overcome by good education and good work and therefore good employment. Thus the private sector has a very important role to play in dealing with inequality by basically supporting good economic policy in the economic field that will result in duration of employment, through training—on-the-job training—which will result in middle classes which are the support of a modern society. (Latin America forum)

———————————

> If the generation of youngsters that are now going through school does not understand what the value of individual freedoms are and human rights, we may have a long journey in developing the country back into a specific success story like it used to be in the fifties, sixties, and seventies. (Latin America forum)

The difficulty, as these quotes indicate, is that education is fundamental to many aspects of social and economic development, and yet many nations are unable or unwilling to invest the necessary resources. Recall the European executive quoted earlier (in discussing the immigration challenge):

> We have this huge state debt, and a lot of our budget is really being misused to pay back interest on this debt, instead of investing it into education and things that look forward, rather than paying off the past. (Europe forum)

The Rise of State Capitalism

Another matter that generates uncertainty about the sustainability of market capitalism is the emergence of large economic powers that are not deeply rooted in the modern traditions of market capitalism. Our business leaders frequently mentioned Russia, China, and India as nations whose actions might disrupt the global economic system or systematically distort the operation and functioning of the global capitalist market system. The challenge was neatly summed up by an executive at the Europe forum:

> If Chinese companies or Russian companies—which are being financed in different ways and which have different governance rules—if they come and play a significant role outside of Russia and China in the world . . . we wouldn't be on a level playing field. So clearly, that is not acceptable . . . If . . . either China or Russia go to what we know as capitalism, then they will be in a transition period. But if this transition period is too long, or if they choose a different model, as Russia seems to be doing currently, then we have a real problem, and we have to manage this interaction. And we shouldn't be naive and believe that naturally everything . . . will go well because everybody will recognize the supreme value of market capitalism. I know some of these countries may decide for some time, or even a long time, to play a different game. And if they play a different game, we should be careful. You cannot use the rules of football to play soccer. So you should make sure that people either play by the same rules or that you manage the interfaces between different games. (Europe forum)

Leaders in Europe were particularly concerned about the competitive impact of state-owned companies with access to government funding to make acquisitions and to invest in developing technologies under circumstances that would not be economically feasible for market-driven firms:

> And we are confronted with the competition coming from countries who are not playing with the same kind of rules. So we play chess, and they play baseball with no ball and just a bat. So that's the situation we are confronted with, and we have to find the solutions for the future. (Europe forum)

The Asian business leaders took a more optimistic view:

> The opening up of China and India means that two of the largest underutilized workforces in the world are now being admitted to

participation in the global workforce. This can only increase productivity globally and, other things being equal, should lead to significant improvements in growth, productivity, and standard of living for most people in the world. (Asia forum)

The challenge, as seen by many outside Asia, is that nations traditionally use relations with other nations as a mechanism for self-advancement. The trading system and the environment involve *all* nations; both require cooperation among nations for their maintenance and improvement. Yet, several major countries have managed their economies in ways that exploit the openness of the free-market system, using managed exchange rates, state-funded overcapacity, dumping or managed exports of scarce commodities, and asymmetric market access. This characterization could apply—at least in part—to Germany and Japan from 1950 to 1980 as easily as it could apply to China and Russia today. But today's leaders, especially those from the developed world, are not sanguine that the tactics employed by the giant BRIC countries can be absorbed into the global market system.

Executives at our European forum, in particular, offered various examples of what they saw as three contrasting types of capitalism: industrial capitalism, focused on goods and services; financial capitalism, focused on trading; and state capitalism, in the form of Chinese state-owned enterprises, the Russian energy sector, and sovereign wealth funds investing trillions in various forms of real assets:

> The main issue is nationalism. People have the control of their future; they try to build a state, and to build that state, they have to control the economy, the industry, and everything. They want to achieve equality . . . We cannot blame Japan for having done what they have done. Japan would not have been where they are today if they had not started by having a system which was directed by the state. The same with Korea. The same today with China . . . They have to control the system, and they have to control how they can build a middle class. (Europe forum)

The preceding executive's observation provoked this response:

> This is a tough reality, and these are some of the hard facts that we have to look at. The hard fact is that if you are chief of state

of China, you don't care about the rules of the Americas or other high-technology countries which you compete with. You would try to take most of that technology and the knowledge in order to modernize your country. But your task is not to make GE richer. Your task is to make the population richer and to create the infrastructure in your country. That's the task of the chief of state . . . So we have a dual situation. When we are in a shrinking world, which is the world of true capitalism, and the expanded world, where we have the world of state capitalism, which is controlled or governed by objectives which have nothing to do with the classic objective of the capitalism, which is "I'm a state and I'm trying to build my country," . . . then competition is distorted. (Europe forum)

Radical Movements, Terrorism, and War

Another significant and complex group of concerns involves the challenge of maintaining sufficient peace and security for capitalism to prosper. Free-market exchange on a global scale requires a level of general security adequate to permit flows of goods, services, and capital, and a climate of sufficient calm that investors and traders can be confident of arrangements that extend into the medium- and longer-term horizons. Yet many worry that radical movements and systemic conflict between people and perhaps between parts of the world with widely differing views of how societies should be organized are on the rise and may lead to a "clash of civilizations" that breeds sustained levels of disruptive conflicts. The market system cannot function effectively in the face of continuous, debilitating, and destructive armed conflicts and continuing scattered attacks on assets (shipping, extraction, infrastructure, and so on) whose safety and availability are essential to the successful operation of capitalist exchange.

The problems of terrorism and armed conflict were seen as more serious by executives from some regions than from others. For example, the issue was not seen as critical in Latin America:

The problem of terrorism, in the worldwide image that you know, for me, is an important issue. We have had many experiences in many places in the world, so you know terrorism can affect the society. Fortunately, in the case of Latin America, it is not very close to us. We don't live in that world, though any kind of terrorist act can influence in a negative way what's happened in Latin America. (Latin America forum) [The speaker was from neither Colombia nor Mexico.]

In Asia, the focus was more on flash points that could trigger armed conflict and war:

I'm personally more concerned with the human aspects of the conflicts that may come along in the future and that could impede the healthy growth of market capitalism. You know, protectionism and conflicts among nations in East Asia is still a concern. From North Korea on to Taiwan Straits and into the India-Pakistan border, all these are flaring points which may, if anything serious happens, impede the flow of trade and flow of business. (Asia forum)

Evolution and Pandemics

In 1918 and 1919, a peculiarly virulent flu virus with an extremely high death rate—especially among otherwise healthy young people between the ages of fifteen and thirty—swept through communities around the globe. In some locations, 10 to 25 percent of those who became infected died, often within twenty-four to forty-eight hours. In the wake of the epidemic, many communities were economically and socially devastated. Minimum estimates are that 50 million people died worldwide; credible estimates range as high as 200 million deaths. Notably, this pandemic arose in a world significantly less interconnected (through air travel, cross-border trade, and so on) than our world today. Recalling this, our participants identified the potential of emergent disease as the tenth significant threat to free-market systems.

Our participants cited the impact of HIV/AIDS as one example. Where, as in countries like South Africa, the infection rate of AIDS has reached high levels, the impact on family income has been devastating. The consequence of the death of young adults in agricultural areas is visible from the sky as the jungle reclaims farm areas. Were pandemics such as severe acute respiratory syndrome (SARS), which was also noted in a number of our discussions, or swine flu to grow out of control, the effects could be equally dramatic.

Especially in our Asia and Europe forums, these examples were seen as a warning that biological evolution, particularly of viruses for which there is little natural immunity in human populations and of drug-resistant bacteria, is an ongoing phenomenon that could once again—and fairly suddenly—create a devastating pandemic. Such a global epidemic might so disrupt trade and financial markets that the worldwide economic system would collapse. One executive's comment indicated how the fear of sudden, catastrophic events can override concern about long-term challenges:

> I can't afford for the bird flu to strike. I can—I hate this, but
> I can—breathe bad air for a few years. (Asia forum)

Inadequacy of Existing Institutions

As our participants discussed the preceding lines of argument about forces that might impinge on the continuing success of capitalism (or, worse, severely disrupt it or ultimately cause it to be unsustainable), they frequently discussed why current institutions—both national and international—seemed inadequate to addressing these challenges. Much discussion therefore centered on whether existing institutions can be expected to meet these challenges. In the process, our participants identified a number of inadequacies in existing institutions as mechanisms for coping with the scope and scale of the negative forces being identified.

While these perceived inadequacies taken individually do not on their own constitute a threat to capitalism, their systemic impact was thought to be very problematic. We heard that present arrangements aren't working and that new ones and new institutions are needed. In effect, an eleventh threat is that the institutions currently on the landscape and ostensibly designed (at least in part) to make the existing system of market capitalism sustainable will be unable to counter the ten active threats identified above.

Several interrelated reasons were offered for viewing existing institutional arrangements as inadequate:

Business governance. Our participants were concerned that while the problems they were discussing would take time to resolve, the horizons imposed on companies by financial markets were short and possibly getting shorter. The perceived source of the problems varied. Leaders in the United States spoke of financial markets but also of the intensity of global competition. They said they knew how to manage on a global basis, but it meant constantly moving where the ability to create value was greatest—which in contemporary circumstances was not often the United States:

> You can talk to any of the international CEOs today, and I would suspect they would say, "I know what to do." And as a corporate head, I redeploy my assets, and I redeploy how I operate or how I set my company to operate based on the current rules, and I know where to go, how to do it—and the fact that it increasingly disadvantages the United States is not something I'm very comfortable about as a citizen. (U.S. forum)

In a similar vein, an executive in Hong Kong pointed to financial market pressures as a barrier to tackling the larger problems:

> Businesspeople in today's world are under tremendous pressure to produce short-term results. You know, there's this tyranny of quarterly results that most businesspeople have to account for, and that makes it difficult to find businesspeople who are prepared to dedicate the time and commitment to working on these broader issues. (Asia forum)

In Latin America, the challenge was seen to come from the instability of government. If a Chávez lurked around the corner, it was hard to take a long point of view:

> In the case of Latin America, the main threat is that unfortunately, many governments . . . see the scenario just in the short term. They don't have the vision in the longer term. So they are thinking, you know, in the next political term, the next political horizon, could be four years, could be five years, could be

six years. But if you want to have the country in a growing trend, you need once again to have a longer-term scenario, a longer-term horizon. (Latin America forum)

In Europe, there was more concern with the emergence of financial capitalism that seemed to be very powerful and not congruent with the needs of the commercial and industrial sectors. Recall the European executive quoted earlier:

> Private equity groups, in many instances, are playing a useful role, but they are shortening the horizon of companies. So how do we make it consistent that we can have this flow of capital going to private equity and that we still have kind of a long-term development of the economy, of innovation, research, et cetera? (Europe forum)

> Governance starts with our own internal governance. And one of the things that we should educate leaders to do is not to cave in. I mean, there are a lot of constituencies in the financial sector. There are a lot of constituencies everywhere. And one of the things that I find shocking is when the board talks only about short-term value creation or hedge-fund activism. People should not cave in. (Europe forum)

National governments and institutions. In many locations, national governments were regarded as either incompetent, distracted, or corrupt—and, therefore, unlikely to play a sufficiently positive role in defending and supplying the infrastructure of capitalism. By *infrastructure of capitalism,* the business leaders meant the enforcement of rules and contracts, widespread belief that free-market exchange creates social value, an education system that provides skills and opportunities, a social safety net and income distribution process that prevents populist revolution, and so on. As quoted earlier, one participant in Hong Kong spoke clearly in this regard:

> Well, what we want is effective governance that has the interest of the society at heart, rather than being a looting process in which a few people are able to claim everything. And there are

various different governmental schemes that might be able to produce that. I don't think we want to treat good governance as exogenous. (Asia forum)

This view was shared by others in Hong Kong and elsewhere:

It is precisely that we don't regard it as exogenous. We regard it as the outcome of things that smart people in the society do. (Asia forum)

And as we observed earlier (in discussing the rule of law), one Latin American participant urged business to take a stronger role in holding governments to account:

There is a role for the private sector to monitor how government goes about spending its money. And I think creating and supporting watchdog organizations that monitor government spending and have a regular report on government spending in depth . . . would be very valuable. Because our governments, I think, get away with a lot of spending that is unaccounted for. And I think that is a very important source of problems. (Latin America forum)

In New York, a U.S. executive expressed both frustration and resignation:

So let me just name a few of the threats that I think are serious threats to market capitalism. Number one is politicians, because politicians create the rules that we all have to live by, and the politicians responding to voters can create rules that could be very, very damaging to our form of capitalism here in the United States. (U.S. forum)

In Europe, the view was that firms need to push nations toward international governance. There was impatience that firms could not even agree on a step of that sort:

If the business community of the developed countries, first stage— let's forget, for the time being, China and India. If the business community of the developed countries is not able to express a few joint views about the stronger international governance and the few programs, it means, on the contrary, that we are perfectly happy with the present situation, where we put our destiny in the hands of national governments that understand nothing about the issues that we have been discussing since yesterday night. So is it yes or no? Are we happy or not? Full stop. (Europe forum)

We can do very little without interaction of society, but we can do a lot to create an interaction with society. (Europe forum)

International and multilateral institutions. International institutions—including development organizations, the international trade system, and others—were regarded as having three significant liabilities as instruments for addressing the active threats to capitalism. First, went the argument, they are not managed particularly well; they are bureaucratized, bloated, and self-interested. Second (and perhaps related), many felt that existing international institutions have been systematically undercut by the lack of cooperation from important national governments—most notably, the United States, Russia, and China. Finally, and perhaps most crucially, many observers noted that the main international institutions on the landscape today were never designed to deal with the issues that are now arising or with the threats to economic progress identified in our conversations. These organizations were, for the most part, designed in the post–World War II era to facilitate trade flows among industrialized countries and to create opportunities for investment and development in less developed regions. While existing institutions may or may not have functioned effectively in coping with the perceived challenges for which they were designed, they certainly weren't designed to handle, for example, worldwide threats of environmental collapse resulting from a failure to manage environmental damage and climate change.

One business leader traced the current situation to the post–World War II era:

I just want to try as a provocative, stylized fact about capitalism, that there is a period after the Second World War and up to, say, nineteen ninety, which you might call the heyday of market capitalism, in which we had basically nation-state-based firms. Most businesses had a location: nation-states. And there was a pretty happy arrangement . . . that the nation-states basically gathered prosperity by virtue of the firms that they had, and the firms worked with their national governments. And over the course of this period, business became international in a way that the governance structure never was and isn't yet. And so now you have a whole bunch of international forces operating in the private-capital markets . . . And you still have nation-states, but you have international business. And there's a lack of alignment, in effect, between those forces. And we don't really have yet—we haven't yet evolved—a mechanism for managing in that larger world that business has come to inhabit but that the rest of the world hasn't. (Asia forum)

Our informants, in other words, perceived a significant *mismatch* between the design, goals, and performance of national and international institutions on the one hand, and the scope, scale, and nature of the perceived threats to capitalism on the other:

I think the only way is to have different, much stronger international governance . . . Is there anything which can make this international governance a reality? And I believe that if we look at what's happening around us, there are a few elements which should lead to better international governance. For example, the trade issues obviously show the need for an international governance system. Climate change is one issue where it will be completely clear that if there is no international governance, it's going to throw out of balance the whole economic system . . . And then the last one, which is terrorism, which is the fact that governments cannot control the international flows of people, of crime in general, financial crime. This shows that if there is not much stronger international governance, terrible things happen. (Europe forum)

When you think about the rules, the institutions that make the rules and enforce the rules obviously [are] what we need to focus on. I submit that today's multilateral institutions which have been set up some fifty or more years ago are really set up for a totally different world versus the one that we have today. There is the need to take a look at the world as it exists today, the needs of today's world, and the multilateral institutions that would be needed for today's world. And I think that is, frankly, a very pressing task. (Asia forum)

———————————

The business world has internationalized in a way which the government world has not. There is, in effect, a mismatch between those two. And that, at least to me, frames some of the issues that we ought to talk about, in terms of what the business world will do about anything. (Asia forum)

———————————

One of the things that's concerned me for a while is that in this age of terrific political polarization, there don't seem to be honest brokers anymore. There don't seem to be people above the fray who everybody respects and [who], if they reach a judgment, it will be seen as fair, objective, and bipartisan. Things seem to be divided into camps, and even the most innocuous statement can be attacked almost without any facts. So it is worth looking for institutions that we may have or probably may even need to create in order to regain some legitimacy to talk about these issues in a fact-based and dispassionate way but also one that will have credibility. (U.S. forum)

As the authors of this book, we are sympathetic to these arguments; we agree that multilateral institutions need to be reformed and strengthened. But we also agree with some of the other business leaders at our forums who saw these same challenges differently, not as an occasion for governmental or multinational institutional reform, although that might be helpful, but *as challenges to be addressed by business enterprise.* Because we work at a business school and are impressed with the capabilities of well-managed corporations, we were intrigued with this point of view. We do not believe that all the problems that were identified in our discussions can be resolved by business. But our discussions have led us to the hypothesis that were the major business participants in the global economy to examine the forces that we have discussed, they would see commercial opportunities, not just problems. Part Two of this book is devoted to this hypothesis. One executive deftly summarized the point near the end of our discussions in New York:

> The question that should be asked at this conference is not how we protect the gains of global capitalism and deal with the threats. It is how we understand and create corporate structures that can actually take advantage of all the opportunities that exist in these economies while at the same time being part of the solution. (U.S. forum)

Conclusion:
Risks—But Also Opportunities

Participants in our forums saw the ten disruptive forces and the lack of effective institutions to address these problems as breeding grounds for potentially serious threats to market capitalism. They discussed how conflicts in these areas could give rise to complex chains of cause and effect—natural, political, social, and economic—that could undermine the global market system or the conditions necessary for its effective functioning.

We cannot place accurate probabilities on the various outcomes the business leaders imagined. Some of the envisioned scenarios may indeed seem quite remote or even unimaginable from where we sit today. And—to paraphrase the variously attributed and widely quoted quip—predictions, especially about the future, are notoriously difficult.[9] So we are not suggesting that our business leaders' concerns should be taken as a guide to what is going to happen or even what might happen (although the participants in the Europe forum were uncannily accurate about what a financial meltdown might look like). Rather, the concerns expressed in our forums, and the data on which the fears are based, are indicators of risks that need to be recognized and managed. Even if the likelihood of devastating climate change, another financial system collapse, and a populist revolution appears to be low, the magnitude and seriousness of their potential impact on the market system—and on individual companies operating within that system—are sufficiently high that principles of prudence and risk management dictate that these concerns be given serious attention.

The financial crisis has taught the importance of planning for statistical outliers—so-called tail risks and Black Swans—and of recognizing interdependencies among what normally appear to be unrelated phenomena. As elaborated by proponents of the Black Swan theory, high-magnitude events that are impossible to predict using scientific methods because they are so rare have played a disproportionate role in human history.[10] And the possibility of such events tends to be systematically under-recognized because of psychological and other biases. These lessons apply no less to risks arising from the workings of the world's social, political, and environmental systems than to those arising from its financial system.

If some concerns voiced by the forum participants seem remote, other concerns are already in evidence. Consider the populist governments, global warming effects, and immigration problems discussed earlier in this chapter. Our research—and that of others—suggests that the eleven areas identified in our forums are real sources of risk to the system and its participating members. From a risk-management perspective, then, these are areas that all companies of any size should include on their risk screens and dashboards. A business leader in Hong Kong put the point simply:

> We need to get out in front of these problems and to preempt any breakdowns. (Asia forum)

But our discussions also pointed to another possible perspective on these eleven areas. Yes, there are serious threats to the future of global market prosperity, and dealing with them requires a series of changes by national governments and multinational institutions. But as one of our earlier-quoted New York participants said, in many ways these challenges—at least some of them—can also be viewed as opportunities for business, especially for large enterprises. Consider the challenge of three billion unskilled workers in the developing world. This is a staggering opportunity for those companies that figure out how to bring those workers into the system as suppliers and customers.

Before we turn to that argument and, more generally, to the role that companies can play in strengthening the market system and combating the disruptors identified in our forums, it is helpful to step back and see the complex of forces discussed in this chapter as part of one ecological system. We will take up this idea in chapter 4.

Seeing the Threats as
Systemic

THE ELEVEN LINES of argument presented in chapter 3 may seem to be discrete and self-contained. But if market capitalism is viewed in relation to the larger sociopolitical system in which it is embedded, many, if not all, of the concerns voiced by our executives appear to be interrelated and to lie at the interface between the market system and the larger system that supports and legitimizes it.

Before turning to strategies for addressing the challenges raised by our business leaders, it is useful to review this complex of forces in its totality—as part of one ecological system or, to quote a forum participant who heads a large public-sector investment fund, as part of "one integrated operating system":

> The market doesn't sit in isolation from some philosophy and some culture. You know, the philosopher David Hume had a very simple three-point system which was about the right to property, its transference by consent, and the enforcement of promises. That means that no open market system can exist unless there's a government that truly believes that and puts in place a set of rules that allows that to happen. If they do, the history suggests that that will work well. So I never like to separate in my mind the notion of a private sector over here and a public sector over here. They're actually one integrated operating system in which you need huge collaboration. And I think business,

of course, must pursue its own interests to play its role, but it has to find a way of marshaling people around future possibilities, the consequences of things not working, to get collaborative action with governments, regulators, and other people. And we have to regard people in government and in regulation and the public service as part of our team. And they must be highly recognized for the significant role that they play. (Asia forum)

A better understanding of the bigger picture will reveal important relationships among the potentially destabilizing forces identified in our forums and suggest ways to make the market system more robust. It will also provide a framework for identifying possible interventions to improve the system's performance and foster its sustainability.

Although sustainability is often discussed in purely environmental terms, we frame the issue somewhat differently. We agree that environmental protection is a critical priority, but, as we will explain, the market system's durability depends more broadly on its ability to engage and deliver positive results for an ever-growing number of the world's citizens. To be sure, this means better management of capitalism's damaging environmental and other impacts. But it also means amplifying and disseminating the benefits of capitalism more widely. Put in marketing terms, if capitalism is the product, then society is the customer whose satisfaction is ultimately at stake.

In this chapter, we construct a picture of the larger sociopolitical ecosystem in which market capitalism is embedded. We show how the lines of argument advanced in our forums relate to one another and to the larger ecosystem, but we also discuss the market system's dependency on the larger system of which it is part. The analysis we offer here was inspired and informed by what we heard in our forums, but the synthesis we present goes well beyond those discussions and was constructed after the sessions. It has not been seen (or commented directly upon) by the business leaders who participated in our dialogues.

We start by showing market capitalism as a circle at the center of our picture, as in figure 4-1; later in the chapter, we will say more about what's inside this circle. For now, it can serve as a reference point around which to construct a view of the larger system. We will first

FIGURE 4-1

array a series of elements of the larger ecology around this core, then turn to the content of the core, and finally describe how we see these various elements as causally related.

The Outcomes:
Results Driven by the Market System

When the market system is working well, it produces many beneficial outcomes. Wealth and economic growth are by far the most frequently discussed, measured, and celebrated. As noted in chapter 1 and elaborated by economists from Adam Smith to the present, the market system creates value for society in many ways—through more efficient uses of resources, enhanced consumer welfare, increased national prosperity, and improved standards of living for the general citizenry, to mention a few. This wealth, in turn, can be used to advance other aims—military, political, scientific, intellectual, cultural, artistic, athletic.

But the system's benefits include much more than economic growth and prosperity. We might talk, for example, about its propensity to encourage innovation—which arguably has intrinsic value independent of its economic contribution. And the system's tendency to promote self-reliance can be beneficial for personal development. For individuals, the market system offers opportunities to create and amass personal wealth and, in turn, to realize their chosen way of life. For a multitude, it provides personally satisfying work. In these ways, capitalism also promotes individual liberty and human creativity as well as social diversity and development along many dimensions. A few of the positive outcomes flowing from the market system are noted in figure 4-2.

FIGURE 4-2

As our forum discussions revealed, however, the consequences of capitalism are not all beneficial or even benign. Depending on the effectiveness of the institutions that mediate and regulate its functioning, the market system also generates a range of negative consequences for society. These consequences (some of which are noted in the right section of figure 4-3) can be significant, and besides their direct impacts, they may have negative indirect effects as well. If left unattended, these consequences can combine with other destabilizing forces and intensify the ten active disruptors discussed in chapter 3 (whose effects are shown graphically at the bottom of figure 4-3).

Three of the eleven lines of argument examined in the previous chapter centered on negative consequences of this kind and on their contribution to potentially disruptive forces. One argument focused on capitalism's tendency, at least as currently operated, to produce— or to reinforce—extreme disparities of income and wealth. Even when these disparities are not the result of fraud or coercion, they can breed doubt about the openness and legitimacy of the system and generate hostility among those who feel excluded or unfairly treated. The aggrieved and excluded may, in turn, look to the system's opponents for redress or revenge—or merely for a better way of life.

Another line of argument focused on the market system's damaging effects on the natural environment, especially on air, water, climate, and reserves of nonrenewable resources. As discussed, these negative environmental impacts can undercut the market system via

FIGURE 4-3

both natural and sociopolitical mechanisms. Pollution, for example, can damage people's health and well-being and, in some cases, whole communities' livelihood. These injuries, in turn, fuel demands for compensation and corrective action—demands that, if not addressed, can lead to social unrest and political activism against markets and their proponents. As described earlier, indifference to the environment also puts capitalism at risk of disruptions on a much larger scale—from the collapse of natural systems to the breakdown of global agriculture or the flooding of heavily populated coastal zones because of rising sea levels.

Yet another line of argument centered on financial system instability. Many of our business leaders questioned society's tolerance for the recurrent boom-and-bust cycles that capitalism—again, as currently practiced—seems to generate. While financiers and bankers may joke about the inevitability of a financial crisis every few years, the negative impacts reach far beyond the financial world, wreaking havoc on the lives and livelihoods of innocent parties across the social and economic spectrum. Unlike well-heeled financiers, most people want and need a higher level of stability and predictability than the system has delivered in recent years. One danger, particularly if volatility increases, is political pressure leading to overregulation that hamstrings the system—or even outright rejection of the system by the broader society.

Exogenous Forces:
Outside Influences on the Market System

Not all of the potential disruptors that worried our executives derive solely from the system's negative consequences. Some, like major natural catastrophes, arise from sources that are completely exogenous to capitalism—although the impact of these catastrophes, which often disproportionately affect the poor, is, importantly, endogenous. Other influences that could disrupt belief in the market system or undercut its functioning have mixed origins. Religious fundamentalism and organized international piracy, for example, arise mainly from external sources but gather strength from negative impacts of the system itself.

Of the ten direct lines of argument we have discussed, three concerned forces that are wholly or partly exogenous. These are depicted in figure 4-4 (along with several other examples that did not arise directly at our forums).

As noted earlier, our leaders worried, first, about the potential disruptions that could arise from wholly external forces such as biological evolution and pandemics. Many cited the emergence of HIV/AIDS in the 1990s and the SARS crisis of 2003 as cases in point. The air traffic shutdown precipitated by the cloud of volcanic ash wafting over Europe in the spring of 2010 is a further reminder of nature's power to cripple trade and markets worldwide. After only a few days, plants were announcing temporary closures for lack of parts shipments,

FIGURE 4-4

agricultural exports from Africa to Europe were down significantly, and commentators were predicting dire economic consequences if the volcano continued to erupt periodically.

A second line of argument about largely exogenous forces that leaders raised in our forums focused on the threat from radical movements and terrorist groups that are ideologically opposed to capitalism and bent on its defeat by any means possible—including random violence and armed conflict. Although the threats from terrorism and radicalism come largely from outside, the market system's negative consequences give leaders of these movements a more compelling platform and help them gain adherents and sympathizers.

A third argument advanced by our forum participants, the potential disruptions arising from the adoption of state capitalism in newly emerging economic powers, is also largely but not entirely exogenous. For many nations, these state-led and often nationalist ideologies appear to provide a way to catch up with and perhaps even to surpass nations that have long been successful competitors in the global market system. For some nations, an additional appeal of state capitalism lies in market capitalism's perceived shortcomings and on past injustices—real or perceived—that capitalism and capitalists have visited on their countries. Many Chinese, for example, harbor deep resentment over humiliations they believe China has suffered at the hands of foreign capitalist powers. Similar sentiments can be found in Latin America, Africa, and other parts of the world.

The Antecedents: Preconditions for the Market System

A further set of concerns raised in our forums centered on what we term the market system's antecedents. By *antecedents*, we mean the preconditions that confer legitimacy on the system and enable its functioning—particularly the underlying institutions, social and political conditions, and resource flows that the system requires (figure 4-5). Our business leaders expressed concern about breakdowns or inadequacies in critical antecedents in each of the three categories shown in the figure.

Antecedent Institutions

The market system presupposes a legitimate and effective governing authority that can, in turn, legitimate the market's activities and perform functions essential to its operations: maintaining peace and stability, upholding the rule of law, protecting public health, providing

FIGURE 4-5

for public education, and facilitating transportation and communications, to name just a few of the most critical.

As we have discussed, many executives cited weaknesses in the rule of law and a rising tide of government corruption as threats to the system. Although the law's importance for economic development is widely recognized, many countries have yet to establish a fair and effective system for law enforcement or an independent judiciary. Bribery and its kin—extortion, kickbacks, embezzlement—seem to be increasingly widespread, with all their well-known distorting effects on markets, investment, and competition. The threat to property and security from organized crime has become global, but regulation and law enforcement continue to be fragmented by jurisdictional boundaries and hampered by competition among authorities within and across countries. This combination of corruption, disdain for law, and ineffective enforcement severely compromises the law's role as a facilitator of commerce and protector of the market system's integrity.

Antecedent Social and Political Conditions

In the absence of certain social and political conditions, the market system cannot function effectively—and in some cases, it cannot function at all. Weaknesses in these areas, moreover, can increase the system's vulnerability to the disruptive forces we have already described. For instance, if people do not understand the system or if they do not believe that markets produce equitable results, they may question whether market capitalism is an appropriate model, or they may be unwilling to accept markets as mechanisms of social production. People may thus be more receptive to radical ideologies and political movements aimed at dismantling the system and replacing it with something considered more equitable. Or, to take another example, a modicum of respect for diversity is necessary to enable commerce and to prevent conflict among people with differing ethnic, national, religious, and other identities and backgrounds.

As noted earlier, inadequacies in public health and education were another focal point of our forums. Our leaders worried about shortages of skilled labor and the necessity of good health and education for the economic and social progress of nations. As discussed, public health and education have direct links to productivity. Indeed, the market system's effective functioning is heavily premised on educated and informed decision making by all participants—be they consumers and employees, or investors, executives, and government officials. Poor health and lack of education, moreover, can be significant barriers to mobility and to individuals' full participation in the system, and both tend to exacerbate the income and wealth disparities that fuel discontent and generate hostility to market capitalism as a whole.

Antecedent Resources

The system is further premised on the availability and flow of resources—of people, raw materials, capital, information—to fuel the processes of production, distribution, and consumption that lie at its core. Two lines of argument in our forums focused on the flows of resources and people—particularly on the rise of protectionism and the challenges of migration. These forces, many of our executives feared, would slow down growth and development in some of the world's neediest regions. As we discussed, the state of trade in energy is particularly problematic, given energy's centrality to almost every facet of modern life. But our leaders worried, more generally, that growing protectionist sentiment would lead more and more nations to erect trade barriers and other restrictions on the flows of people, raw materials, goods and services, information, and other resources necessary for a vibrant market system.

These three groups of antecedents—effective and legitimate institutions, supportive social and political conditions, and an abundant flow of resources—in effect constitute the necessary foundations of market capitalism. The market system can perform at a high level only if these antecedents are in place and maintained over time. In their absence, the system works poorly or not at all.

The Central Core: The Market System Itself

We come back, then, to the core of this sociopolitical ecosystem—the market system itself. Although our forums did not delve deeply into the inner workings of this core, it is important to recognize that the market system is itself complex. It comprises many interrelated markets and subsystems that must function effectively to generate the beneficial outcomes (and minimize the negative outcomes) that capitalism is capable of producing.

As shown in figure 4-6, these components of the market system include markets for labor, capital, and raw materials. Through these markets, firms purchase the inputs they need to produce the goods and

FIGURE 4-6

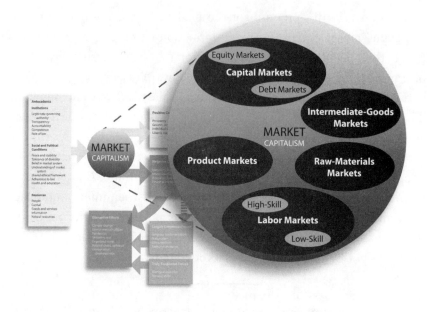

services that constitute the major benefits of the system. These markets, in turn, consist of differentiated but interrelated submarkets for varying skill types and levels in labor markets, different instruments in capital markets, and so on. Intermediate-goods markets allow firms to trade among themselves (*business to business*) so that businesses do not each have to take each product they produce from the raw-materials stage all the way to the final consumer. Firms are thus able to focus and specialize, thereby enhancing their own productivity and efficiency and that of the overall system. The markets for final goods and services allow consumers to find and purchase the outputs of this system.

The Infrastructure:
Institutions Internal to the Market System

The market system is much more than this collection of markets and submarkets, however. It also comprises an extensive set of institutions that permit these markets' existence, regulate their functioning, and mediate their outcomes. Here, we have in mind the customary practices and ethical standards that shape market behavior as well as the organizations and agencies that define these norms and create the structures through which markets operate.

The markets that allow production, distribution, and consumption cannot function independently of this institutional infrastructure. Like the operating system that shapes how a computer works, this infrastructure also shapes how markets work. Without laws defining and authorizing limited liability corporations, for example, the market for corporate control would not exist and many product and labor markets would function very differently. Or, to take another example, strong self-enforced norms allow participants in some markets to make billion-dollar trades on the basis of verbal agreements. In other markets, even minor transactions can be effected only through extensive documentation.

The elements of this institutional infrastructure are many and varied. Some of its key agencies and organizations are shown in figure 4-7.

FIGURE 4-7

Obviously, government plays a large role in creating and maintaining the market system's internal institutions. Government bodies perform a variety of crucial functions that include establishing the laws and rules under which businesses are formed, licensed, operated, and governed; establishing standards and definitions (of weights and measures or communications network protocols, for example); providing for the enforcement of contracts; and implementing a variety of public laws and regulations aimed at prohibiting fraud, ensuring fair competition, and maintaining safety and security.

Many private-sector and nongovernmental entities also play crucial roles. Industry associations define technical standards (e.g., for electrical plugs and fittings and for rules of accounting and reporting) that allow coordination and improve information, thus dramatically reducing costs to both businesses and consumers. Voluntary associations also set standards for professional performance and ethics, enhancing the trust and credibility business partners and consumers place in the transactions covered by the associations' rules. Business and other professional schools also play a role by preparing would-be market actors and regulators to be effective participants in the system. The business media provide transparency and disseminate vital information that lubricates the system and makes it function more efficiently.

These roles often interact across sectors in important ways. In the United States, for example, the nonprofit Financial Accounting Standards Board establishes standards for accounting and financial disclosure; these are given the force of law by being recognized by the Securities and Exchange Commission, an agency of the federal government.[1] Similarly, when businesses come together in industry associations to set voluntary standards that allow compatibility of devices (e.g., when manufacturers of optical disc drives agree on uniform standards and formats for physical size and information-storage densities that allow information written on one computer to be accessible on another), governments allow these actions, which might otherwise be viewed as illegal collusion.

Within this context, individuals and firms also shape how markets function. Through their governance structures, decision-making processes, pay practices, and performance metrics, firms influence not only their own behavior but also that of rivals and other parties in their network of stakeholders. When the innovative practices of a firm take hold and are adopted widely across industries and sectors of the economy—when the practices are institutionalized, in other words—they, too, become part of the market system.

Taken together, these institutions shape the behavior of specific markets, actors in markets, and the market system as a whole. To the extent that these institutions succeed in reducing the incidence of coercive, fraudulent, and exploitative behavior, they enhance the likelihood that market transactions will be—and will appear to be—honest and fair. In the absence of these conditions, market participants would struggle for a basis on which to trust the system, and exchange would largely or completely collapse. The near standstill in the credit markets at the height of the financial crisis of 2008 suggests how such a collapse might occur.

The institutional infrastructure, thus, dramatically influences other outcomes of the system—and the balance between positive and negative outcomes with which we began this chapter (see figure 4-3 for a summary). In response to the lines of argument from our business leader forums, these institutions can collectively foster more (or less) attention to the environmental impacts of market activity and promote greater (or less) financial stability; likewise, they can encourage (or discourage) broad participation in the system and widen (or narrow) disparities in how the wealth created by the system is allocated. But as discussed, our business leaders made clear that neither the institutions internal to the market system nor the societal institutions that precede it seem capable of tackling these issues effectively today.

Feedback: Drivers That Close the System

How the market system works and the consequences it generates depend, then, in significant measure on the institutions that permit and regulate its functioning. When the market system is performing well, it generates strongly positive consequences that, in turn, sustain the preconditions that made it possible in the first place. Figure 4-8 illustrates this relationship as a positive-feedback loop across the top of our overall system diagram. Strong positive performance of the system will reinforce beliefs in it, supporting and sustaining its foundational elements.

FIGURE 4-8

The negative consequences, however, also have implications for the antecedent foundations. As outlined earlier, the negative outcomes feed a series of potential disruptors—such as climate change, resource depletion, pandemics, political chaos, revolution, terrorism, and other influences—which in turn will tend to undercut these foundations. This dynamic is shown in figure 4-8 by the negative-feedback loop at the bottom of the diagram.

The System as a Whole:
Is the Market System Sustainable?

The market system is thus at the center of two feedback loops. The positive consequences that flow from functioning markets create positive feedback that reinforces and supports the antecedent institutions, sociopolitical conditions, and resource flows necessary to sustain the system, while the negative consequences feed into disruptive effects (which may also be caused by exogenous factors) that undercut and weaken these same antecedents.

If market capitalism is understood in this way, the question of its sustainability can be broken down into a series of considerations that encompass, but go beyond, the environmental, social, and governance factors often associated with the term. According to the logic of our discussion, the market system's sustainability has to do with the following factors:

- How effectively the positive consequences are translated into forces that support and reinforce the antecedents

- How powerfully the negative consequences create and drive disruptors, and how seriously the disruptors undercut the antecedents

- How powerfully the exogenous influences drive the disruptors and undermine the antecedents

- How successfully the antecedent institutions, conditions, and resource flows withstand the disruptors that threaten to undercut them

- How effectively the mediating and regulating institutions manage this complex of forces to ensure that the balance tilts toward the positive forces and that the negative forces and potential disruptors are held in check

It is important to recognize that the overall system we have described—complete with its internally driven feedback loops and its exogenous forces—was not *designed* or *built*. Instead, it *formed* as the system of market transactions and the mediating institutions were developed and evolved. As a result, there is no grand design or simple intention driving the system—and no group or institution is in charge of the overall system, its functioning, or its outcomes.

Who, then, will feel responsible for trying to make this overall system more value-creating and sustainable? Who would be in a position to intervene in any part of this complex of forces to shift its balance toward the positive feedbacks and interrupt the chain of negative forces? What strategies could they develop? What actions should they take?

We hypothesize that the market system will be more sustainable—that is, more likely to endure and more resistant to the destabilizing influences we have discussed—when the following criteria are met:

- Its positive consequences are substantial, visible, and equitably enjoyed.

- Its negative consequences are minimized, managed, and equitably borne.

- Its antecedent institutions, sociopolitical conditions, and resources are robust and plentiful.

- Its resistance to exogenous threats is high.

- Its mediating and regulating institutions are effective in managing and maintaining these conditions.

By the same token, the system will be less sustainable when these criteria are not met or are only weakly satisfied.

Put differently, the system's performance depends on the extent to which these criteria are met. But the question then arises, who is responsible for ensuring that the capitalist system performs at a high (and ever-improving) level—and who will monitor and address dysfunctional influences when they arise?

In the remaining chapters in this book, we take up the role of business as a part of the answer to these questions.

Part Two

How Business Can Lead

5

The Business Response

W
HAT, THEN, should be done about the challenges facing market capitalism? And what, specifically, is the role of business in this effort? In our conversations, we heard answers reflecting a spectrum of views. Although executives in our forums did not use our terminology, their positions clustered into four broad categories that we term *business as bystander*, *business as activist*, *business as innovator*, and *business as usual*.

In this chapter, before offering our own view, we take a closer look at these four positions. Although we find none of them entirely satisfactory, each contains some important insights. A closer look will help us construct a fifth position—*business as leader*—and suggest an alternative understanding of what business can do to help address the potential disruptors and strengthen the market system.

In what follows, we try to give a fair presentation of each view, although, as will become clear, we do not agree with all the points made. Indeed, on some issues, the differing views are in direct conflict with one another. In spelling out these positions, we draw on comments from our forums and sketch some of the classic arguments and rationales offered for each.

Business as Bystander:
Leaving Solutions to the Government

At one end of the spectrum are executives who see little, if any, role for business in addressing the challenges facing market capitalism. This group includes executives, like the one quoted earlier, who view these challenges as "above my pay grade" or lying outside the sphere of legitimate business activity. For these individuals, the potential disruptors may be important, but they are best dealt with by someone other than business—most typically, by government. As an advocate for this position put it, "The world would be a better place if business stayed out of these issues. The best solution is a well-functioning government pursuing social justice."

This view, which we call *business as bystander*, has its roots in neoclassical economic theory and nineteenth-century liberalism. Starting from the proposition that business is—and should be—about the pursuit of financial self-interest, proponents of this view often frame the challenges to market capitalism as public-goods problems. As defined in standard textbooks, *public goods* are socially valuable goods whose enjoyment cannot be easily restricted to those who are willing to pay for them. Once created, public goods can be enjoyed by all, and additional beneficiaries can be served at little incremental cost. A classic example is a clean environment, but other examples might include a stable financial system, social justice, and the rule of law.

According to this perspective, markets are an effective mechanism for providing society with *private* goods and services—those whose benefits flow mainly to the private parties who purchase them and for which the beneficiary can easily be required to pay. But the market is problematic as a delivery mechanism for public goods and services.

One difficulty is that public goods can be produced and maintained on a scale adequate to meet the public's need only through the coordinated actions of many parties. No single firm or group acting alone can generate clean air, social trust, or respect for law—and it is unlikely that a sufficient number of individual firms will spontaneously cooperate for these ends.

Providing public goods, moreover, is costly, and recouping the cost is often difficult since, by definition as noted above, those who are unwilling to pay cannot be easily prevented from enjoying the benefits. Public goods, in other words, are susceptible to the free-rider problem. Many beneficiaries will not pay if they can access public goods for free, and it may not be possible to attract a sufficient number of willing payers to cover the necessary cost.

A firm that voluntarily undertakes to do its share to provide a public good thus runs the risk of putting itself at a disadvantage relative to its less public-spirited rivals. A company that scrupulously follows the letter of the law, for example, will often incur higher costs than one that is only selectively obedient. And at the same time, unless the volunteer firm is joined by others in a large-scale and well-coordinated campaign, the ultimate contribution to meeting the public need is likely to be negligible.

The logical conclusion is that some higher authority is required to compel collective action to supply the desired public good and to ensure that the costs of providing it are equitably borne. Since governments are the only agents with the authority and legitimacy to play this role, it follows that governments are the proper agents to address public-goods problems and, moreover, that business efforts in this domain are likely to be both costly and futile.

Seen from this perspective, business efforts to promote public goods may also be challenged as a usurpation of governmental authority or an illegitimate interference in the democratic process, particularly if the goods at issue are not (yet) highly valued by the broader society. Once threats to market capitalism are framed as public-goods problems, the conclusion that they should be dealt with by government follows almost inexorably, by the logic of this perspective. Several of our business leaders seemed resigned to this stance, even though they were not particularly happy about it. "The power is in the hands of the government," noted a European executive when asked what companies could do about threats to the market system.

In our sessions, proponents of the business-as-bystander view also questioned the business community's competence to handle the political and public-policy issues raised by the problems identified. Executives may know about sourcing inputs and achieving operational efficiencies, commented one participant, but what do they know about designing a regulatory system or reducing poverty? Echoing this

sentiment, a former CEO who was quoted earlier candidly acknowledged the limitations of the typical executive's expertise. Most executives, he observed, know how to deploy their assets or structure their
operations based on current rules, but few know how to go about
making a contribution to worldwide stability.

Business, moreover, is not organized to work in a cooperative fashion, especially on global concerns. "The business community is completely disparate and desegregated," noted one participant, likening
it to the Austro-Hungarian Empire. And few executives have the
patience needed for the lengthy discussion and airing of views that
are a necessary part of tackling public issues. "Businesspeople are not
very good at coping with differences of opinion and different ways of
looking at things," said one executive, citing his own experience in
discussions of public issues among his peers. "In a diverse group, they
grow impatient."

Many proponents of the bystander view are deeply skeptical of
business morality as well. This attitude flows in part from a theoretical
framework that posits purely self-interested behavior by market actors.
But the bystander group's skepticism also finds support in examples of
self-serving corporate behavior, overreaching, and outright misconduct
by companies and executives that regularly appear in the news. Rev-
elations of widespread fraud and deception in the mortgage market
prior to the financial crisis, for example, only reinforced this group's
conviction that business is driven by greed and cannot be trusted to
consider the public interest.

Bystander advocates also point to the recent growth in corporate
lobbying as further evidence that business is indifferent to the greater
good. According to the Center for Responsive Politics, business was a
major contributor to some $3.5 billion spent on lobbying the U.S. fed-
eral government in 2009, up from $1.4 billion ten years earlier.[1] Lobby-
ing expenditures at the state level in the United States have historically
been about half that at the federal level.[2] Although the amount of
dollars spent says nothing about the positions taken, most bystander
advocates believe that business lobbying is—and can only be—wholly
self-serving.

As a recent case in point, one speaker cited what happened when
the private sector was invited to participate in the Basel II process on

capital requirements for financial institutions: "The private sector took government to the cleaners." The result was lower capital requirements for financial institutions, which, combined with the high leverage adopted by many banks, made the banking system even more vulnerable to the meltdown of 2008.

Such examples all feed into a view, prevalent in the bystander camp, that businesspeople lack the motivation and commitment required to think broadly about the public good. To paraphrase the conclusion of the speaker quoted above, if you wanted to choose people to set the broad direction of public policy, you'd be better off selecting a random set of individuals from the phone book.

Even if they wanted to, companies would be unable to take a more public-spirited stance, say business-as-bystander advocates. Executives are fiduciaries for their shareholders, and spending money to benefit the public beyond what the law requires would violate these duties—or so it is often argued. Shareholders, moreover, would surely balk at the use of corporate funds for what was described as "pursuing social passion with shareholders' money." An Asian executive spoke candidly about his unsuccessful efforts to engage executives in discussions of major public issues: "Frankly, most of them say, 'Hey, look, my primary responsibility is to my shareholders, my board, and my business.'"

Such shareholder-based arguments for corporate noninvolvement in addressing threats to the market system often assume that shareholders, as a group, are opposed to such involvement. Investors are thought to be interested first and foremost in maximizing their short-term financial interests. Since efforts to foster the system's long-term health are presumed to be antithetical to these interests, it follows, according to this view, that companies would be both wrong and foolish to take a more active stance. The business-as-bystander advocate often cautions that executives who take sustainability issues seriously are likely to be shown the door—they may even be charged with breach of fiduciary duty and sued for their trouble.

On the business-as-bystander view, the role of business in addressing the challenges to capitalism is largely a negative one—to get out of government's way. More dramatically, some proponents of this school of thought hold that business should stop lobbying, stop making campaign contributions, stop trying to influence public policy, and stop seeking tax breaks. In other words, business should let government do its job and should not meddle in policy making.

More positively, companies should focus on producing the goods and services that markets require and, in so doing, generate as much wealth as possible. In the words of one executive, "What we should do—the best contribution we can make—is to run our companies and make them as efficient as possible."

Business as Activist:
Shaping and Promoting Government Solutions

Another group sees a very different role for business—not as a bystander waiting for government to act, but as an activist spurring and guiding governments toward policies and programs that will strengthen the market system. Like advocates of the bystander view, proponents of the business-as-activist viewpoint frame the challenges to capitalism largely as public-goods problems and see governments as the principal actor in addressing them. But members of this group are far less sanguine about the ability of governments to effect the needed changes. Largely for this reason, executives in this camp argue that business can and must become more actively engaged in shaping and influencing public policy.

This group's pessimism about government stems in part from the limits of national authority. As business leaders in all regions pointed out, the problems facing capitalism are largely international. The prime illustration is climate change, which affects the globe and is caused by greenhouse gases that defy jurisdictional boundaries and cross borders with impunity. But other challenges, such as ethnic conflicts arising from mass migration or financial system weaknesses arising from differences in national regulations, are essentially international as well.

Unilateral action by national governments can go only so far toward addressing these issues. As one executive said, "We know that trade and investment issues, climate change issues, terrorist issues, financial crime issues, are issues that cannot be handled at the national level. They can only be handled at the international level. Unless we develop this international framework, we have the risk that there will be backlash against the very concept of capitalism itself."

Yet many executives doubted that governments unaided would rise to the challenge. Even if national leaders are otherwise inclined to collaborate on international solutions with their counterparts in other countries, their ability to do so is limited since they are, after all, elected by, and accountable to, a national citizenry. With many voters feeling that globalization threatens their livelihood if not their national identity and their country's sovereignty, democratically elected leaders are understandably loath to tackle issues that touch these sensitive areas. As a European executive noted, "Even if you are a national politician who is worried about something that's going on in the international environment, it's often very hard to develop a local constituency, particularly for any kind of sacrifice that you would be asking for on behalf of some larger global gain."

Indeed, numerous executives in our sessions voiced concerns about the rise of protectionist sentiment in many countries. Citing the business community's considerable experience with internationalization, leaders in the activist camp saw a crucial role for business in developing proposals for dealing with volatile international issues. And many thought it would be easier for business to agree on a path forward. Migration, for instance, was seen as "an area where it will be much easier for companies to reach consensus than [it will be] for governments." Similarly, climate change was identified as an issue for which "it's probably easier to get agreements between national companies and NGOs" than among governments.

"Short-termism" was cited as another obstacle to effective government action. As several discussants observed, short election cycles and long campaigns do not encourage long-term thinking. In some countries, politicians' time horizons seem to be even shorter than those of corporate executives. And good policies put in place by one administration can be quickly undone by a successor administration with different goals and priorities. Despite the pressures of quarterly reporting and short-term investors, participants in our forums felt that businesspeople, as compared with politicians, had more flexibility to embrace the long-term orientation needed to develop and implement policies to strengthen the market system.

Many business-as-activist proponents also question government's competence to devise the needed reforms and worry that policy makers lack the necessary knowledge. One U.S. business leader's comment was typical: "Our politicians don't really understand the dynamics of the global economy and the implications for business and for their constituents' issues such as jobs, health care, and standard of living." In our discussions, executives shared their fears that misguided governments acting alone would weaken the market system and make problems worse through misguided or overzealous regulation or by expropriating private property.

Although concerns about government competence were more pronounced in some regions than others, these worries were nonetheless widespread. Indeed, as noted earlier, one U.S. executive called politicians "the number one threat to capitalism," explaining that "politicians create the rules that we all have to live by, and politicians responding to voters can create rules that could be very, very damaging."

Some in the activist camp pointed to resource constraints as another reason that business must work closely with government. Governments cannot invest in improving the market system—or even take on more limited tasks that fall clearly within their purview—because they are simply stretched too thin. Arguing that business is needed to help cover the shortfall, a European executive described the situation in his own country by way of example: "A lot of our budget is really being misused to pay back interest on this [huge state] debt, instead of investing it into education and things that look forward, rather than paying off the past."

Proponents of business as activist point to the moral failings of bureaucrats and politicians as further reason that business cannot simply step aside and leave the care and protection of the market system to governments. If advocates of business as bystander take a dim view of business morality, advocates of business as activist take an even dimmer view of political morality. Citing abuses of authority and high levels of corruption in governments around the world, many executives expressed deep distrust of the public sector's motives and commitments. Recall the Latin American executive quoted earlier: "We are not trusting [of government], and there is a reason why." Other data suggests similar views among thousands of executives polled by the World Economic Forum. Over the past decade, these annual surveys have shown that executives consistently rate the trustworthiness of politicians as low or very low in more than half of the countries examined.[3]

While our CEOs saw specialized multilateral institutions as partial solutions to the deficiencies of national governments, these leaders were also pessimistic about the capacity of existing multilaterals and development organizations to deal effectively with challenges facing the system. As noted earlier, executives from all regions viewed these institutions as hobbled by bureaucracy, inefficiency, and public distrust; poorly designed for the problems of today; and lacking in support from major countries such as the United States, China, and Russia. Existing institutions are also perceived by many in the developing world as one-sided in their agenda. As expressed by an executive at our Asia forum in Hong Kong, "Internationally, in my view, the weakness [of] and the challenge to most of our multilateral institutions is that they are perceived as not serving the interests of all humanity."

Executives in the business-as-activist camp called on their fellow business leaders to speak out for better international governance. Business, they argued, should be more supportive of efforts to build new and improved multilateral institutions to tackle problems such as climate change, financial system stability, and international crime. "I think that businesses around the world not only have a role but have a responsibility to think about this," urged an Asian executive referring to the mismatch between the design of existing multilateral institutions and challenges facing the market system today.

Others called on business to advocate more strongly against protectionism and in favor of free trade and to speak up for national policies to combat the problems of rising inequality. In our Latin America forum, for instance, executives stressed the importance of policies that promote training and employment as a counterweight to rising inequality. In other forums, discussions focused more on tax and education policies as a lever on this problem. Similarly, on other issues, the business-as-activist participants in our forums saw opportunities for business to put its voice behind greater transparency and other constructive suggestions for improvement.

In addition to expressing the voice of business more clearly and forcefully, many in the business-as-activist group argued that business should take a leadership role in opening up discussions of critical issues with other segments of society. In Europe, for example, participants suggested that business leaders might initiate discussions with the Greens on climate change and with trade unions on international trade and investment. Such efforts, even if "very difficult and slightly subversive," to quote one executive, were seen as crucial for building a decentralized social network with the power to shape public discourse and opinion.

Some in the business-as-activist camp saw business taking the further step of forming ad hoc consortia or standing organizations to develop public policies for consideration by the relevant governmental bodies. An advocate of this approach urged similarly that such groups should be "a little more embracing of people who don't usually talk together: union leaders, NGOs, people from the political world, and businesspeople . . . I'm more of a believer that with the right people in the room you can get pretty close to the truth and therefore pretty close to some practical lines of possible legislation."

Alternatively and more modestly, business-sponsored consortia could help define the range of policy options available and contribute to public understanding of the choices at issue. These organizations, our executives suggested, might also conduct or sponsor independent fact-finding and research. In our Latin America forum, we heard support for even a further step—business-sponsored watchdog organizations to monitor and report on government spending.

While urging greater business involvement in the policy arena, the business-as-activist group nonetheless sees government as the central and most important actor for strengthening and supporting the market system. The role of business is critical, but it is secondary to the role of government. Business can propose, advocate, sponsor, and support solutions, but, ultimately, governments must act for these solutions to take effect.

In viewing government as the central actor in addressing threats to capitalism, activists are like the business-as-bystander group discussed earlier. Activists part company with their bystander cousins, however, when it comes to lobbying and other efforts to influence public opinion and public policy. While bystanders argue that such efforts are inappropriate attempts to distort democracy and to usurp government authority, activists see the use of influence techniques as a legitimate exercise of free expression and a necessary response to the threats facing capitalism both nationally and internationally. "I don't think we want to treat good governance as exogenous [to the market system]," noted one proponent of a more activist stance. "We regard it as the outcome of things that smart people in the society do." But activists are not confused about their authority. As one executive put it, "The only authority that any business group has comes from its leadership. There is absolutely no authority whatsoever other than that."

Business as Innovator: Addressing Challenges Directly

Yet another group of executives at our forums saw business as more than a supporting player to government. This group envisioned business as a force for change in its own right, taking direct action to address the emerging threats and challenges to the market system. Advocates of this perspective, which we call *business as innovator*, tended to frame the disruptors and dysfunctions more as practical problems to be solved on a company-by-company basis than as broad public policy issues requiring government solutions. As one executive put it, "It's companies which are over and over and over again at the front line [and that] pragmatically have to deal with [these] very profound problems."

For the business-as-innovator group, improvements to the market system will be driven not by governments and public policy changes but by firms and individuals developing innovative business models and improved management practices. Where bystanders and economic theorists see public-goods problems, the business-as-innovator group sees unmet needs and unrealized opportunities for business leadership. One participant, for example, pointed to the vast numbers of people currently excluded from the market system around the world and especially in emerging-markets countries. By developing new business models and new organizational structures, she argued, companies could "actually take advantage of all the opportunities that exist in these economies while at the same time being part of the solution."

In contrast to those who stress the need for governments to compel coordinated action, proponents of business as innovator view social and economic change as a bottoms-up phenomenon that is better understood through a cultural or social lens than a legislative, regulatory, or public policy lens. The innovator group points out that government action is almost always a lagging indicator of social, economic, and technological developments and that these developments are themselves the result of experimentation and risk-taking by pioneering thinkers and entrepreneurs. Moreover, governments can act only after ideas have gained wide acceptance, since otherwise, political support would be difficult to mobilize.

According to the innovator view, new ideas and practices gain adherents not through legislative fiat but through the power of positive example or what social scientists term *positive deviance*. Business as innovator readily acknowledges that no single firm or business leader acting alone can solve problems that cut across the system. Nor do individuals and firms have the sovereign power of government to compel a collective or coordinated response to these problems. However, individual companies can, by example, inspire others to act and, through the force of competition, spur innovation and improve practice throughout an industry or a sector and, in the best case, drive a "race to the top."

From the perspective of innovators, government is, at most, an enabler. Whatever incentives or rules the government may put in place, the decision to act or react lies with the private sector. And it is the private sector that transforms policy goals and objectives into the concrete activities that affect people's lives. As one member of this camp put it, "Governments can make policies and pass laws, but it is ultimately business that creates jobs and provides employment."

An advocate of business as innovator illustrated the point with the example of poverty: "When we talk about roles, often the problem of poverty is seen as the problem of government. You know, just educate them more, give them a little more health care, and pretty soon, they will get on board. The reality is that the single biggest problem of poor people is that they don't have enough money. And that sounds like a tautology, except that if poor people have the capacity to earn, then they will send their kids to school, they will use the health clinics, and they will vote for private-sector, market-oriented governments." In other words, the solution to poverty lies ultimately in developing business models that create more jobs. Government programs to provide education and health care are important, but on their own, they will not solve the fundamental problem confronting the poor—namely, the lack of employment.

Innovators tend to be optimistic about the prospects for business-generated solutions to many of the problems and challenges outlined earlier. Taking inspiration from history, they point to technologies that have revolutionized how companies operate and transformed how societies function. This group cites the speed with which new management practices and business models have traversed the globe in recent decades as evidence that business can transform itself without the need for government intervention. Indeed, many leading multinationals operate their facilities to higher standards of safety, employee relations, and environmental protection than required by local law and regulation in many of the jurisdictions where they do business.

By and large, the innovators share with activists a generally pessimistic view of government. For innovators, though, a particular point of concern is the overly broad nature of mandates that typically issue from government bodies. Government policy making is just too cumbersome, and the one-size-fits-all directives that often result cannot accommodate the many variations in company size, structure, strategy, and circumstances. Moreover, government officials rarely have the in-depth business knowledge needed to translate general societal objectives into specific company- or industry-level operating procedures. All too often, say the innovators, business gets saddled with costly compliance responsibilities that make no sense for the enterprise and that contribute little to the intended policy objective.

A frequently cited case in point were the internal controls mandates of the Sarbanes-Oxley Act—specifically, the much-maligned section 404(b) requiring auditor attestation to management's assessment of a company's internal controls. Drafted with large companies in mind, these provisions proved costly and difficult for small companies to implement, and many critics argued that the costs for small companies far outweighed the benefits. In a similar vein, innovators worry that government limits on greenhouse gas emissions will have disproportionate impacts on some sectors of the economy and put smaller companies at a competitive disadvantage compared with their larger brethren. Far better, say innovators, for companies to take the initiative in finding creative and competitive ways to limit their own greenhouse gas emissions.

Those who see business as the primary engine of systemic improvement often cite the global reach of business as another reason to favor business-driven over government-driven solutions. With authority that transcends national boundaries, leaders of multinational companies can introduce problem-mitigating innovations that span the globe and engage people of different creeds and nationalities far more quickly and effectively than governments can. Indeed, as one executive stressed, big, global companies are by their very nature forced to "make people work together in a constructive way," despite differences in the attitudes and assumptions people may bring to the workplace.

Global reach and integrated operations and decision making also give large corporations considerable clout. For example, when McDonald's told its french-fry suppliers that it would no longer accept potatoes that had been genetically modified to resist the Colorado potato bug and were thus popular with farmers but controversial with environmental advocates, the response in the potato market was immediate and widespread. The manufacturer quietly withdrew the genetically modified seeds—its first genetically engineered product—from the market shortly thereafter. When Walmart announced that it was seeking products with improved energy efficiency, its suppliers across the globe scrambled to get on board. Implementing similarly significant changes over as broad a geographic area on as aggressive a time scale through government regulation alone would be nothing short of miraculous.

Global companies have the further advantage of access to ideas and talent around the world. Although relatively few multinationals have begun to take full advantage of this access, some are beginning to set up research and development (R&D) centers at key locations in different regions. By building a truly global R&D function, companies can more easily tap into insights wherever they emerge. These companies increasingly view China and India, for example, not just as sources of cheap labor or even as markets for stripped-down versions of products designed in the West, but as hubs of innovation and sources of insight and talent.

Among the business-as-innovator group in our forums, many executives called on companies to take a more active and direct role in addressing the market system's potential disruptors and dysfunctions. Some people urged more investment in new technologies with the potential to mitigate looming environmental, energy, and health-related problems. Others emphasized the need for new business models and structures to help alleviate poverty and give the disenfranchised a real stake in the market system. Still others called for more humanistic management practices, changes in executive compensation, and reforms in corporate governance to better moderate the system's outcomes and better manage systemic risk.

Members of this group also called for changes in the dominant patterns of business thinking. Executives' tendency to ignore the environmental and human impact of their decisions, argued some, needs to be replaced with a more sustainable way of thinking. As expressed by one executive, this means replacing a single-minded focus on profitability with a richer set of decision criteria—one that includes profitability but also recognizes the limits of our natural resources and the profound consequences that business decisions can have for people's lives. This executive urged others to pay more attention to impacts on employees, customers, and members of the community as human beings and not just economic actors in a marketplace.

Other participants called for a comparable shift in the thinking of investors whom they perceived as overly focused on the short term and indifferent to the broader consequences of their investment decisions. Many felt it would be difficult to change the mind-set of business executives without a parallel change in investors. Commenting on innovations that could help alleviate poverty, for example, one executive urged that a successful effort "means not just changing the mentality of the business executives that have to make the decisions but also changing the mentality of the investors, the shareholders of the businesses where these executives are working."

Importantly, the business-as-innovator proponents saw their proposals for addressing the challenges to capitalism as fully consistent with the wealth-creating role of companies. Unlike bystanders, who, in keeping with their characterization of the disruptors as public-goods problems, tend to presume a conflict between the good of the firm and the good of the system, innovators are more apt to assume that creative thinking and entrepreneurial effort will generate solutions that simultaneously advance the good of both. Similarly, bystander proponents often take the disruptors as evidence that profitable private-sector solutions to these problems do not exist, while innovators simply believe that such solutions have not yet been invented.

Indeed, some innovators see bystander thinking itself as a serious threat to capitalism. As one proponent of business as innovator put it, "I think the biggest threat to market capitalism is that large corporations in the United States and in the emerging markets will not figure out that they need to be part of the solution."

Business as Usual: Taking Crises in Stride

The three groups described above all argued that a successful attack on forces threatening to disrupt the market system would require fundamental changes in how business functions. Proponents of the bystander view called for business to withdraw from the law- and policy-making arena and to end its efforts to shape public policy to its own ends. The business-as-activist group called for the opposite—a more robust and informed effort by business to engage with government and shape policy, albeit with a focus on the public interest rather than just the narrow self-interest of particular companies and industries. The business-as-innovator group called for a range of reforms in the internal operations of business—the development of new business models, more investment in new technologies, the adoption of new ways of thinking and making decisions.

A fourth and smaller group, however, felt that the disruptors would be addressed without the need for focused attention or fundamental change. We call this stance *business as usual.* Proponents of business as usual did not dispute the evidence of problems and challenges. But they felt the seriousness of these problems was overstated and that the capitalist market system, as it currently functions, is fundamentally sound. Over time, argued members of this group, the issues needing attention would take care of themselves through the normal workings of existing government, business, and other institutions.

The business-as-usual group included those very few who were generally untroubled by the problems identified by others in our forums, as well as those who saw the problems as worrisome but not particularly threatening to the market system. One speaker, for instance, characterized the growing gap between rich and poor as a serious moral problem and, therefore, an issue deserving of much more attention from both the public and the private sectors, but he did not see it as a threat to the market system.

From the business-as-usual vantage point, episodes like the 2008 financial crisis are taken as evidence of the market system's remarkable capacity for self-correction. Human behavior being what it is, booms and busts are an inevitable part of the system's functioning, and the pain associated with periodic busts is more than offset by the wealth created during the corresponding booms. Proponents of this view tend to believe that efforts to moderate this cycle—and, more generally, efforts to adjust the system to address other destabilizing forces—are likely to generate new and potentially worse problems, and their benefits are unlikely to outweigh their costs.

Although proponents of business as usual tend to be pessimistic about particular efforts to improve the market system, they are nonetheless optimistic about the system's overall ability to improve over time. They point to the enormous changes that market capitalism has undergone throughout its history. Contrast, for example, working conditions in the factories of late nineteenth-century America with those in today's Six Sigma workplaces. Advocates of business as usual see changes like this as part of an inevitable and impersonal evolutionary process rather than the product of leadership and focused effort. And they are confident that this same evolutionary process will enable the market system to overcome or adapt to the challenges ahead.

Business as Leader: Forging Solutions Through Innovation and Activism

As this discussion indicates, the positions taken by the participants in our forums reflect wide differences in outlook and experience. Most leaders agreed with the broad outlines of the problems presented, but described them in different language and approached them from different vantage points. Some took a top-down perspective; others saw the issues from the bottom up. As discussed earlier, leaders applying a public-goods frame reached very different conclusions from those adopting an entrepreneurial frame. Participants' comments revealed a wide range of beliefs and assumptions about other topics—the dynamics of social change, the sources of executive authority, the morality of business and government, and the capabilities of business and government, to name just a few.

Taken together, however, their perspectives suggest that business has a crucial role to play in addressing the various forces that threaten the market system. We agree. And in the proposals put forth at our forums, we see an intriguing menu of possibilities for business-led action to do so. While we came away from our discussions with a heightened awareness of the challenges that must be overcome, we also developed a richer appreciation of the possibilities for leadership to address these challenges.

Our principal conclusion is that business can and must play a central role in sustaining the market system and improving its performance for society. Borrowing elements from each of the perspectives above, we see this role as multifaceted—part innovator, part activist, part bystander, and even, in some respects, carrying on with business as usual. (Even though we call for significant changes in business behavior—and, in this respect, differ from the proponents of business as usual—we also emphasize that many of the "usual" skills and capabilities of business, including the ability to innovate, are crucial for meeting the challenges ahead.) We call our view, which incorporates the most convincing aspects of the various schools of thought on the role of business in market capitalism, *business as leader*.

To be more precise, our vision calls for business to continue doing what it does well and, at the same time, help raise the market system's functioning to a higher and ultimately more sustainable level through innovations in business operations and activism for good government and sound public policy. The activism we envision respects the authority of government and seeks to uphold the democratic process. As we will discuss in chapter 7, this constructive engagement between business and government, while not unprecedented, is nonetheless a far cry from the kinds of lobbying and influence tactics that the public—and the bystander school—associates with business today.

Unlike those who say that business should sit on the sidelines while governments address the system's problems, we believe that business has much to contribute both directly through its own activities and indirectly through inputs on critical policy and regulatory questions. Moreover, we are not persuaded that governments can do the job alone. Even apart from the resource constraints that governments are facing around the world, governmental capacity is limited. Although most business executives know little about public policy (as bystander advocates rightfully argue), most governments have limited knowledge and expertise when it comes to developing effective policies on climate change, financial regulation, poverty reduction, and other challenges discussed at our forums.

The activist and innovator schools correctly argue that policy makers and regulators need a practical understanding of the private sector to shape the sector's activities. The recent financial crisis is yet another example of what can happen when the complexities of business outstrip the understanding of regulators and policy makers. At the same time, BP's early handling of the 2010 oil spill in the Gulf of Mexico did little to inspire confidence in the private sector's capacity to address the large-scale environmental and other challenges facing the market system. Neither sector—public or private—has a monopoly on the expertise and knowledge that will be needed. Rather, as acknowledged by many business leaders in our discussions, both sectors will need to acquire new knowledge and build new competencies to address these challenges successfully.

Nor is the public sector morally better equipped for these tasks than the private sector, as suggested by the bystander camp. Regrettably, as the daily news attests, no sector is immune to the forces of corruption. Public-opinion surveys consistently report low levels of trust in both government and business. Surveys of Americans conducted by Gallup in 2010, for example, indicate that big business and the U.S. Congress are the country's two least trusted institutions. Only 19 percent of Americans expressed "a great deal" or "a lot" of confidence in big business; only 11 percent, in Congress.[4] Other surveys show that across the world, people regard business and their country's national legislature as the institutions they least trust to act in society's best interests.[5] According to some polls, the highest levels of public trust in business and government to do what is right can be found, perhaps surprisingly, in China.[6] Taken in its totality, the evidence indicates that both sectors face serious credibility challenges that, if unaddressed, will increasingly compromise their effectiveness as purveyors of solutions to the challenges we have outlined.

Of course, the role of governments in making the market system stronger and more resilient is crucial. Our call for business to take a leadership role in this effort in no way diminishes the importance of government. As noted earlier (and will be discussed more fully in chapter 7), there are some things that only governments can do, and the business-as-bystander proponents make a useful point in emphasizing the limits of voluntary action by private-sector actors. While at least some of the disruptors represent near-term business opportunities for forward-thinking companies, government involvement is sometimes necessary to level the playing field or to provide incentives for desirable activities that would otherwise be prohibitive for individual companies.

In summary, though the task of improving the market system's performance for society is necessarily a multisector effort, business must take a leadership role in driving this effort. But what, specifically, can business do? In the next two chapters, we suggest some possible avenues. Chapter 6 examines what companies can do on their own and considers the innovators' notion that the market system's potential disruptors contain the seeds of business opportunity. In chapter 7, we explore what companies can do when they work with and through governments, other business and industry groups, and the nonprofit sector.

Leading Through Innovative Business Models

A S WE HAVE explored in earlier chapters, two sets of forces—one from outside the economic system and one arising naturally from within it—have jointly created a series of large-scale challenges that threaten the foundations and future of the global market system. Threats come from many sources: the lack of education and opportunity in some areas, the rise of radical political movements in others, environmental degradation and climate change worldwide, growing disparities in the distribution of income and benefits flowing from the system in many countries, and failures of governance across critical sectors. The challenges are large and growing. And as we have also discussed, effective countervailing forces—and institutions that produce and direct those countervailing forces—have yet to arise or at least to become complete and effective. From this vantage point, the prospects for significantly ameliorating these constellations of negative forces appear bleak.

One possible source of countervailing force is business itself. To what extent can this growing array of threats to the market system be addressed through actions by individual firms and entrepreneurs? Many would say that the challenges are too great and too massive in scale for individual firms to have a significant impact. And many argue that governments and multilateral institutions are ultimately the only actors capable of managing risks of this magnitude and that the proper role for business is to get out of the way and let governments do their job.

This assessment, however, misses the mark. Companies and entrepreneurs *can* make a material difference. By aligning their activities with the needs of a sustainable economy and bringing their distinctive skills and capabilities to bear on these disruptive forces, companies can help strengthen the system and put it on a more secure footing. In answer to worries that such efforts might be a competitive handicap or a disincentive for investors, we see evidence that at least sometimes, these efforts can actually help drive innovation, growth, and profitability.

In this chapter, we review some examples of companies that have pursued innovative business models with the potential to help address some of the systemic challenges identified in earlier chapters. These examples illustrate four generic approaches suggested by the model of the market system introduced in chapter 4. As shown in figure 4-8, interventions to strengthen the system can take a variety of forms. One is by amplifying the system's positive consequences—for example, extending its benefits to new and previously excluded groups. A second is by mitigating its negative consequences—for example, reducing damage to human health and the environment. A third is by seeking to counteract or interrupt exogenous threats—for example, strengthening resistance to health and security threats from without. A fourth is by reinforcing the antecedents necessary for the system's effective functioning—for example, introducing improved methods of governance and capital allocation.

The examples that follow lend credence to the business-as-innovator view that at least some of the challenges to capitalism have within them the seeds of business opportunity. This is not to say that realizing these opportunities is easy or straightforward. As our examples show, even the most sophisticated companies and executives may need to acquire new knowledge, build new capabilities, or cultivate new ways of thinking and doing business to build successful business models around these opportunities. Nonetheless, these examples demonstrate that individual and firm-level actions *can* help mitigate some of the brewing threats if business leaders are willing to innovate to that end.

Mitigating the Negatives:
General Electric and Ecomagination

Consider "ecomagination," General Electric's signature environmental effort. Conceived in 2004, ecomagination was aimed at driving innovation and generating superior returns by tackling some of the planet's biggest problems—energy efficiency and harmful environmental impacts. Within five years, the initiative accounted for more than ninety products and services and some $18 billion in revenues.[1]

As CEO Jeff Immelt tells it, GE was going through its annual strategic planning review in June 2004 when the management team realized that six of the company's core businesses were deeply involved in environment- and energy-related projects. The appliance business was exploring energy conservation; the plastics business was working on the replacement of PCBs (polychlorinated biphenyls, once widely used industrial compounds found to be harmful to health and the environment); and the energy business was examining alternatives to fossil fuels. Other businesses were dealing with emissions reduction, resource scarcity, and energy efficiency. Far from reflecting a deliberate strategy on GE's part, these projects had all been initiated by GE in response to demands from its customers.

When these common issues surfaced across different lines of business in the midst of its planning process, the group realized that something was going on that GE needed to better understand and possibly become part of. Immelt announced that he wanted to learn about greenhouse gas emissions, and the company set about educating itself on critical energy and environmental issues. Meetings with leading customers were arranged, and the management team launched a study of the science behind climate change. "We went through a process of really understanding and coming to our own points of view on the science," recalled Immelt. At the same time, GE deepened its engagement with government officials and regulators on environmental issues and hired a consulting firm to help it understand the NGO landscape. This same consulting firm would eventually help GE identify promising products and services for its environmental portfolio.

As the management team gathered information and perspectives from external sources, GE also looked inward. A review of the company's technologies and technical capabilities revealed some important gaps that needed to be filled. The culture, some managers felt, needed to become more innovative and more externally focused. At several points in the learning and self-evaluation process, Immelt shared the management group's findings with GE's board of directors. He wanted board members to understand both the financial and the social aspects of the "green is green" message that was emerging and to be comfortable with the strategy that was taking shape.

After nearly a year of information gathering and analysis, the management team settled on an environmentally focused strategy that would cut across five or six key businesses. Immelt had become convinced that the world was changing dramatically and that climate change was a "technical fact." He believed that GE could prosper by helping its customers improve their environmental performance.[2] Some of his deputies disagreed, but Immelt was ready to put people and resources behind these ideas. The new strategy was dubbed "ecomagination" for its links to economics and ecology and its echo of GE's "imagination at work" tagline. As Immelt made clear, ecomagination was not a feel-good effort or just a rebranding move—it was aimed fundamentally at driving growth and innovation.

With dedicated funding in place, Immelt tapped one of the company's promising young leaders as the program's first manager. In characteristic GE fashion, the leadership team wrestled with finding the right metrics to guide and measure success. "If I stood up and talked about this as something we wanted to do without any output metrics, nobody would follow," noted Immelt, referring to GE's rigorous use of metrics as a company hallmark. He also stressed the importance of a program that could be easily understood and replicated: "It's got to be repeatable, it's got to be learnable, it's got to be teachable, and it's got to be something that investors can understand we are doing across the company."

The management team ultimately chose four core metrics, but only after extensive discussion and analysis over six months. As originally framed, the initiative would be assessed by R&D spending, growth in revenue from eco products, increased customer activation, and reductions in GE's own greenhouse gas emissions. Reductions in water use and heightened public engagement would be added later.

GE set targets for doubling its R&D investment in clean technologies to $1.5 billion per year by 2010 and growing revenues from eco products to $20 billion by 2010. (The target was later raised to $25 billion for a time and then reset back to the original $20 billion.) In its own operations, GE set out to cut greenhouse gas intensity—a measure of emissions against output—by 30 percent by 2008 and to cut absolute emissions by 1 percent by 2012 (as compared with what would have been a 40 percent increase in a business-as-usual scenario). These corporate goals were broken into subgoals and parceled out across the relevant businesses.

To fill gaps in its technology portfolio, GE put together an investment program that included in-house R&D efforts and a sizable venture fund to invest in innovative environmental and energy solutions. By investing in early-stage ventures in core areas such as renewable energy, water use, carbon management, and smart-grid development, GE enlarged its innovation network and forged relationships with a cohort of creative entrepreneurs and scientists. The company also formed an outside advisory board of energy and environmental thought leaders. Members of the advisory board offered a valuable external perspective on the company's efforts and shared with the heads of GE businesses insights on emerging issues and opportunities.

Immelt's team recognized the importance of the evolving policy framework to the ultimate success of its strategy. Rather than leaving matters to chance, GE joined forces with a select group of other U.S. companies and environmental NGOs to develop a proposed framework on climate change. As discussed more fully in chapter 7, the United States Climate Action Partnership (USCAP) issued a call for action in late 2006, laying out a set of principles and proposals, including support for legislation to cap carbon dioxide emissions. Immelt's answer to critics of this foray into the policy arena was succinct: "We are much better as a company getting ahead of [climate change policy] than we are pretending like it doesn't exist."[3]

As ecomagination got under way, Immelt found himself walking the fine line between staying ahead of the market but not so far ahead that it would alienate some of GE's biggest customers—not all of whom were as convinced as Immelt about climate change and the need for legislation capping emissions. With those more skeptical customers, some of whom were personal friends, Immelt's approach was one of candor and transparency. "You are going to hate this," he told one particularly close but dubious customer who ran a major utility. "I'm going to make it so the public utility commission [says] you've got to do coal gasification—but I'm transparent and you're going to know every step of the way what we're doing."[4]

When ecomagination was announced in May 2005, investor reactions were mixed. Some analysts deemed the strategy "sensible and intelligent" and pronounced the individual products well aligned with market demand.[5] Others, however, questioned whether the strategy could be made to pay—and whether the environmental markets that Immelt envisioned would actually materialize. For those who had lived through earlier periods of environmental concern, the current enthusiasm was just that—a passing enthusiasm.

By 2010, GE had overcome much of the early skepticism about its new direction, though the global slowdown after the financial crisis of 2008 had hit the company hard. GE stock lost nearly half its value in the crisis. Nonetheless, the company met its original goal of doubling its annual investment in clean technologies by 2009 (a year ahead of plan) and exceeded its original targets for reducing its own greenhouse gas emission. Taking a page from its playbook for customers, GE adopted many of its own new technologies and mobilized the efforts of employees at fifty GE facilities around the world. The result was a 41 percent reduction in greenhouse gas intensity by 2008, well above the originally targeted 30 percent by 2008. A major contributor was media and entertainment company NBC Universal, where a number of television and movie production studios embraced the go-green message by adopting comprehensive programs to save energy and reduce their carbon footprint.

Even in the absence of U.S. legislation capping carbon emissions, GE was also on track to achieve its original goal of at least $20 billion in revenues from ecomagination products by 2010. And, noted Steve Fludder, ecomagination's head until mid-2010, GE's eco products were among its most profitable. Contrary to widespread expectations that the financial crisis would kill the company's environmental business, the crisis actually proved to be something of a boon. Virtually all the postcrisis stimulus packages put in place by governments around the world included a significant environmental component earmarked for just the kinds of projects that GE was prepared to deliver, thanks to ecomagination. GE won contracts for a range of major infrastructure projects aimed at laying the foundations of a new energy future: clean-coal demonstration plants, renewable energy generation, electric-grid modernization, and many others.

Although the cumulative environmental impact of ecomagination innovations was difficult to assess, GE pointed to significant improvements in a number of areas—such as increased fuel efficiency for jet engines and avoided carbon dioxide emissions from using wind power. GE had grown its wind turbine business, purchased from a post-bankruptcy Enron, from $200 million a year in 2002 to $6 billion for 2008. The company calculated that the nearly twelve thousand wind turbines it had installed around the world were avoiding 32 million metric tons of carbon dioxide emissions annually, compared with traditional U.S. grid sources. By its estimates, GE had also improved turbine reliability by 11 percent, creating another $2 billion in value on a net-present-value basis for the turbine owners.

From a certain perspective, the ecomagination story can be seen simply as a continuation of GE's hundred-year-plus tradition of using manufacturing and process excellence to improve the efficiency and performance of the technologies it offers the marketplace. But Fludder sees it as much more. From his vantage point, ecomagination has allowed GE to create new solutions that individual business units, left to their own devices and following their historic focus on pushing products out the door, would not have been able to develop. "By bringing the outside in and mobilizing the company to address a major multiconstituent problem in society, ecomagination has helped transform GE's relationship with the world," he noted. "The initiative has shown that you can make money and make the world a better place at the same time."

Extending the Positives:
China Mobile and the Digital Divide

China Mobile, China's largest telecommunications operator and the listed subsidiary of state-owned China Mobile Communications Company (CMCC), is another company that has prospered by addressing a potential threat to the system. Through the rural communications strategy that it launched in 2004, China Mobile has helped narrow the gap between China's urban rich and rural poor and extended the benefits of participating in the market system to millions of people. At the same time, the rural communications strategy has helped fuel the company's own growth and profitability.[6]

The catalyst for the company's efforts to bring mobile phone service to China's rural regions was the Chinese government's Cun Cun Tong ("connect every village") program. First launched in 1996, when China's telecoms sector consisted of two state-owned operators and when China Mobile had not yet come into existence, the program was aimed at providing universal service to China's then 850 million rural citizens and, more generally, at promoting rural economic development. In practical terms, this meant providing service to hundreds of thousands of unserved villages, including a large proportion of the country's estimated 740,000 administrative villages at that time and its more than 2 million natural villages. (An *administrative village* is China's smallest unit of political organization; it typically comprises from one to twenty *natural villages*—defined as a grouping of more than twenty households.)

Given China's vast territory and rugged terrain—encompassing the mountains of Tibet as well as the deserts of Xinjiang and Inner Mongolia—the Cun Cun Tong program was an extraordinarily ambitious undertaking, especially for a country and industry in the throes of rapid transition on so many other fronts. Few, if any, believed that truly universal coverage could be achieved given the last-mile problem. Still, with an estimated seventy thousand administrative villages still unconnected at the end of 2003 and the wealth disparity between China's rural and urban populations growing ever more pronounced, the government decided to step up the effort. In 2004, the Ministry of Information Industry (MII) relaunched Cun Cun Tong and set a target date of 2010 for reaching the remaining villages. In furtherance of its efforts to foster social harmony and more-balanced growth between urban and rural areas, the Chinese Communist Party also incorporated the new goals into its eleventh five-year plan for 2006 through 2010.

Each of China's then six state-owned telecommunications companies, including CMCC, was charged with providing at least two phone lines to an assigned number of unconnected villages. The government would provide support in the form of expedited approvals, tax credits, and access to energy, but each operator was responsible for funding the necessary infrastructure—principally base stations—and providing connectivity to its assigned number of villages. As the largest of China's telecoms companies, CMCC was tasked with the largest share.

By the time of Cun Cun Tong's relaunch, China Mobile was traded on both the New York and the Hong Kong stock exchanges and had become the world's eleventh-largest telecom operator by market capitalization.[7] In the period following its listing in 1997, the company had focused on acquiring various provincial networks from its parent CMCC and building up its subscriber base in China's cities and densely populated eastern seaboard regions. By 2004, China Mobile owned wireless networks in all of China's thirty-one provinces, autonomous regions, and directly administered municipalities. Its subscriber base, mostly in the cities, numbered some 200 million, up from 45 million in 2000.

At China Mobile and other operators, the Cun Cun Tong directive was met with grudging acquiescence. For a company whose annual revenue and net income growth had averaged some 30 percent and 25 percent, respectively, between 2000 and 2004, the prospect of having to build networks in remote areas with low rates of phone traffic held little appeal. Analysis of the company's scant rural business— then less than 3 percent of subscribers—led many at China Mobile to question whether the investment required by Cun Cun Tong could ever be made to pay. "Everyone had doubts about how the poor could afford such an expensive item and how the company could reduce the cost enough to generate a profitable expansion," recalled a company adviser.

Moreover, by 2004, China Mobile's management had a much bigger problem than Cun Cun Tong. With mobile phone penetration rates in China's cities as high as 80 percent—and even approaching 100 percent—in some cases—the looming question was where the company was going to find its next 200 million customers. The new chairman and CEO, Wang Jianzhou—also the new chairman and chief executive of CMCC—challenged China Mobile's strategy group to find an answer. The group soon realized what, in retrospect, would seem obvious: that future growth would come from the countryside. Instead of viewing the government's Cun Cun Tong program as a burden that had to be borne and something of a distraction from the company's main business activities, key members of the strategy group began to see it as a platform for the next phase in China Mobile's own growth and development.

With Cun Cun Tong recast as the foundation of a new rural communications strategy, the group turned to the challenges of execution. How to implement the new strategy was far from self-evident, given the vast territory to be covered and the uncertainties about the acceptance of wireless communications in the rural areas. The picture was further clouded by other risks involved in building the extensive network to a scale large enough to achieve even theoretical profitability. Using the idea of innovation competitions, Wang challenged the heads of the company's thirty-one provincial subsidiaries to come up with new ideas for the business. The provincial heads, in turn, challenged their subordinates to do the same. In keeping with the company's customary practice of testing new ideas with pilot projects, China Mobile launched a series of pilots to test various approaches to marketing and distribution. Some regions set up flagship stores; others tried franchisees. Some also experimented with independent sales agents like those the company was already using in the cities.

Ultimately, management went with an innovative distribution system that reached deep into the countryside. Unlike many other companies that had tried to penetrate China's rural regions, China Mobile recognized the importance of establishing outlets at every level of the country's administrative structure—not just the 31 provincial capitals and nearly 2,900 county seats, but all the way down to the nearly 41,000 townships (or township-level entities) and more than 735,000 administrative villages (down from the earlier number because of consolidations and recategorizations). Under the slogan of "one store per township and one agent per village"—an approach crafted by a provincial operator during the experimental phase and then replicated across the company—China Mobile set up a vast but low-cost distribution system, encompassing company-owned stores at the county-seat level, both company-owned and franchise stores at the township level, and a network of more than a million independent sales agents at the village level. To help minimize turnover and build strong ties with customers, the company tapped respected local citizens and village leaders as store managers and agents whenever possible.

By the end of 2005, the rural communications strategy was taking off and voices of doubt inside the company were receding. Even the investor community, which had been highly skeptical of the strategy when it was announced, had started to come around. While meeting its Cun Cun Tong obligations in 2005, China Mobile also added another 42 million subscribers, about half in rural areas, and grew its revenues by 26 percent. As networks were constructed in rural areas, farmers and merchants quickly saw the benefits of basic voice and texting services. For this group, the mobile phone became an essential tool of daily commerce. By keeping costs low—through its low-cost distribution system, low-cost handsets, and customized pricing—China Mobile was able to make its services affordable for the average rural resident.

Drawing from its ongoing research and innovation efforts, China Mobile soon began to add new services tailored to the needs of rural customers. One early success was a rural information network that users could access through their mobile phones or through special information terminals. The network provided farmers with critical information about topics from weather forecasts and agricultural prices to pest management and job opportunities. The network also provided access to agricultural experts knowledgeable about various regions or specific crops. Much of this information had never before been available, and farmers quickly made use of it to gain more-accurate price information and to better time the delivery of their crops to market. In some cases, they were able to cut out costly middlemen entirely by communicating directly with wholesalers and factories.

From 2006 to 2010, the rural market continued to be a significant driver of China Mobile's growth, accounting for over half of the company's newly added subscribers each year. Innovations such as more-convenient payment systems, complimentary life insurance with certain offerings, and solar-powered charging stations where subscribers gathered to recharge their phones and socialize with one another fueled this growth and put China Mobile ahead of its rivals.

By late 2010, China Mobile had signed up more than 220 million rural customers and held an estimated 76 percent share of the rural market for mobile phones.[8] Enlisting the next segment of rural residents would no doubt require further innovation and be more difficult still. But China Mobile's rural communications strategy had paid off for the company—revenue and income grew at an average annual rate of 17 percent and 21 percent, respectively, between 2005 and 2009—while at the same time narrowing the digital divide and helping millions of rural citizens increase their incomes and improve their standard of living. Whatever difficulties the company might face in the future, this achievement, too, explained one China Mobile manager, is "a kind of profit."[9]

Combating External Threats:
Cipla and the HIV/AIDS Pandemic

India's generic-drug maker Cipla Limited has led the way—albeit not without controversy—in fashioning a business model for delivering antiretroviral drugs (ARVs) to some of the world's poorest regions.[10] Also known for its antibiotics, anticancer drugs, and anti-asthma inhalers, including the first chlorofluorocarbon-free inhaler made by an Asian company, Cipla entered the ARV business in 1998. By 2005, this business had expanded to nearly 150 countries and an estimated 25 percent of the total ARV market.[11] By 2009, Cipla was the world's largest supplier of ARVs (as measured by units produced and distributed), and its drugs were being taken by as many as 40 percent of the HIV/AIDS patients undergoing antiretroviral therapy worldwide.[12]

Cipla CEO Yusuf Hamied Jr. recognized the threat posed by HIV/AIDS earlier than many. Alarmed by the rapid spread of AIDS in India, Hamied announced in 1992 that Cipla would begin producing AZT, an anti-HIV/AIDS drug made and sold in the United States by Burroughs Wellcome at prices of nearly $10,000 per person for a year's dosage. At the time, India's intellectual-property system allowed for patents on drug-making processes but not on drug products, so Cipla was legally permitted to reverse-engineer AZT and produce generic AZT capsules using its own novel manufacturing process. The company did just that. Priced at only $2 per day, the Cipla therapy nonetheless proved too costly for India's AIDS patients. After an unsuccessful attempt at persuading the Indian government to buy and distribute the drugs, Cipla withdrew from the AIDS market.

Meanwhile, the number of AIDS cases in India and elsewhere continued to grow. In 1998, Cipla reentered the market, this time with a different combination of drugs but again reverse-engineering products developed by multinational pharmaceutical companies. By this time, South Africa's infection rate was skyrocketing. (In 2000, a quarter of all deaths in South Africa were attributable to AIDS, and the number of infected individuals was expected to reach nearly 5 million in 2002.) With the country's annual per-capita income at just over $2,500, few South Africans could afford the $10,000 per year that the multinationals were asking for their ARVs. Facing this dire situation, South African president Nelson Mandela gave effect to a new law that allowed for the import or manufacture of generic anti-HIV/AIDS drugs on payment of a licensing fee to the patent holder but without the patent holder's prior approval. Even though experts argued that the law's provisions on compulsory licensing and parallel imports were similar to those in other jurisdictions and consistent with international patent agreements, Mandela's actions set off a firestorm.[13]

Many of the global pharma companies saw Mandela's move as a threat. With business models predicated on huge investments in the discovery and development of blockbuster drugs to be sold at premium prices in the industrialized world, the major multinationals were ill equipped to meet the challenge presented by a pandemic afflicting patients who could not pay the prices the industry had come to expect. And the companies worried that compromising on prices for the developing world would put further pressure on prices in the developed world—already a controversial issue—and ultimately erode the intellectual-property system on which their business models depended. Nearly forty companies filed suit against Mandela and the South African government, arguing that high R&D costs made it impossible to reduce the price of ARVs. The move only heightened the pressure from NGOs and world health authorities. In early 2000, the World Health Organization (WHO) called on the leading global pharmas to join forces in a collective effort to increase access to anti-HIV/AIDS drugs. The result: several companies offered discounts of up to 50 percent. Still, at $6,000 annually, the price remained out of reach for most afflicted Africans.

As Hamied watched the controversy unfold, he saw the situation in Africa as both a humanitarian disaster and an opportunity for Cipla to intervene. In early 2001, he announced that Cipla would offer to sell its triple-therapy ARV "cocktail" using a three-tiered pricing structure of $1,200 per person annually to wholesalers, $600 to governments, and $350 to the Geneva-based nonprofit Médicins Sans Frontières. The announcement made the front page of the *New York Times* and catapulted Cipla onto the world stage. According to Hamied, Cipla would neither make nor lose money on the proposal; the average of the three prices would allow it to break even. After seeking a license from the patent holders and getting no response, Cipla applied to the South African government for a compulsory license. The World Health Organization subsequently qualified three Cipla units to supply anti-HIV/AIDS drugs, making it the first Indian company to receive WHO certification.[14]

Hamied's offer angered many global pharmas, but it demonstrated to the world that ARV drug prices were malleable. Within months, the multinationals' lawsuit against South Africa's government was dropped, and several European and U.S. companies announced price cuts of their own. As prices came down, generic-drug makers, NGOs, and some leading brand names entered into negotiations with volume purchasers. But Cipla's prices were typically lower, and many purchasers preferred its once-daily cocktail for reasons of patient compliance. Between 2003 and 2006, Cipla's ARV business grew to an estimated 35 percent of its exports.[15] The largest portion of the company's ARV exports went to countries in Africa under high-volume, low-margin contracts with governments and foundations. (A decision taken during trade talks in late 2001 gave less developed countries in Africa and elsewhere until 2016 to comply with the World Trade Organization's intellectual property rules, and as noted, opposition to South Africa's new law permitting parallel imports and compulsory licensing had been dropped.) In India, Cipla continued to be the leading supplier of ARVs, with an estimated 51 percent of the market in 2009, according to analysts.[16]

Cipla's ability to sell ARVs at affordable prices depended on its distinctive low-cost business model.[17] In sharp contrast to multinationals that concentrated their efforts on developing new blockbuster drugs and selling them in rich countries at premium prices, Cipla focused on bringing down the cost of existing drugs and making them more widely available to the less well-off. Through its innovative approach to pricing—an issue that multinationals had long declined to consider—Cipla allowed purchasers to segment themselves into tiers while the company saved on its own financing and inventory costs.[18] The lowest prices were available to those willing to prepay and preorder in bulk, assume shipping and customs responsibilities, protect against raw-materials price inflation, and indemnify Cipla from patent suits. By working with governments, foundations, and aid organizations, Cipla kept its marketing and administrative costs to only 9 percent of total expenses, compared with 33 percent for the multinationals.[19]

Without question, Cipla and other generic companies benefited greatly from the multinational firms' investments in discovering and developing these drugs, bringing them to market, and creating demand in the medical community. But Cipla and its generic brethren also created markets for these drugs where they had not previously existed. In so doing, the companies extended treatment to several million people with HIV/AIDS in low- and middle-income countries—an estimated 5.2 million were receiving treatment in 2009, compared with 300,000 in 2002—and helped moderate the broader health and economic effects of one of the world's most lethal epidemics.[20] Economists have estimated that losses in gross domestic product for a typical sub-Saharan country with an HIV rate of 15 percent could be as high as 4 percent per year.[21]

Cipla's role in expanding access to ARVs is all the more remarkable considering that during this same period, the company grew overall sales and income at an average annual rate of more than 20 percent, making it a favorite among investors. Between 2002 and 2009, the company's average annual return on equity was more than 25 percent. With changes in the protections afforded to intellectual property in the least developed countries (LDCs) scheduled to take effect in 2016, Cipla will no doubt face significant challenges. Indeed, the company's sales growth slowed considerably in 2010, partly because of fewer ARV exports.[22] Still, Cipla's role at the forefront of the HIV/AIDS crisis has made the company a worldwide name and an attractive partner for many of the multinational drug companies now looking to expand into emerging and less developed markets.

Meanwhile, Cipla's bold actions also helped catalyze reforms in World Trade Organization rules for trade in lifesaving drugs for the world's poorest regions, and many global pharma companies have joined the effort to combat HIV/AIDS. With only 18 percent of the estimated 33.4 million people with HIV/AIDS worldwide receiving ARV therapy as of 2009, the opportunities to become involved would appear to be plentiful.[23]

Reinforcing the Antecedents: Generation Investment Management and Sustainable Investing

Generation Investment Management illustrates a fourth type of intervention suggested by the model in chapter 4: strengthening the antecedents of the market system. Founded in 2004, London-based Generation is a boutique asset-management firm that invests in companies whose business models are aligned with the needs of a sustainable global economy. The firm's flagship product is a $6 billion global equities fund that takes long positions in publicly traded companies. At any given time, its holdings include thirty to sixty companies that have been selected using the firm's innovative investment process. The fund's goal is to outperform the MSCI World Index by 9 to 12 percent (on a three-year rolling-average basis).[24]

The idea for Generation grew out of a meeting in 2003 between David Blood, then CEO of the Goldman Sachs asset management division, and former U.S. vice president Al Gore. At the time, Blood was preparing to leave Goldman Sachs to pursue his interests in sustainable development, and Gore was seeking advice on an investment. In the course of the meeting, Blood and Gore discovered that they had much in common. Both were deeply concerned about challenges facing the global economy. Blood was most focused on poverty, and Gore on climate change, but the two men were convinced that these and other global trends were closely linked and would present major challenges for business and society in the years ahead. They also found common cause in their concern over "short-termism" in the capital markets. Both believed that short-term investing only aggravated the larger societal problems that worried them and was a poor investment strategy in any case.

Shortly after their initial meeting, Blood and Gore decided to join forces to launch an investment firm that would put their ideas to the test and potentially offer a better way to manage money. Their basic premise was that companies able to manage the challenges presented by the changing global context would outperform for investors over the long term. In addition to Blood and Gore, the seven founding partners included Gore's former chief of staff, two of Blood's former colleagues from Goldman Sachs, a leading expert on sustainability research, and an experienced investment manager with expertise in the health-care sector.

The founding partners spent the first half of 2004 forming the new firm's leadership team and hiring a staff of investment professionals. As a foundation for building the capabilities needed to execute on their novel investment premise, they sought to attract professionals with a mix of skills and perspectives. About two-thirds of the firm's sixteen original investment professionals came from traditional asset management backgrounds, and one-third from the newer field of sustainability research.

With the team in place, the group turned to the next challenge— translating their investment premise into an actual day-to-day investing process. It was clear from the start that the models and analytics used by traditional investment professionals could not readily accommodate the social, environmental, and other factors the Generation team thought important. But the founding partners were also wary of creating an organization in which the traditional analysts and the sustainability researchers operated as two separate camps—a common situation in asset management firms that added sustainability researchers to their staffs without rethinking their overall investment process.

As a first step toward creating an integrated investment framework, the managing group set up working partnerships between those with traditional investment backgrounds and those schooled in sustainability research, government, or the nonprofit sector. For more than a year, before beginning to manage any money from third parties, these groups worked side by side to learn each other's concepts and methods for analyzing companies and industries. To the founding partners, one of the firm's most significant early accomplishments was the integration of these different skill sets into a structured investment process that would be used by all analysts, whatever their original discipline.

By the time Generation began accepting third-party money in late 2005, it had developed an innovative approach to investing that integrated sustainability factors and fundamental equity analysis at each stage. By necessity, the process required that all of the firm's investment professionals learn the fundamentals of traditional equity analysis as well as the fundamentals of sustainability research. In practical terms, this meant that a sustainability researcher had to earn a financial analyst degree, and a financial analyst had to master the techniques of sustainability research.

Generation's investment process starts with identifying what the firm calls *sustainability themes*—major trends and developments affecting the global context of business. To help identify and stay abreast of these themes, the leadership team created an outside advisory board of global thought leaders and experts in a range of domains—from capital markets and information technology to human rights and environmental science. Twice a year, the advisory board meets with Generation partners and analysts to share insights and review the investment implications of large-scale changes in the global business context. Key themes explored by this group have included climate change, water scarcity, poverty, pandemics, demographic flows, corruption, and corporate governance.

These themes then form the basis of Generation's sustainability research agenda. Using many sources that investors have not traditionally tapped, analysts develop thematic white papers that examine the likely impacts of a given theme for different businesses and industries. For example, a white paper on anticipated water shortages would identify intensive water users, like beverage makers, for which a shortage would represent a major risk. The paper would also identify sectors such as developers of desalination or wastewater treatment technologies, for which water shortages would represent a significant opportunity. Building on the white papers, Generation analysts then create industry roadmaps that focus in greater detail on long-term trends and specific sustainability issues for particular industries. These roadmaps, which also incorporate more traditional forms of industry analysis, seek to chart how industries are likely to evolve and to identify the companies that are best positioned to thrive in the projected context over the long term.

For individual companies, Generation then develops a sustainability profile to assess how well the company is positioned in relation to the risks and opportunities arising from the relevant themes. This assessment focuses on the company's core products and strategies and on the themes most material to that company's specific business and industry. In evaluating a bank, for instance, Generation looks at the bank's culture, leadership, and risk and incentive systems, as well as whether it considers environmental and social risks in its lending practices—but not whether it recycles paper. The aim is not to catalog all possible sustainability impacts for a given company, but to evaluate how well the company is addressing risks and opportunities—including second-order risks and opportunities arising from changes in regulations and social attitudes, for example—that are material to its business and strategy over the long term.

In deciding whether to put a company on its focus list—a list of companies it would like to own, subject to price—Generation looks more closely at each prospect's business quality and management quality. In each category, analysts again consider a mix of sustainability and traditional factors. For instance, in evaluating business quality, Generation analysts consider traditional factors such as a company's competitive position, pricing power, and technological strength, as well as sustainability factors such as the company's use of energy, handling of waste, and impacts on the quality of life, especially for poorer segments of the population. Similarly, when assessing management quality, the team looks at traditional factors such as the management team's record on execution and talent retention as well as sustainability factors such as its record on corruption and its leadership on environmental issues. In each instance, a company is evaluated on the factors that the Generation team deems most relevant and most material.

For companies that make it to Generation's focus list, the decision to buy—or sell—involves a careful evaluation of the company's price and value. Even though Generation focuses on long-term trends and how well companies are positioned relative to those trends, its portfolio managers are highly disciplined when it comes to buying and selling. A significant change in management quality or business quality, or stock price movements that exceed predetermined value ranges, may trigger a decision to sell. At the same time, Generation engages with management, votes proxies, and generally seeks to act as a responsible long-term owner.

Consistent with its investment philosophy, Generation has adopted sustainability practices in its own operations. Partners invest in the global equities fund on the same terms and conditions as clients, paying the same fees and adhering to the same policies, including the one-year lock-in period for investments. The firm actively manages its carbon emissions and purchases offsets on an annual basis. In general, Generation seeks to govern itself by the leadership and management principles that it applies to companies on its focus list. Compensation is based on both annual performance and rolling three-year averages. As a holiday gift one year, the firm gave employees home energy checkups.

About 90 percent of Generation's $6 billion in assets under management comes from institutional investors in the United States, Europe, and Australia. The rest is from wealthy individuals. Clients pay a base fee related to asset values to cover costs and a performance fee if the fund outperforms its benchmark. Although Generation does not publicly disclose its holdings or its performance (it discloses these only to clients), the company is rumored to have weathered the financial crisis exceptionally well and met or exceeded its performance goals in recent years.[25] But only time will tell whether the fund's underlying investment premise is robust and whether the targets can be met consistently.

Perhaps the firm's most important contribution to date, however, has been its innovative investment model. Blood, for one, is convinced that integrating sustainability factors into fundamental equities analysis allows Generation to make better investment decisions. For the founding partners' ambitions to be fully realized, however, the model will have to influence investing methods more broadly so that capital flows and corporate resources are more consistently directed toward uses aligned with the needs of a sustainable global economy.

The Path from Problem to Opportunity

These are just a few examples of companies that are finding business opportunities in the challenges and potential disruptors identified by our business leaders. Many other cases could be cited. Indeed, numerous books have been written about the opportunities presented by the world's environmental challenges or those presented by poverty—especially by populations at the "bottom of the pyramid" living on less than $2 per day.[26] The successes of organizations like Enterprise Solutions to Poverty (ESP),[27] an adviser to India's ITC on the e-Choupal initiative described in chapter 1, and the increasing flow of venture capital into green tech, smart consumption, and other environmentally promising fields provide further illustrations.[28]

Such examples are important for at least two reasons. As noted earlier, they lend credence to our claim that at least some of market capitalism's weaknesses and vulnerabilities contain the seeds of opportunity. They provide evidence that slogans like "green is green" cannot be dismissed as wishful thinking and that business *can* play a role in strengthening the market system while still delivering profitability in the short term. But perhaps more important, these examples point to some of the skills and capabilities that may be needed to realize these opportunities. As the case studies in this chapter make clear, the path from systemic problem to corporate opportunity is not always clear and the journey may call for new ways of seeing the world and doing business.

The business potential inherent in many of the problems we have been discussing may be difficult to discern, in part, for structural reasons. Market solutions are relatively easy to envision when demand is evident and supply is nonexistent. In the paradigmatic situation, an entrepreneur emerges to develop a new product or service to satisfy this unmet demand. The entrepreneur typically does not need to worry about creating the infrastructure needed for markets to function—since this is presumed to exist—and instead can focus more narrowly on securing funds, developing the technology, and mobilizing people to carry out the business plan. However, in the examples discussed in this chapter—and more generally when the issue is finding market solutions to systemic threats and problems—some features of the standard situation may be absent. As a result, the opportunity may not be readily apparent and the entrepreneur may face obstacles that seldom appear in the more conventional scenario.

A recurrent theme, as illustrated by the case examples, is the absence of a clear and visible market demand. In some cases, demand is inchoate because the underlying problem is not yet well understood. When problems are complex and manifest themselves slowly over time, the felt need for solutions emerges slowly as well. It takes time for evidence to accumulate and understanding to spread. Climate change is a good example, but long lead times are a characteristic of many other threats and disruptors identified by our business leaders. Even after a problem is widely recognized, market signals may still remain weak. As marketers have long known, action almost always lags awareness. And this natural lag is exacerbated by well-documented human tendencies to shun complexity, postpone difficult choices, discount the future, and deny weakness. Success in combating these tendencies requires extra efforts to educate the prospective market and careful attention to timing. Like Jeff Immelt at GE, entrepreneurs seeking to build a business around solutions to problems with long lead times must walk a fine line between being ahead of the market but not so far ahead as to alienate their customers and potential customers.

In other situations, the need for solutions may be acute, but market signals are weak for other reasons. Would-be customers may lack the ability to pay, for example, and therefore not appear as prospects through the lenses typically applied by marketers. As seen in the Cipla case, people with HIV/AIDS in Africa are a prime example. Their need, while evident, did not express itself in the form of market demand, and global pharma companies did not naturally view Africa as a potential market, given the continent's low income levels. Indeed, few companies in any industry would view the indigent as potential customers, and fewer still would see poverty reduction as an element of their corporate strategy. Recall that many questioned how poor Chinese farmers could pay for China Mobile's cell phone service. Yet, as the Cipla and China Mobile cases illustrate, addressing poverty and would-be customers' inability to pay are crucial for transforming many systemic problems into business opportunities. To bring indigent citizens into the system as paying customers, a company needs somehow to overcome the affordability obstacle—by increasing prospective customers' purchasing power, reducing prices to levels they can afford, or finding a proxy such as a government or another third party to pay on the ultimate users' behalf.

In still other situations, the business opportunity may be difficult to discern because would-be customers are physically remote or otherwise disconnected from the infrastructure necessary to support their participation in the market. The villagers of rural China, without access to land lines and mobile phone networks, are one example. But many other potential participants in the market system are excluded by their lack of access to transportation, communication, energy, banking, governance, or other essential support structures. To realize opportunities involving potential customers like these, entrepreneurs must find ways to overcome such access barriers—often by working with governments or other third parties to fill the gaps in needed infrastructure. China Mobile was fortunate to have its state-owned parent's assistance in funding and building the base stations necessary to operate its mobile network across rural China.

Perhaps the most challenging obstacles, however, are the conceptual barriers—habits of mind and mental models—that leaders must overcome to gain support for their ideas. The executives profiled in this chapter had to contend not just with the standard resistance to change that accompanies virtually all innovation. They also faced deep-seated resistance based on fundamental beliefs about the role of business and how it should be conducted. Recall the reactions to Immelt's idea of building a business around mitigating environmental externalities. To many, it was unclear whether this was a space that GE could—or should—claim. Like Cipla's challenge to the intellectual property system, China Mobile's focus on reaching the rural poor and Generation Investment Management's integration of sustainability factors into investment analytics, GE's proposed new business model ran up against widely held assumptions about what business could or should be doing.

Success in overcoming these obstacles and building viable businesses calls for leaders with an uncommon set of skills and attributes. They must be able to challenge orthodoxy without alienating the orthodox. They must see markets and opportunities where others see nothing or see only problems. Even while pursuing innovative business models that throw basic assumptions into question and upset familiar arrangements, they must at the same time maintain their organization's competitiveness and perform their usual functions as business leaders—allocating resources, motivating and developing people, answering to investors and boards of directors, and so on.

In many respects, these leaders are quintessential entrepreneurs. They are imaginative, energetic risk-takers who put themselves and their companies on the line for an envisioned future. In each instance, they successfully mobilized the human and financial resources needed to pursue an innovative strategy. In "pursuing opportunity without regard to resources currently controlled"—to cite our colleague Howard Stevenson's widely quoted definition—they exemplified the essence of entrepreneurial activity.[29] But these individuals are a very different breed from the garage-shop entrepreneur focused on developing a new product or technology or the startup entrepreneur who launches a new business with the intention of exiting at the first opportunity for a public offering.

These leaders are also skilled in the subtle arts of general management. They are masters at directing and coordinating the activities of their organizations—to cite another classic definition.[30] But unlike the archetypal general manager described in Chester Barnard's seminal text, *The Functions of the Executive*, these leaders see their companies as actors on a world stage with the potential to influence the lives of people and communities around the globe. They are attentive not just to their organizations but also to the larger system within which their organizations operate. They understand that the health of their organization depends on the health of this larger system. And they possess the skills needed to interact with other participants in this system.

In other words, these leaders are also diplomats. They are comfortable engaging with constituencies beyond the organization and its investors and even beyond the private sector. Successful execution of the strategic plan in each of the cases discussed required an understanding of public policy and government affairs. Leaders in each company were called on to engage with a range of public-sector actors, including governments, multilateral institutions, NGOs, and civic leaders at various levels.[31]

The leaders in our case examples each pursued a very different type of innovation: a new environmental business at GE, a new distribution system at China Mobile, a new marketing model at Cipla, and a new investment process at Generation Investment Management.

But in each case, the motivating insight came in significant measure from an awareness of larger systemic needs, trends, challenges—and consequent opportunities. To translate these insights into workable businesses, these leaders capitalized on well-honed business skills and capabilities—their own and those of their organizations. None were novices in their field; in fact, all were highly accomplished. At the same time, they and their organizations had to acquire new knowledge and learn about issues well beyond their customary domains. Immelt and his team at GE, for example, immersed themselves in the science of climate change. China Mobile experimented with different distribution models through pilot projects across China. The investment team at Generation dedicated a year to learning new analytic techniques and developing a new investment process. To ensure ongoing engagement with the wider world, both GE and Generation established standing advisory boards of outside experts as part of their organizational models.

These examples suggest that success in building a business that addresses these larger issues calls for an expansive outlook and an enlarged skill set. The ability to learn quickly about new domains, think creatively about systemic problems, and work across different sectors of society—these are essential skills for functioning in this arena. But to be useful, these skills must be anchored in fundamental business and management know-how. As ecomagination head Steve Fludder put it, "If you're going to go after a big multiconstituent societal problem and make a business out of it . . . [you have] to really think about how to take that big problem . . . and treat it like a market opportunity and use your traditional instincts of profit and profitability and making money for yourself and your shareholders and bring that same thinking to these new problems."

CSR or Self-Interest Properly Understood?

Our view that companies should take a broader view and seek to align their activities with the needs of a robust and sustainable market system may strike some as a brief for corporate social responsibility (CSR). But we prefer to describe it as a call for enlightened self-interest—or

what the nineteenth-century French political thinker Alexis de Tocqueville termed "self-interest properly understood" and what others
have called "self-interest rightly conceived."

When Tocqueville toured the United States in the 1830s to explore
the then developing country's progress and assess the effects of
democracy on society, he was struck by what he described as a "near
universal" tendency among Americans to explain their acts of apparent generosity or civic responsibility not as expressions of morality
but as pragmatic actions that would ultimately redound to their own
benefit: "It gives [Americans] pleasure to point out how an enlightened self-love continually leads them to help one another and disposes
them freely to give part of their time and wealth for the good of the
state."[32] Calling the doctrine of self-interest properly understood "the
best suited of all philosophical theories to the wants of men," Tocqueville also saw it as ultimately "their strongest remaining guarantee
against themselves."[33]

The accuracy of Tocqueville's description of these tendencies as
"near universal" is certainly open to question. By other accounts, the
marketplace of that era was awash in commercial fraud and similarly
pernicious practices.[34] Still, the outlook he highlights is similar to that
of forward-looking companies today. Like the Americans encountered
by Tocqueville, these companies recognize that their own health and
prosperity are deeply intertwined with the health and prosperity of
the market system as a whole and, conversely, that a fragile system
presents threats and risks to their companies and to enterprises across
the industrial spectrum. In seeking to moderate forces that threaten to
disrupt the system—or in adopting strategies and behaviors that help
reinforce and strengthen the system—these businesses realize that
they are looking after their own long-term interests as much as they are
performing a civic responsibility.

By putting the accent on enlightened self-interest, we hope to
counteract the tendency to regard efforts to improve the system as
optional—nice, perhaps, but by no means necessary. If the prognoses
presented in earlier chapters are anywhere near correct, continuing
to disregard the health of the market system will be seen by future
historians as the height of folly—a term defined by historian Barbara
Tuchman in her masterful book *The March of Folly* as a ruinous and

costly policy that is mistakenly believed to advance the interests of those pursuing it.[35] Her findings seem all too relevant: "Primacy of self-aggrandizement, illusion of invulnerable status, and obliviousness to the growing disaffection of their constituents are persistent aspects of folly."[36] Unless action is taken to contain the negative forces identified by our business leaders, future generations looking back on today will not ask why proponents of the market system were so uncharitable; rather future generations will wonder why the system's supporters did so little to protect their own interests despite mounting evidence of serious problems.

Moreover, the activities typically undertaken under the CSR banner, worthy as they may be, are not likely to be sufficient—individually or collectively—to address the problems at issue. In most companies that we know, CSR activities are entirely peripheral to the main lines of decision making and management. They are treated as discretionary, and their impact on the targeted problem is typically modest. Although altruism and corporate charity have their place, a sustainable economic system cannot be built purely on self-sacrifice any more than it can be built purely on greed.

Whatever terminology is used, however, the quest for growth and profitability must go hand in hand with respect for the health and sustainability of the market system. As we have tried to show in this chapter, companies and entrepreneurs have a crucial role to play in strengthening this system and improving its performance for society. But innovative and enlightened companies cannot do it all unilaterally. In the next chapter, we will take a closer look at the role of companies as activists for good government and more-effective institutions.

Leading Through
Institutional Activism

I N CHAPTER 4, we proposed a systemic view of the challenge of sustaining market capitalism. We argued that forces within and outside market capitalism itself—its good and not-so-good outcomes, the antecedents that allow it to function successfully (or, indeed, at all), and the disruptions that threaten it—are related to one another, often in self-reinforcing cycles that can either buttress or undermine capitalism's sustainability. We then outlined alternative roles business might play in ensuring the overall system's ongoing success and explored in greater depth the role of business as innovator. We looked at examples of innovations by companies that show how business might contribute significantly to the positively reinforcing cycles of the system and help mitigate the negative ones.

These examples of innovative companies generally centered on innovation in company *strategies* and *business models*. Several also involved new products and technologies. In these domains, success is typically dependent on a company's relationships with its *direct* stakeholders—the employees, customers, investors, partners, suppliers, and others with whom it has a market or direct contractual relationship. Notably, however, most of the innovations we have examined required at least some interventions beyond this nexus of contracts (as this set of relationships is sometimes called). The case of Cipla is a good example. The actions of the company in reengineering its own activities involved a challenge to the existing regime of intellectual property rights, and significant progress depended ultimately on collaboration and collective action with other firms and with multiple governments.

In this chapter, we extend this argument and consider other examples of businesses operating beyond the nexus of direct stakeholder relationships. In addition to requiring innovation in products and business models, success in addressing the challenges we have identified will also require innovation in *institutional arrangements* in the external environment within which firms operate. These innovations, in turn, will require new forms of engagement with *indirect* stakeholders—parties whose participation may be needed to effect change but with whom the company does not have a market or contractual relationship, and over whom it therefore generally has less leverage or influence. We accept the idea of business as innovator and further explore the idea of business as activist, asking, "What forms of activism and what forms of involvement by business might be most important and helpful?"

For those who recognize that much in our systemic conception of threats to market capitalism cannot be addressed by business alone—despite the innovations that businesses will naturally create, such as those described in our examples—a common reaction would be the business-as-bystander position. Such a position proposes that whatever else may be needed must be supplied by collective action. Generally, that would mean action by a government or governments, or perhaps by international organizations created by governments, or by other institutions of society. According to the business-as-bystander view, these collective actions should be mobilized by others—citizens or other interest groups—and the task of mobilizing them, naturally, goes beyond the scope of what businesses can or should do.

We respectfully but strongly disagree with this view. Despite the many useful innovations we eagerly anticipate from business, numerous preconditions for sustainable market capitalism will remain unmet. Business in its usual role will not naturally provide them. Insuring the sustainability of capitalism will require business to take both its traditional roles and a new, broader leadership role. Business cannot simply relegate to government and the rest of society the remainder of what needs to be accomplished. The stakes are too high, the existing mechanisms too weak, and the need for leadership from business too great to have business stand by and simply wait for others to act.

In this chapter, we explore both the role of business acting by itself and its role in activating and guiding the other necessary players in this crucial drama as it continues to unfold. In its new role in society and especially with government, business must play a constructive part in defining and addressing issues at the *system* level.

Beyond (Academic) Conventional Wisdom About Capitalism

Academic economics (as presented in textbooks) has long focused on an orthodox view of the purest form of capitalism. In this understanding of free-market systems, the focus is on action at the firm and individual consumer level. Firms operate without collusion in competitive markets (in purchasing the factors of production and in selling their goods), with complete information about prices (present and future); consumers with fixed preferences choose with full information among competitively supplied products to maximize their individual welfare. By the theorems of welfare economics, such a system can be shown to have one or more equilibria from which no arrangement of exchanges will make all players simultaneously better off—that is, any other arrangement that leaves some better off will, of necessity, make others worse off.[1]

Conventional economics adopts this Pareto principle as the standard for evaluating public welfare. At equilibrium, resources are said to be used *efficiently*—if the system were then shifted so that some people received, for example, better education, others would have to reduce their consumption of some other valued good or service. That might, from some perspectives, be better on balance, but from such a point of equilibrium, any move would involve both winners and losers, and the economic approach to judging outcomes by the Pareto principle does not have a mechanism for balancing the gains against the losses. Instead, each of these equilibria is said to *maximize* public welfare, and this narrow and somewhat peculiar form of maximization is commonly offered as a general justification for maintaining free, open, and competitive markets.[2]

While this argument is correct on its own terms—it is, in fact, validated by mathematical proof—its terms are decidedly narrow. As applied to real-world situations and policies, it is flawed both theoretically and empirically. From a theoretical perspective, a good deal of the logic hinges on a very special definition of public welfare. The definition assumes that public welfare is determined solely by the self-perceived individual welfare of the participants and is incomparable across individuals. (Thus, the only standard of improvement would be an improvement for all; it is assumed to be impossible to determine whether gains to some and losses to others might constitute an improvement.) If we allow for a broader definition of social welfare—a definition that allows the evaluation of trade-offs among individuals, recognizes that some members of society are in effect nonparticipants in the market, or includes externalities and third-party impacts—then the competitive equilibria of the conventional model no longer necessarily maximize welfare.

From an empirical perspective, the pure orthodoxy of market capitalism again breaks down. Viewed within a more general frame (with more realistic assumptions), the proof of welfare maximization does not hold. Where consumers have preferences that are not fixed in advance (and instead, for example, can be altered by advertising); where many markets are far short of being fully competitive; and where individual agents commonly lack important information about goods, services, and prices (current and future), competitive markets cannot be guaranteed to produce the best—or even good—outcomes. And considering that some members of society are nonparticipants in the market system and that there are externalities (like pollution and congestion) flowing from the actions of market participants, "pure" capitalism can create some very undesirable outcomes indeed.

Broadly speaking, there are two ways out of the dilemma that these observations create for those who wish to argue that the market capitalist system is good for the general public welfare. First (and the most common argument among academic economists) is the *as-if* or *close-enough* argument—that actual markets function in ways that are close enough to the assumptions of the orthodox capitalist system and hence will produce results similar to those that it would obtain if the conditions were perfectly met. In addition, this argument requires the presumption that the *policy prescriptions* that can be derived from the orthodox pure model will remain approximately correct (and, hence, are likely to be among the best policies to adopt).

For example, the close-enough argument was essentially what free-trade advocates used to urge the acceptance of the North American Free Trade Agreement (NAFTA)—that even if the assumptions used to prove the public welfare theorems in the economics literature on free trade did not strictly apply to the United States, Canada, and Mexico situation (which they most certainly did and do not), the parties could nonetheless be confident that free trade would be good for all. This view can be challenged in light of the theory of the second-best, which holds that when a single assumption of a model is violated, one can no longer be sure that the best policies in the resulting second-best world will even lie in the same direction (let alone have similar magnitudes) as those derived from the first-best model. Nevertheless, academic economists and others argued strongly for NAFTA on the basis that it is "generally well known" that free trade is good, on balance, for all participants.

Free trade may indeed generally be a good policy in the aggregate, and gains may significantly exceed losses (perhaps even in every participating country), but this cannot be proven by reference to mathematical results in models of purely competitive free trade. Free trade, as actually operated under NAFTA and other agreements, certainly results in significant transfers and losses for some participants as well as gains for others. And even among those who gain, some gain distinctly more than others. In many other examples of the as-if or close-enough assumptions, the results are the same: the prescriptions may hold, but they may also not, and it is difficult to tell for sure when they will.

The second way to address the dilemma of the divergence of the real world from the pure orthodox model is to appeal to an external mediating system—generally, government and social institutions—that can oversee, regulate, and address the difficulties posed by the unfettered market system. Even in the narrowest orthodox system of capitalism, there is a nearly universally agreed-on role for government. Adam Smith produced the classic list of governmental duties: national defense to protect the nation and its economic system from outsiders, antitrust to protect consumers and society from collusion among businesses, and contract enforcement (including anticorruption measures) to protect all participants from scoundrels. But when we approach the market system with assumptions that are more realistic, other important challenges must also be attended to. To put it another way, to function effectively in the real world, market capitalism must be embedded in an effective governmental system, one that allows—presumably through an accountable (and, hopefully, democratic) political system—for the regulation and mediation of the system and its effects and one that permits the determination of which trade-offs of welfare among different parties are, on balance, worth making.

The expanded list for this external mediating structure—be it government or civil society or a combination—is increasingly extensive. In the wake of the 2008–2009 financial crisis, no one should further doubt the need for a regulatory system that insures the functioning, transparency, and stability of the banking system. In the presence of widespread threats flowing from climate change, few still doubt the need for collective action to reduce ongoing human activity that pushes global climate away from its former range. In a world where large-scale migration is a reality, national and, arguably, international arrangements for regulating flows of people are increasingly essential, and existing paradigms may be outdated. Where capitalism's effects include generating increasing disparities in income between rich and poor, mechanisms for addressing inequality may be essential, and again, existing mechanisms may not be adequate to the task. In all these areas, standard business innovation (through the development of new products and services as well as new business models and strategies) may be relevant and important, but is unlikely to address fully the evolving challenges—and the stakes for business in the short run and for the successful sustaining of the market system in the long run are very high. Moreover, they are all areas where the existing processes of government and civil society may be inadequately coping with the challenges and may be failing to define and successfully grasp the opportunities.

All of this argues for a significant redefinition of the appropriate role of business in identifying these issues, in activating others to address them, and in participating with others to redesign elements of the system and to operate it more successfully. As we have shown, companies can make a significant contribution by adopting innovative strategies and business models that are aligned with the needs of a sustainable system. By playing a role that it has always played as an innovator and a developer of new products, services, business models, and strategies—but with a sensibility attuned to the larger, systemic issues—business can successfully and profitably make a material difference to the capitalist market system's health and improved functioning.

But even if individual companies continue to innovate at a significant pace, it hardly seems likely that this by itself will be sufficient to rid the system of the threats identified in our forums. Thus, in addition to expanding its remit as an innovator within its own operations, business will need to see itself as an innovator in the broader institutional context as well. Practically speaking, this means that companies will also need to become more active participants in guiding the market system's healthy development and engaging with other parties to address issues that cannot be dealt with by individual firms acting alone. Leaders will need to become more involved in working with industry and national and international groups and will need to become more attuned to the interrelationships among different parts of the system.

For many, as we heard in our forums, the activist role is far less familiar—and less comfortable—than the innovator role, for reasons that are quite understandable. It is a role that business has played only infrequently—at least recently—and that runs counter to the current prevailing ideologies (both left and right). Many companies and business leaders, moreover, are currently poorly equipped for such a role. But activism may be so crucial to the sustainability of business as we know it that businesses and business leaders must now figure out how indeed to play that role successfully. What, then, might be the most important and threatened areas of the capitalist system for business to help address, and what role or roles might business take in helping to sustain the vital elements of the market capitalist system?

As we analyze how business might currently respond to the unmet challenges of sustaining the best elements of market capitalism (and mitigating its downsides), many historical examples show promising directions or provide models that could be expanded upon or adapted. Although current circumstances call for significantly greater business activism than we have recently seen—so that contemporary historical models do not seem entirely up to the task—some of these models nevertheless offer some insight into how to cope with broader systemic challenges.

Before we turn to some of the positive models, however, it is worth briefly considering some negative ones—ways in which companies and industries have sought to protect or advance their own narrow self-interest at the expense of the wider society (and system). If business is going to organize itself to have, on balance, a broader and more positive presence in reshaping the institutions and conditions necessary to support a well-functioning capitalist system, these negative models need to be consciously avoided as we try to build on the more positive historical modes of action—and, perhaps, invent new ones.

History We Do *Not* Want to Repeat

Unfortunately, there are many unhappy historical models of business actively and effectively organizing itself to defend or advance its own interests at the expense of the broader society. A broad literature in economics covers *regulatory capture*—the development of political power by regulated entities, which use the regulators to protect and extend their own market power. An intriguing, century-old example is the regulation of railroads by the newly formed Interstate Commerce Commission (ICC). The standard historical interpretation is this: the railroads' monopoly led to high freight prices and frustrated economic growth, a situation that eventually spawned a political movement that created the ICC, which regulated freight rates and ultimately broke the monopoly of the railroad barons. This would seem, on its face, to demonstrate how the standard processes of collective political action worked to rectify a miscarriage of the market mechanism, with government rising to the challenge of regulating market misbehavior. An alternative reading of the history, however, provides a starkly different view. According to some historians, increasing competition in the railroad industry was already breaking the market power of the barons; new competitors were undercutting established rates, reducing the profitability of the railroads. Far from being imposed by reformers, according to this view, the ICC was accepted by the railroads precisely because it was a way of providing regulatory stability—which is to say, as a way of *maintaining*, not breaking, the monopoly power of the existing railroads. (Subsequent legislation to "reform" the ICC and protect consumers and workers would later lock the railroads into an untenable long-term position.)

Examples of business activism for its own perceived interests are easy to find throughout history. American automobile companies—in the heyday of their economic, market, and political power—lobbied successfully in Congress and elsewhere against the imposition of more aggressive fuel-efficiency standards in the 1980s, arguing among other things that higher standards would create an unfair advantage for their foreign competitors. Essentially, this amounted to the argument that U.S. companies were already behind in the development of more efficient engines and could not innovate as successfully or as quickly as their foreign competitors. Lobbying for what was tantamount to a policy of protection of domestic industry—at the height of its competitive standing in global markets—may have been perceived by the businesses that undertook this as a way to protect their interests, but if so, the interests in question must have been very short term indeed. The ultimate effect of this policy seems to have further retarded the pace at which American companies undertook innovations in fuel efficiency— innovations that were eventually demanded by the market in the face of higher gasoline prices. As a result, the policy probably contributed to the recent near demise of American automobile manufacturing.

Recent history also shows how Enron made lobbying against government restraints on its energy and trading businesses a cornerstone of its business model. The company's extensive lobbying organization was largely successful in its efforts to avoid or remove government scrutiny over key aspects of its operations. For instance, Enron successfully blocked government efforts to regulate its derivatives trading business and won exemptions that allowed it to operate an electricity auction without federal oversight. The company also won special treatment under investment and securities laws—treatment that facilitated its use of the special partnerships that were central to its overextension and ultimate demise.[3] In view of the widespread damage done by Enron's spectacular collapse in 2001, it might be reasonable to ask whether a bit more application of the so-called wise restraints that make people free would have been better for the company and for nearly everyone else as well.

Parallel examples abound—indeed, the great majority of the multibillion-dollar Washington, D.C., lobbying industry appears to be focused on pressing similarly narrow interests. Consider two striking recent illustrations. Oil-production companies apparently lobbied successfully against requirements to install multiple redundant backup devices (specifically, to equip blowout preventers with a second "blind shear ram") at undersea wellheads to shut off oil flows in the case of blowouts.[4] In the aftermath of the 2010 BP oil spill in the Gulf of Mexico, this decision looks shortsighted not only from the perspective of society and the environment, but even from the perspective of the oil-production industry itself, which seems likely now to confront both delays in production and significant additional regulatory and cost burdens. To take another example, Wall Street and other financial firms successfully lobbied for regulatory changes that created the conditions that generated—or at least permitted—the recent worldwide financial market meltdown. This same group of interests has now been almost completely unhelpful in suggesting ways to improve the integrity of that system. Instead, the financial industry has been resisting essentially all new or additional regulatory requirements and to date undertaking few, if any, reforms in its own internal governance. Again, neither the initial lobbying nor the ongoing defensive lobbying seem wise from a long-term business perspective, and even less so from the perspective of the larger society.

Many of the historical models of business engagement with government, then, are not particularly positive about the ability of business activism to protect market capitalism from the kinds of challenges we have identified throughout this book. Nor do these examples suggest that simply putting greater reliance on government will work. Witness, for instance, the disappointing performance of the U.S. Minerals Management Service in failing to protect the Gulf of Mexico and its coastline from BP's Macondo well blowout in the spring of 2010, in part by not enforcing its own rules requiring oil companies to submit proof that the key components of their blowout-prevention systems actually work. Not only do these forms of business and government performance fail to exemplify how we might make more progress going forward, but they actively need to be prevented and avoided.

History We Want to Build On

Fortunately, alongside the negative models we have just discussed, there are positive models, too. Such positive examples can provide a springboard for business leaders wanting to engage their businesses further in sustaining the system of market capitalism. These examples show business leaders taking action to improve the system locally, nationally, and internationally.

CED and Postwar Planning for Full Employment

In 1942, the Committee for Economic Development (CED) was formed as a private, nonprofit, nonpolitical association of business executives for two purposes: mobilizing U.S. business to plan for a quick conversion to a full-employment economy after World War II and conducting fundamental research on policies to promote high levels of employment in a free economy.[5] The CED was headed by two experienced businessmen: its chairman, Paul G. Hoffman, former president of Studebaker Company, and its vice chairman, William Benton, an advertising executive who had sold his stake in the Madison Avenue firm of Benton and Bowles to become the University of Chicago's vice president.

Already well acquainted by 1942, Hoffman and Benton had found common cause in their belief that the nation would benefit from greater collaboration between business and academia. Before the war, they had begun to sketch out plans for a unique (at the time) association that would bring together leading executives and scholars to tackle some of the nation's most vexing economic problems. Hoffman put unemployment at the top of the list. In his years at Studebaker, he had come to believe that widespread unemployment was the country's most serious problem—"a social disease gnawing at our vitals," he called it. He was troubled that in 1941, after ten years of struggle, the country still had 8 million unemployed, and he was even more troubled by the argument, advanced by some, that a free economy could never find an answer to unemployment. Hoffman believed that progress might be made if only the problem could be looked at objectively, without regard to politics. He approached Benton and the University of Chicago's president, Robert Hutchins, with the idea of establishing a group that would conduct fundamental research on this and other issues central to maintaining a free economy.

Plans for the proposed group, to be called the American Policy Commission, were thwarted by the outbreak of war, but they were revived when Hoffman became involved with a proposal that was taking shape in the U.S. Department of Commerce. Even as the war effort was still ramping up, some forward-thinking officials were beginning to worry about what would happen when it was over. The specter of another depression—armies of unemployed, shuttered factories, shortages of essential goods—loomed large, especially for those who had lived through the 1930s. Somehow the country would have to find productive jobs for millions of demobilized veterans and provide a steady flow of orders to keep America's factories humming as hostilities ended and wartime contracts were canceled on a grand scale. Failure to do so, some predicted, would mean 30 million Americans out of work and the worst depression the country had ever seen.[6] It could also mean political pressure to extend the government's war powers over industry and manufacturing.

As part of its effort to avert another economic breakdown after the war, the Commerce Department proposed the creation of an independent committee of public-spirited business leaders to stimulate and direct a broad investigation into postwar private-investment opportunities across the country. Given that no existing organization, public or private, was prepared to take the lead on such an extensive field project, a new group would have to be formed. The Secretary of Commerce had in mind a group that would bring together big and small business with the aim of working toward the "full, prompt restoration of our American standard of living; the steady maintenance and continual enhancement of this standard; and the efficient, effective employment *for these purposes* of all persons able and willing to work."[7] The department would provide technical assistance, but the committee's funding would come from the private sector, and its operations would be wholly independent of government once it was set up and its initial roster of forty-five core members chosen.*

When the appointed organizers asked Hoffman to head the proposed committee, by then named the Committee for Economic Development, he accepted on condition that Benton be appointed vice chairman. Benton, in turn, agreed to serve only if a research group similar to the American Policy Commission that he and Hoffman had been working on before the war was incorporated into CED on an equal footing with the planned field program. The Secretary of Commerce gave his approval, and CED was born, with the dual mission of postwar planning and research on employment.

Hoffman and Benton insisted that CED's research be objective and that CED itself avoid, in Benton's words, "being stamped as a business-pressure group, concerned with business first, rather than the public first."[8] CED's nonpartisan mission was reflected in its certificate of incorporation as well as its bylaws, which, according to one commentator, were written to protect CED from the vice of "kept economists."[9] The bylaws provided that each research project would be approached from "the standpoint of the general welfare and not that of any special political or economic group" and that each project would bear directly on public policies designed to foster "the attainment of high and secure standards of living for people in all walks of life through maximum employment and high productivity." The bylaws also provided that all materials would be subject to thorough debate among the members and granted dissenters the "right of a dissenting footnote" in reports issued by CED.[10] As a further safeguard, CED established a research advisory board of eminent economists and social scientists.

CED's early research indicated that attaining a high level of postwar employment would require an increase in production of some 30 to

---

*Donald David, then dean of Harvard Business School, was a member of the CED's first research committee. In addition to Hoffman and Benton, who served ex officio, the research committee also included five corporate executives, the chairman of the Federal Reserve Bank of New York, and the president of the Federal Reserve of St. Louis. "Jobs for 55,000,000 Is Post-War Plan: Business Men Organize for Economic Development When Peace Has Been Made," *New York Times*, January 2, 1943.

45 percent over what it had been in 1940, while the number of jobs would have to increase by 10 million. These targets translated into a postwar gross national product of around $150 billion, with jobs for 53 to 56 million people. To many, these figures seemed little more than a pipe dream. To meet the challenge, CED launched a further program of research and embarked on a field campaign to stimulate governments and businesses in communities across the country to begin canvassing their postwar opportunities. Local chairs were appointed, and affiliate committees were set up in three cities as test sites to determine how best to engage small businesses in making their maximum contribution to reemployment and to develop an experience base for rolling out the campaign nationally. Regional, district, and town-level chairs were named; they, in turn, set up local committees. Early field research revealed that few employers had given any thought to the problems they would face at war's end. Although some derided CED's campaign as a "national planning effort," Hoffman argued that to the contrary, it was simply an attempt by business to stimulate high employment and maximum productivity after the war. Between 1942 and 1945, committees were organized in nearly three thousand communities. More than seventy thousand businesspeople served as voluntary members.[11]

By January 1946, only months after Japan's surrender and well before most expected, the United States had achieved close to full employment. It was impossible to say what would have happened in the absence of efforts by CED and many other organizations that turned to postwar planning as time went on, but the results seemed to speak for themselves. CED counted 52 million workers in civilian jobs, compared with the 53.5 million that it considered full employment and had been expecting to achieve only by September 1946. Moreover, earnings were on the rise and only slightly below the wartime peak, and production of civilian goods was up from 50 to 75 percent over the previous six months.[12] In three short years, CED had proven the value of its approach to research and become a trusted voice of business.[13]

In January 1947, with the country's conversion from war production largely accomplished, CED reorganized itself, shutting down the field organization that had been created for the postwar planning campaign and launching a new two-year research program aimed at developing policies that would help maintain production and employment at high levels.[14] CED would later play a crucial role in mobilizing U.S. business behind the Marshall Plan for rebuilding Europe, and CED's research continues to this day to inform public debate on pressing economic and business issues, including most recently corporate governance and health-care reform in the United States.[15] But the business community's involvement in postwar planning for full employment stands out as an example of how business leaders can think creatively about the broader environment and what business can do beyond the boundaries of a single firm or single industry group to help strengthen and sustain the market system.

Cleveland Tomorrow

During the postwar period, the city of Cleveland, Ohio—along with many other Midwestern U.S. cities with a major reliance on heavy manufacturing—underwent a cataclysmic downward shift in its economic and social circumstances. A stable and reasonably prosperous city in 1945, it had by 1978 witnessed high-income flight from the central city, the disappearance of half of its manufacturing jobs and over a third of its population, the decline of its school system, a rise in structural unemployment and in crime rates, a deterioration in race relations and the outbreak of urban riots, and the embarrassment of its Cuyahoga River becoming so choked with industrial pollutants that it famously literally caught fire in 1969.[16] The culminating disgrace—and what turned out to be the catalyst for business leaders to self-organize into a collective and ultimately highly successful effort at turnaround—was the city's default on its municipal bonds on December 15, 1978, making it the first major U.S. city since the Great Depression to declare bankruptcy.

The rebound was slow, and it had many contributing drivers—but a central force in conceiving and activating a new strategy for the city was a collection of CEOs of major firms from the area. Galvanized into action by the default—a strong wake-up call that the situation had deteriorated to the point of real crisis—business leaders came together and fundamentally redesigned their relationship to the city government and to the city itself. Weak and dysfunctional government could—and would—no longer be seen as an advantage to business and would no longer be tolerated; business leaders worked to find political candidates whose leadership could raise the quality of government, improve services, and rebuild financial integrity. Companies loaned executives to a new mayor to help find ways to improve city services and operations.

Having thus begun to address the political and governance issues confronting the city—and helping government develop its capacities to address these issues—business leaders turned to the task of revitalizing the city's economy. Forming a task force to analyze the forces that had generated the city's economic decline and to recommend new directions, business leaders founded a new organization called Cleveland Tomorrow, a nonprofit that opened its doors in 1982 with a small staff and thirty-six local company CEOs as members. The understanding—a compact of sorts among the CEOs—was that they were coming together to diagnose and address the still-significant challenges facing Cleveland. As heads of the major businesses in the area (membership required $300 million in revenues or a similar level of influence in the community as indicated by other aspects of a company's presence in the region), the members understood that they would need to support—financially and otherwise—new initiatives to revitalize the economy. The members also realized that they had sufficient positions of influence in their companies to guarantee the ability to generate the necessary resources.

The group of CEO members constituted the board of directors—and as a CEO-only organization, members could not send a delegate to attend meetings on their behalf. Given busy CEO schedules, this meant that not every member was present at each meeting, but it also meant that people with decision-making ability and influence were present at the creation of the strategy and willing and able to play their assigned roles in the tactical execution of that strategy. The purpose was not representation of business interests—rather, it was to bring together people with influence and resources who could formulate and see to the execution of a focused, coherent, and effective strategy for revitalization.

Over the next fifteen years, this group helped to generate a remarkable renaissance. By the time of its bicentennial celebration in 1996,

Cleveland could boast of a series of awards as a livable city, a revitalized economy, a fiscally solvent government, and a rejuvenated outlook.

The role taken by business in helping to catalyze and guide the changes that produced this transformation goes far beyond the usual interpretation of social responsibility or corporate citizenship. It was surely in the interest of these companies that the city in which they had major investments undergo a turnaround—but for many of them, it might have been simpler and less risky to move their investments elsewhere. The engagement by these CEOs in producing the turnaround appears to have been motivated not only by their own and their company's economic self-interest, but also by a deeper form of commitment and loyalty to the city and region, and a willingness to work personally and professionally on a project with deeper meaning and value. And their ability to self-organize—admittedly, in the face of a wake-up crisis—to undertake this agenda is at least one example of how more extensive leadership from the business community can act on behalf of a broad and collective interest.

Level Up, Not Down—Dealing with Corruption

In the early 1990s, a coalition of multinational companies from the United States and Europe came together to tackle the growing problem of bribery and corruption in international business.[17] Their effort had originated a few years earlier in opposition to a different group of U.S. companies that had sought to water down the U.S. Foreign Corrupt Practices Act (FCPA). Enacted by Congress in 1977, the FCPA set the United States apart from other industrialized nations by making it a crime for U.S. companies and issuers of securities in U.S. markets to bribe overseas government officials to win or keep business. (Other U.S. laws already prohibited bribery of officials at home.) Antibribery advocates hoped that other nations would follow suit, but none did. Rather than criminalizing illicit payments to foreign officials by their transnational companies, other countries continued to turn a blind eye to overseas bribery; some even permitted their companies to treat bribes as tax-deductible business expenses. Arguing that the restrictive law was causing American companies to lose billions of dollars in orders to foreign competitors, some U.S. multinationals sought to level the playing field by rolling back the FCPA.

In their effort to marshal allies for their lobbying effort, the group soon hit a snag. Approached to join, one company balked. At GE, general counsel Ben Heineman acknowledged the validity of the competitive argument, but he questioned the proposed "solution" in view of the damaging effects of bribery and corruption—not only on markets and competition, but also on national development and poverty reduction. He concluded that his company and the business community more generally should seek to "level up, not level down." The real solution, he believed, was not to weaken the FCPA but to "internationalize" it and try to raise standards for all multinationals headquartered in the industrialized world. This solution would benefit companies subject to the FCPA and countries plagued by corruption. Internationalization would be helpful both to his company's immediate interest by creating a level playing field on which the company could compete on its merits and to the company's broader interest by supporting the rule of law in emerging markets. Equally important, internationalization would benefit business and society at large by fostering greater integrity in competition and by avoiding the hypocrisy of clandestine deals and false bookkeeping that undermined efforts to foster a culture of integrity within the company. Any other approach, he felt, would be self-defeating over the long term. Put simply, in his words, "corruption is terrible for business."

Thus began an eight-year campaign involving U.S. and European corporations, in conjunction with antibribery advocates across the globe. To keep the process nimble and nonpartisan, Heineman assembled a small, ad hoc working group rather than channel the effort through a large, existing industry organization. He reached out to peers at both European and U.S. multinationals to take on what everyone knew would be a long and arduous task and to work closely with like-minded groups and individuals in both the public and the private sectors around the world. The organizers decided on a two-pronged strategy: establishing an NGO to conduct research and shine a spotlight on corruption, and advocating the passage of an Organisation for Economic Co-operation and Development (OECD) convention against overseas bribery on the model of the FCPA. If adopted, a convention would require all members of the OECD—twenty-five countries at the time—to enact national laws similar to the FCPA. As envisioned, the two prongs would reinforce one another. Exposing corruption to public view would help build support for an anticorruption convention, and a convention would provide a clear standard by which to assess and report cases of foreign bribery in the developed world.

Working on a parallel but initially independent track, German lawyer Peter Eigen had begun developing plans for Transparency International (TI), a new NGO to tackle international corruption. Eigen's twenty-five years at the World Bank had given him firsthand experience of corruption's insidious impact on developing nations. He was seeking to build a broad-based group of development professionals, government officials, and international business leaders to mount a serious effort to build more effective anticorruption systems around the globe. Eigen was particularly eager to enlist support from the international business community, and the multinational working group saw Eigen's planned NGO as a promising candidate for the organization they envisioned. GE seconded one of its lawyers to work with Eigen's team.

In 1993, with support from like-minded companies and from many other groups, Transparency International opened the doors of its headquarters in Berlin. In keeping with its organizers' belief that effective reform would require focused action at the national level, TI embarked on a major effort to build a network of national chapters in all parts of the world. Like the headquarters organization, each chapter was organized with multisector support including business, professional, academic, civic, and other groups. Prominent among supporters of the U.S. chapter were U.S. multinationals that had been behind the anticorruption drive.

Meanwhile, the anticorruption group pressed forward on the second prong of its strategy. In May 1994, the OECD passed a recommendation calling on member countries to take effective action to combat the bribery of foreign officials. Working with government officials and with TI chapters that had by then been established in the OECD member states, supportive multinationals helped raise the profile of the recommendation and urged that it be taken seriously. In 1996, the OECD committee on fiscal affairs recommended that all OECD states deny the tax deductibility of bribes, and another OECD working group began developing proposals to criminalize the bribery of foreign officials. The next year, in the spring of 1997, twenty European CEOs issued a letter in support of the convention, and in December, the OECD voted to adopt it—thus obliging member states to criminalize overseas bribery by their corporations. The convention took effect in twenty countries in 1999.

As this example shows, companies working together and in collaboration with others can effect positive change in important institutions—and create *new* institutions. By mid-2010, the OECD convention had been adopted by thirty-eight countries, each of which had enacted national laws prohibiting foreign bribery by their corporations, and the OECD Working Group on Bribery had established a highly regarded peer monitoring process. Meaningful enforcement programs had been established in five of the world's eight largest exporting countries, some of which, like Germany, had treated foreign bribery as a tax-deductible business expense only ten years earlier. (In late 2008, for example, Siemens paid more than $1.5 billion in fines and penalties for violations of German and U.S. antibribery laws.) Transparency International had grown to approximately one hundred national chapters and local partners and was recognized worldwide as a strong and influential voice against corruption. Among many other activities, TI published a well-known index of perceived corruption in countries around the world and issued annual reports comparing the enforcement of antibribery laws in OECD countries.

Of course, an OECD convention alone is hardly a cure for global corruption. Implementation and enforcement of the convention have a mixed record, and as evidenced in our business leader forums, corruption continues to be a significant threat to the market system and a tax on development in many nations. A prohibition on bribery by developed world companies is only one piece in the complex process of change needed to establish transparent and accountable institutions dedicated to the rule of law. Still, the OECD convention must be counted as a major breakthrough in establishing a common legal framework among industrialized countries.

The business-led campaign to build support for the convention played an important role in its adoption and, perhaps most crucially, in changing the terms of the debate. Prior to the push for the OECD convention and the creation of TI, commentators, if they addressed bribery at all, tended to dismiss it as inevitable, as a "cultural difference" to be tolerated, or even as a useful lubricant for economic activity. Today, the consensus has shifted; bribery is broadly considered a societal ill, a blight on the economy, a serious public policy concern, and a legitimate area of research and inquiry. The fight against corruption now has a prominent position on the international agenda—in developed nations, in international financing institutions, and, importantly, in many emerging markets.

Scenario Planning in South Africa

During the latter part of the 1980s, a great struggle was under way in the Afrikaans-speaking white community in South Africa over the future of the country. The new leader of the politically dominant Nationalist Party, F. W. de Klerk, had argued, first gently and then increasingly forcefully, that the oppressive apartheid system must be dismantled and that South Africa must inevitably make a transition to a broad-based democratic system or face ruin. As the 1980s drew to a close with Nelson Mandela still in jail, however, many in the white community disputed the necessity for revolutionary change, continuing to believe that the system of white economic and political privilege could be retained with only modest reforms. In this very emotionally, politically, and racially charged setting, a small group of business and civil society leaders in South Africa convened a broader collection of leaders from business, government, and civil society to undertake a systematic analysis of the future of the South African economy. Using the process of scenario analysis developed by Royal Dutch/Shell, they crafted a series of alternative paths forward, illustrating in great detail the long-term economic implications of a variety of policy choices. In developing their forecasting models, the group included every major sector of the economy (export industries, mining, agriculture, energy production, water, transportation, housing, etc.) and considered their interdependencies. The group looked at the capital investment and labor force development that would be required to extend basic services like electricity, water, housing, transportation, and education to the ethnic majority population, which had historically been systematically denied these services.

The scenarios revealed stark and, to many, startling projections. No matter what reasonable assumptions were made about how the system would evolve under a continuation of apartheid, the economic future was bleak. Scenarios predicted shortages of skilled labor and an inability to compete effectively internationally, with the result being a long-term decline in living standards even in the privileged community. Alternative scenarios that involved significant investment in infrastructure, education, and training to extend services to the currently disenfranchised community, by contrast, were cautiously optimistic. The challenges were significant—these paths involved heavy investment to extend basic services much more broadly—but the prospects for a brighter future were realistic even if daunting. With these analyses in hand, the group then embarked on a process of public education, holding forums throughout South Africa to discuss the implications of their analysis.

Both in the development and in the presentation of the scenarios, the group was undertaking a process that might be called *public deliberation*—open and broad discussion of circumstances, possibilities, policies, and consequences. A design feature of public deliberation is that it would bring together a wide range of leaders from different parts of the society and different sectors of the economy to help develop models that underlay the predictions that would be developed. During those discussions, some people who had previously focused narrowly on their own business or sector may have come to see how different parts of society and the economy interacted with one another, forming an ecological web in which changes in any one part would affect others. This process was described by participants as a fundamental education in the realities and complex dynamics of the social, economic, and political system, and it eventually led to a reasonable consensus, among a very disparate group of leaders, about the key choices facing the country—and the consequences that would ensue if the right choices were not made. Having thus achieved a degree of common understanding, the group was in a position to extend the deliberation to a broader audience through the public presentations of its findings. The group thus made presentations to current and incipient government leaders (including both de Klerk and his cabinet and, separately, to Mandela and his shadow cabinet in waiting), to civic associations, to business groups, and to anyone else who was willing to listen.

There were many civic-minded groups operating in South Africa in the late 1980s seeking to help the nation make a peaceful transition from its apartheid past to a one-person, one-vote democratic future; many of these groups were preparing different scenarios and arguments about paths to the future. Though it is impossible to determine what the individual effects of these different efforts may have been, these and many other efforts collectively resulted in a relatively rapid and successful transition to real democracy—something that had been widely predicted to be an impossibility. The scenario-planning process driven largely by business leaders seems to have contributed to showing South Africans (especially resisters in the white Afrikaans-speaking community) that the apartheid system was on an unsustainable economic trajectory. By constructing realistic scenarios and presenting them widely, business helped South African society find a path forward that people could understand, accept, and, ultimately, endorse.

Undertaking this effort required the development of what was essentially a new institution—a group of leaders who came together from across several industrial sectors and civil society to invent a new device for public deliberation, convened themselves and others (supported by a technical staff that could conduct analysis), and deliberated among themselves and with others. This intervention lay well beyond the realm of what individual firms could do. It was clearly political— not in the sense of supporting a candidate or party, but in the sense of explicitly trying to shift the politics associated with a transition to democracy by showing that the paths that did not involve transition were economically bleak. The institution seems to have generated some important public learning—both for its participants and for those who participated in its presentations—and thus helped to create a broader acceptance in South African society of the necessity for, and positive prospects of, a more revolutionary political change than might otherwise have been possible.

The U.S. Climate Action Partnership (USCAP)

In January 2007, ten market-leading businesses, including energy producers and energy sector suppliers, came together with four leading
environmental lobbying groups and climate change research organizations to issue the results of a yearlong study and consensus document
about a series of principles for legislative action on climate change.
Formed as the U.S. Climate Action Partnership (USCAP) with the
express purpose of positively influencing legislation in the United
States to address global climate change, the founding member organizations involved in USCAP seemed like strange bedfellows. Groups
that had for years heavily criticized corporate environmental policies
in general and the policies of energy-producing firms like BP America
and PG&E in particular suddenly were allied with some of the very
firms they had been castigating. Still, over time, USCAP added several
additional leading firms from the energy and manufacturing sectors,
broadening its base and potential influence.

The theory behind this somewhat uneasy coalition seems to have
several elements. First, it was obvious to all that little progress had been
made in formulating and taking action on sensible policies to mitigate
the worst environmental consequences of energy development and use.
Second, energy producers and other companies involved with the energy
sector (as suppliers or as significant consumers) recognized that policies
were likely to be made in this domain, and that joining with environmental organizations to propose and support sensible policies might be
better than having less sensible policies imposed on them. Third, for
their part, environmental organizations realized that for them as well,
the best might be the enemy of the good—that is, by being unwilling
to compromise on the nature of climate-change-mitigating efforts, they
had so far wound up with virtually no progress at all. Finally, parties on
what had been the two opposing sides probably recognized that if they
could come together and forge a consensus on what kinds of climate
change legislation might make sense, they would collectively be hard to
resist and, consequently, might well have more influence on the actual
shape of policies by being inside the coalition than by staying outside it.

Whatever the motivations, the coalition was nearly unprecedented
in its ambition essentially to negotiate a consensus legislative position

that all the disparate members of the group would pledge to support. Not convened by government, but instead self-organized, the group was designed to have significant influence both within each of the formerly opposing sides and in political circles. Or to put it another way, the group was in a position to provide air cover for politicians who could use the group's eclectic nature and previously broad range of policy views as a reason to support the resulting suggested legislation. The group's membership of very disparate interests lent credibility to the idea that the positions that emerged from it might indeed be good for society as a whole. If this many organizations, coming as they did from their very different perspectives and interests, supported a position, then perhaps the position was indeed a public-interest-serving compromise.

USCAP had come together to articulate a series of design principles that in its view should guide policy. In particular, the principles developed and supported *cap and trade* as an important component of any significant approach to limiting and managing greenhouse gas emissions (GHGs). The basic idea of cap and trade is to establish overall limits on the amount of GHGs that companies or other entities are allowed to release. *Initial endowments* (permits to emit specific amounts of GHGs) would be distributed to companies, which are then allowed to trade these permits through a market. While some members of the USCAP coalition might prefer a regime in which there were no limits to GHGs and no charges associated with emissions, they might nonetheless accept the likelihood of some form of limitation, and given that there will be limitations, these members may prefer a market mechanism for allocating GHGs among firms. Similarly, while some of the environmental organizations might prefer much more severe limits on GHGs or a fee imposed for emitting any GHGs (rather than granting initial endowments), these organizations might recognize that such an outcome is unlikely politically. Consequently, the environmental groups may also prefer to shape the process of limitation and allocation.

Thus, even though the participants in USCAP might disagree significantly among themselves about what the ideal regime may look like, they could nonetheless find common ground around designing the best system for managing GHGs within the domain of what is politically feasible. USCAP's 2007 report "A Call for Action," the consensus document issued after a yearlong study (and, no doubt, long hours of debate and discussion), had thirty-three signatories. Twenty-eight of these were corporations (including leading energy, chemical, mining, and manufacturing firms), and five were environmental and climate research organizations. The document was indeed remarkable for its forging a set of action proposals and establishing guiding principles with real content.[18]

Obviously, the details of a cap-and-trade system will matter greatly. How initial rights are recognized or distributed, for example, has significant implications for the amount of funds transacted in the permit marketplace and for who collects them. The ability to participate in shaping these policies—and the likelihood that a coalition like USCAP, because of its composition, would be in a strong position to influence that outcome—may have been one of the great attractions for organizations with widely differing viewpoints.

Perhaps not completely surprisingly, this disparate coalition has proved difficult to keep together. The group was founded at a time when it seemed likely that some form of U.S. and international limitation of GHGs was going to be imposed, and USCAP members then found it possible to work collectively toward devising the best regime for managing such a policy. But although the partnership made good progress on developing a consensus position about necessary actions, when the passage of GHG legislation later became more doubtful, the differences among the members became more pronounced. On February 15, 2010, three of the early members of USCAP announced that they would not renew their memberships—two energy companies (BP America and ConocoPhillips) and machinery manufacturer Caterpillar left the group. While press releases both from the departing members and from USCAP emphasized mutual respect and appreciation for work already accomplished, the departure of the three companies illustrates the challenges of keeping a disparate group together around a set of policies that must naturally be at best a second choice for each member. Nonetheless, the formation and early work of this organization shows that businesses can organize (or be organized) into a deliberative and influential alliance to tackle challenges currently not being effectively addressed by existing governmental and other societal mechanisms.

As we write, the future of the USCAP effort remains in doubt. The 111th Congress enacted what many see as an historic array of major pieces of legislation—but left Washington in late December 2010 without approving any version of the cap-and-trade proposal that USCAP had organized around and sought to advance. The House of Representatives passed a cap-and-trade bill in 2009, but in July 2010, Senate Democratic leaders announced that they did not have the votes to advance the bill in the Senate.[19] So far, the composition and actions of the 112th Congress suggest that this effort will probably not be revived soon. Thus, this task still lies ahead—for business and for the whole of society—but the coalition-building work to date provides an example and a starting point for future work that may contribute to further progress.

A New Domain of Business Engagement: Driving Institutional Innovation

The examples in the previous section—even those that have not come fully to fruition yet—are promising and hopeful. At a minimum, they demonstrate the possibility of cooperation among businesses and the ability of business to help mobilize government action in ways that improve institutions and strengthen the context for business. While these examples do not yet appear to be on a scale or scope that would address the larger challenges to global market capitalism, they may provide models that can be replicated more widely or platforms upon which larger-scale efforts might be built. What our positive historical examples point to—and the prospective examples we present in the next chapter hope for—is business engagement in strengthening the institutional foundations of capitalism.

To make progress of a form and at a scale relevant to the kinds of threats to market capitalism we are discussing, business leadership now needs to move into a new and much broader domain. In the past, a firm's actions were usually focused on its direct production processes and its transactions with its most immediate contacts (customers, shareholders, suppliers, employees, and regulators). In this new domain, businesses would try to restructure the very environment within which they were operating—and to do so in a way that strengthens the future prospects of the market system—and not just their own immediate prospects. An individual firm can, through reengineering its own production process, reduce its own GHG emissions—but it cannot by itself bring about a new regime in which all firms regionally (and even less so, nationally or internationally) will find it imperative to reduce their emissions through urgent innovation. An individual firm may be able to train its own workers, but it probably cannot create a region-wide effort by business and government together to improve materially the prospects of low-income workers who may otherwise feel exploited and inclined to support a populist or revolutionary political movement. And an individual firm may not even recognize its potential role in helping restructure a national education system so that the benefits of capitalism could be more widely shared, especially by the least well-off in society. Having each firm do its part—taking actions that seem reasonable or likely to have a positive payoff for the firm itself—simply has not added up across firms to produce the scope and scale of action needed. Taking on the broader challenge of sustaining market capitalism requires acting intentionally on the larger policy, regulatory, cultural, and social environment within which individual firms carry out their daily work.

Businesses need to engage in *institutional innovation*—innovation designed to shift the system, to reengineer the conditions that individual companies face. By changing the circumstances faced by all firms, thoughtful and effective institutional innovations will create incentives for companies to undertake consistently and forcefully actions that are more aligned with the needs of a sustainable market system. When the CEOs of leading businesses in Cleveland came together to reset the political table and design a strategy for economic renewal, they were reengineering not only the conditions in which *their* businesses operated, but the environment in which *all* businesses in the region operated. When firms came together to try to get every OECD country to adopt laws to prevent its firms from engaging in corrupt practices internationally, they were shifting the environmental circumstances and incentives for themselves, for their competitors, and for powerful political officials in the host countries in which they were pursuing business deals. The actions of the USCAP consortium, though not fully successful, attempted to shift the political landscape, and through it, the regulatory landscape, for all U.S. firms—that is, to produce nothing short of a revolution in how GHGs would be understood and managed by nearly every relevant firm in the country.

Many more, and even greater, efforts will be needed, but these examples point in the right direction. Future business leaders working on social equity, environmental issues, financial system stability, immigration, and other challenges could take similar actions—actions whose intended purpose is to create a new set of rules, regulations, and conditions that encourage all businesses—and others—to strengthen the positive antecedents of market capitalism, reduce the negative consequences that capitalism will otherwise produce and that will undercut its support, and blunt the other forces that threaten to undermine it.

What we are calling for, then, are actions that are larger, broader, more intense, and different in kind from the usual forms of engagement in politics and public policy that we have recently seen by business leaders. These institutional innovations also have little in common with the usual interpretation of corporate social responsibility or corporate citizenship. The level and form of engagement that the examples in this chapter describe lie well beyond the boundary of common business practice in recent years. Institutional innovation will require different skills, different tools, and different organizational structures from traditional business practice.

Requirements of Institutional Innovation

Business leaders who recognize the need for institutional innovation may still have difficulty breaking themselves and their firms out of the old mold of narrowly defined self-interest. But as our discussion has shown, broadening a firm's attention to a more systemic scale can ultimately benefit individual companies as well as the system as a whole. The following four practices will help any business leader to broaden his or her company's outlook and become a more effective institutional innovator in ways that will make market capitalism more sustainable.

First, *business leaders must grasp the central importance of good government*. Historically, much of business activism with regard to government has been defensive, designed to reduce government's imposition of responsibilities on business. Business leaders, perhaps fearing that strong government would impose costly regulation, heavy taxation, or expropriation of private property, have often behaved as if weaker, less effective government were a favor to business. But as we have described, business is embedded in a complex ecology and depends, for its very ability to function and to be sustained over time, not only on its own performance but also on the effective performance of socially useful functions of government. Thus, *business has a profound stake in the quality of government*. One has only to look at the many places in the world where government has almost completely broken down—Kosovo in the early 1990s, for example, or Haiti at the turn of the new century—to see that business in such a setting is nearly impossible. The first priority in having business take its appropriate role in helping to sustain market capitalism, then, is to become a persistent, effective, and unstinting advocate of high-quality, effective government.

Second, *business leaders must develop the motivation to engage with institutional, system-level concerns more broadly and deeply than they generally have done in recent years*. Work in this new domain is difficult and complex—and not necessarily immediately rewarding. Actions taken to reengineer a firm's own processes (to use less energy, for example, or to improve its workers' health and, correspondingly, their productivity) may have a positive short-run payoff and thus may be able to compete more effectively for a leader's time, attention, and resources. On the other hand, the activities in this new domain involve efforts that seemingly distract from other critical priorities (like managing the business itself in a competitive environment—an important everyday concern for all CEOs) and may not always have visible or immediate payoffs. The motivation for this new work will not generally be short-run profits. Business will have to internalize the importance and scale of the threats to capitalism and, from this, develop the motivation needed for a new and sustained set of activities.

Third, *business leaders must create the organizational structures and develop the tools needed for effective engagement in institutional and system-level affairs*. Businesses and business leaders are not necessarily immediately prepared for, or predisposed to, work of this kind. The work will generally involve a level of external engagement and leadership for which corporate officials may not have been trained or selected, and much of it will require the formation of new organizations or structures through which to carry it out. All of these obstacles can be addressed, but it will take effort to build understanding, motivation, commitment, tools, and action.

Fourth, *business leaders must find new ways of self-organizing to promote collective action for systemic improvement.* The structure of business provides little incentive or training in how to go about fostering institutional innovation. Companies in a free-market setting are generally designed to have a strong incentive to produce value as viewed by their customers—that is, an incentive to enhance the self-perceived welfare of the individual members of society who buy their products. Indeed, this is the free market's theory of social value, and it constitutes a large part of our understanding of why free-market activity should be expected to enhance social welfare. Nothing about that system ensures that business will be good at intervening in the larger ecology that sustains the free-market system. And yet, as we have observed in some detail throughout our discussion in this book, business engagement is badly needed. The actions of other parties are insufficient to maintain the market capitalist system, and no party other than business is likely to have the requisite level of interest in the goal combined with the capability to analyze what is needed and to develop and deploy the necessary level of influence.

It remains for business—that is, business leaders individually, those in groups, and the businesses themselves—to develop not only the general interest in sustaining capitalism, but also the individual motivation necessary to mobilize their individual efforts. Business must develop the organizations and tools necessary to understand, address, and influence this outcome—and then actually take the requisite actions.

8
Rethinking the Role
of Business

WE LIVE in extraordinary times. Remarkable social, political, and economic forces are at work in the aftermath of the violent confrontations between fascism, Soviet communism, and democracies in the West. The relative peace since the end of World War II has seen unprecedented economic growth despite a nearly constant low level of regional war. A host of nations—including the People's Republic of China—have chosen to join the market system and have prospered mightily. A global network of enterprise has emerged, linking giant enterprises in major nations with small businesses in emerging nations. Increasingly, the world operates as one economic system.

At the core of this system are independent companies, primarily private companies owned by families or the shareholding public. The controlling managers of these companies have evolved from sea captains and foundry owners to be the stewards of complex enterprises sometimes employing hundreds of thousands of people. The economic scale of the larger of these companies dwarfs the size of many national economies. These companies' leaders are engaged in a kind of management work that could not have been imagined when the corporate form of organization was introduced or even when general incorporation statutes were widely enacted in the mid-nineteenth century.

In this book, we have proposed that for the sake of the system, these enterprises and their leaders need to adopt a new understanding of their role. Plausible forecasts such as those we presented suggest that market capitalism is likely to face serious threats from within and without in the years ahead. Troubling imbalances between positive and negative forces generated by the functioning of the system—particularly the growing income disparities within and between nations and regions—threaten to undermine the conditions necessary for the system's ongoing health and sustainability. As we have discussed, at least ten major forces may disrupt the system, and they are unlikely to be addressed successfully by existing mechanisms and institutions.

Perhaps surprisingly, significant numbers of the business leaders with whom we discussed these forecasts believe that the predictions are quite credible and that some of the disruptive consequences identified are already with us. Many believe that these problems are the most important issues facing companies and are therefore the challenges that Harvard Business School should take most seriously on the occasion of its centennial year as it makes its plans for the coming century.

Our research has led us to a series of radical conclusions. First, the global economy and its social, political, and physical conditions should not be regarded as exogenous to the firms that we study and that our forum participants lead, but instead should be viewed as materially affected by the actions of these firms. Second, these external circumstances therefore *cannot* be viewed as outside the appropriate purview of management. Third, business leaders must, for the sake of the health and sustainability of the very system on which they depend, become better positioned to ameliorate the disruptive forces that may otherwise impinge on market capitalism.

Finally, and most critically, leaders can address these challenges through the core activities of their firms. By appropriately modifying their strategies, some companies can grow profitably through activities that engage more of the billions of unskilled people living in emerging nations so that these people, too, can benefit from the system, and companies can do this in ways that enable rather than undermine the antecedents necessary for the health of the system. Moreover, businesses can prosper by introducing new business models that help ameliorate other critical weaknesses in the market system such as environmental degradation or hypervolatile financial markets.

Throughout their work, business leaders can be motivated by a recognition that continued operation within the existing capitalist market system according to its immediate incentives may, in the longer run, lead to destruction of important elements of that system and that consequently, they have a long-term abiding interest in the design and defense of the system.

Truly Out-of-the-Box Thinking

It is now commonplace to hear business gurus preaching the value of out-of-the-box thought. But almost always what they have in mind is the importance of avoiding getting trapped in conventional ways of framing problems, or of imagining that things can't be done because they never have been done. This advice is captured best in the words of Nobel Prize–winning scientist Albert Szent-Györgyi: "Discovery consists of seeing what everybody has seen and thinking what nobody has thought."[1] It is this kind of thinking that we work hard to inculcate in our students. We help them to understand how to encourage creativity in their organizations and how to recognize strategic threats and opportunities. But all of this goes on within the context of the widely shared box of belief in a narrow conception of the appropriate role of a business leader.

The difficulty posed by this line of thinking is evident in the previously cited comments of the CEO of a very large U.S. corporation who participated in the U.S. forum in New York.

> So let me just name a few of the threats that I think are serious threats to market capitalism. Number one is politicians, because politicians create the rules that we all have to live by, and the politicians responding to voters can create rules that could be very, very damaging to our form of capitalism here in the United States. So that's one major factor. Another factor is, as we've discussed, income distribution. Income distribution [is] a threat

to capitalism through voters putting demands on politicians
and then politicians changing the rules. So that's another major
threat that we face. And then there can also be fear of other
countries and economies, and so a move to protectionism, again
caused by voters and politicians. So I think those are the primary
threats that I would highlight.

When we pushed him as to what business could do, he answered,
"Not much":

> I think there is actually very little that business can do. It's above
> my pay grade. We were talking today about how business can
> lobby and set an example and do all manner of good things to try
> to show that they are very good corporate citizens. But at the end
> of the day, my belief is that while that's important, that's not going
> to sway the rule makers who most often are going to respond to
> voters. Those voters may be well informed, or they may not be
> well informed, but they are voters, and they do carry sway with
> politicians, because the first job of a politician generally is to get
> reelected, and the way they get reelected is to vote in the way that
> their constituents either wisely or unwisely want them to vote.

We live in a democracy. In a democratic society, politicians keep
their jobs by responding to the immediate wishes of the electorate—
and the electorate seldom asks its representatives to do what is needed
to improve the functioning of the system. We heard this repeatedly in
our conversations:

> So education is, I think, one of the most important things that,
> really, governments should drive, but they won't drive, because
> they're dealing with legacies of the past rather than investing in
> the future. So this is clearly, I think, where companies can kick
> in. (CEO of a major European corporation)

Governments won't do the right thing, because they are preoc-
cupied with the past—in this case, our participant had in mind deficits. But in contrast to the American executive's conclusion that little
could be done, the European executive reasoned that business could
and should make a difference. In fact, outside of the United States,

especially in Europe and Asia, we found more sympathy for business in out-of-the-box roles.

> Companies are at the forefront of this struggle because . . . the big companies are exceedingly global and, secondly, they therefore have to make people work together in a constructive way based on an understanding of what happens elsewhere and different attitudes and so on that people bring to jobs and bring to business and bring to the assumptions of their whole behavior. It's companies which over and over and over again at the front line pragmatically have to deal with very profound problems. (European executive who had chaired several major corporations and was now chairman of one of his nation's regulatory groups)

The implications of these differing perspectives—the American's view on the one hand and the European's view on the other—raise serious issues for debate. The U.S. CEO accepts that it is a business leader's role to do the best job he or she can in running a business and through lobbying and testifying to urge on government policies that make sense for the industry and the company. But he defers to elected representatives, the politicians, "to create the rules" and deal with the larger systemic issues. They have the legitimacy that he would lack.

In contrast, the European executive believes that companies have the ability to address at least some of the challenges facing the market system. This executive and others conclude that as a practical consequence, companies "have to deal with very profound problems." Because we believe that inaction will produce precisely the problems that worry the U.S. CEO, we agree with the pragmatic position that at every level of aggregation—firm, industry, nation, and globe—company leaders need to address the disruptors and, where possible, deal with them by incorporating positive action into their strategic agendas.

Challenge: The Question of Legitimacy

We take this position recognizing that it challenges conventional wisdom and theoretical orthodoxy. Many analysts question whether business and its leaders possess the proper authority to play the role we envision. Others say that business is lacking in the necessary skills or mind-set. We agree that companies and their managers will need to develop new capabilities to operate effectively in this broader arena. But outside the United States and perhaps the United Kingdom, many leaders would argue that the challenge is already there. The cases examined in chapter 6 and the positive institutional innovations discussed in chapter 7 provide examples of the kind of capabilities some companies have already developed.

The question of management's authority to play the role we envision often starts from the observation that managers are not elected public officials. By what right, then, can they presume to act on behalf of society at large?

Although we share the democratic sensibilities that motivate this objection, we do not find the objection itself very compelling in the end. As discussed throughout the book, managers of today's large global companies already have a huge impact on society at large. Even if their stated goals and motivations are purely private—to benefit the firm or maximize shareholder value, for example—their decisions have far-reaching consequences for the public, be it the consuming public, the working public, the investing public, or the general citizenry. These consequences, in turn, can either reinforce or undermine the health and sustainability of the market system, which further affects society at large and, ultimately, business itself. We are calling on business leaders to incorporate this reality into their thinking and decision making—and to do so not out of philanthropic concern for the public (though we see no problem with that) but as a matter of enlightened self-interest.

We believe that many sectors of the public would welcome a more robust effort by business to ensure a healthy and well-functioning market system. Few advocates of the system are proud of the behavior that led up to the financial crisis of 2008 or the lack of business leadership in its wake. And many who believe ardently in the system find their faith in it sorely tested by the system's seeming neglect of so many and by the excesses and misdeeds that all too often dominate the business headlines. Tellingly, certain investors and asset managers are waking up to the costs of indifference to the larger, systemic issues and are now calling on companies to disclose the environmental and other societal impacts of their activities. Although some critics might question investors' right to concern themselves with these issues, this is not a new idea. Nearly a century ago, eminent jurist and later U.S. Supreme Court Justice Louis D. Brandeis testified before the U.S. Congress that it was the shareholders' "business and obligation" to ensure that management's policies were "consistent with the public welfare."[2]

Ultimately, however, the matter of legitimacy will be resolved through the test of experience. To the extent that business can successfully play this redefined role—by ameliorating key disruptors and improving the market system's performance—the legitimacy question will resolve itself. By the same token, if business fails to address the challenges facing the system or, worse, helps aggravate them, it may lose legitimacy even for its traditional and more narrowly defined role.

In many regions, as we have noted, business is already on the defensive, seeking to shore up its claim to legitimacy against attacks on both its competence and its morality. The question of the market system's contribution to society is ever present. Recall the observation by the Asian executive quoted earlier: "You cannot achieve a sense of legitimacy . . . if large numbers of people believe that the system doesn't work for them or is unjust to them." As we write, Main Street and Wall Street are continuing to do battle over financial regulation reform in the United States, and public anger over BP's inability to contain the oil that gushed from its underwater well in the Gulf of Mexico remains a vivid and recent memory.

The legitimacy argument thus cuts both ways. Business leaders face legitimacy questions however their role is defined and whether or not they embrace a more systemic orientation. We believe that the business-as-usual course presents the greater risk to business and to the market system. But only time will tell whether companies that adopt our recommended approach will act in ways that benefit the public and earn the approval of society.

New Skill Sets and Mind-Sets

The challenges we have been discussing—the idea that business can and must take a new, creative role in the active defense and reshaping of market capitalism (and the wider political and social systems that make it possible)—has implications for both the role and the required skill set for business leaders. Our argument implies that traditionally schooled managers taught to focus narrowly on driving sales, beating the competition, or pushing new products out the door will need to enlarge their perspective and develop new skills. They will need to be more attuned to the broader sociopolitical and institutional factors that enable the market system to function effectively. Many managers—and even boards of directors—today would find it odd or unusual to discuss the societal and public-policy implications of their strategic decisions. That needs to change. Strategy formulation should be informed by systemic factors, and major strategic initiatives should be analyzed for their systemic impact.

This is not to say that business leaders have not traditionally ventured out into the larger world from within their firms—of course they have and still do. But in the traditional conception of business management, they have often done so principally to represent their own firm's proximate interests—to sell, to buy, to attract investors, to interact with regulators or legislators, and so on. More recently, executives have ventured forth to build strategic partnerships with other businesses and nonprofits and even governments—a step in the right direction—but even in these interactions, the leaders often seem to have been mainly pursuing the interests of their own organization and its owners. They were not, generally speaking, trying to address the larger challenges of the system. That is, most of these leaders conducted their business with no intention of defending, supporting, enhancing, and fixing the larger system of which business is a part.

If corporate leaders are now to operate in this new, tough environment and make progress in helping societies confront the evidently increasing challenges, they will need some new and very different skills. A good deal of the work we envision for new leaders will continue to be within their organizations, where they will develop more inspired business models and strategies—and where they will need much the same skills they have traditionally used (but with an added touch of inspiration and creativity). But much of the new work we envision for business leaders will be *outside* their respective firms, in a milieu in which they have approximately no formal authority and little widely recognized legitimacy—and in which there are major conflicts between their views and the views of other important players about the relevant goals and interests.

Success in this high-conflict, low-authority environment will require executives to present themselves and their interests through advocacy and to organize and lead coalitions through persuasion in a realm far distant from a hierarchical world in which they can command anyone or anything. They must be imaginative about the design and rebalancing of the complex system in which business is embedded. Many executives have formerly viewed the capitalist market system as a given, and as their responsibility only in in the sense that they had to optimize for themselves and their firms within it (but definitely not in the sense that they were responsible either for the health of the system itself or for how it was set up or for trying to figure out how to reconfigure or improve it to produce better overall outcomes). Now, by contrast, they must see this larger system and its defense as a domain central to their own interest—a domain in which they must be effective and responsible agents of change.

Companies that are successful in playing the role we envision will become accustomed to "bringing the outside in," to quote GE's Steve Fludder. In formulating strategy and developing large-scale plans of action, they will routinely seek out the views of outsiders such as policy analysts, government officials, independent experts, and NGO and community leaders. Moreover, the firms will be organized to receive this input in a way that it can be integrated into the company's own planning and decision-making processes.

Leaders of these companies will also be adept at "taking the inside out"—at operating beyond the boundaries of the firm and working with parties and in realms where, as noted, their authority will depend as much on their competence and perceived motivation as on their formal position. They will have an enhanced ability to listen, to grasp multiple perspectives, and then to integrate those perspectives into compelling plans of action. They will be unusually gifted in the subtler forms of influence and conflict management, since they will be unable to rely on the automatic deference of subordinates in those realms. In this world, a capacity to formulate and persuasively explain their decisions on contestable issues will be highly valued.

As we discussed earlier, these leaders will also be independent thinkers who are skilled as both learners and teachers. Because this territory is largely uncharted, creativity in all its forms will be highly developed. What-if sessions and innovation labs—not unlike those familiar to technology futurists—may be common tools for these leaders, but will be aimed at generating innovative ideas for new business models, new organizational forms, new governance structures, and new institutions. Leaders will be good at thinking systemically and traversing different levels of analysis—firm, industry, nation, globe. While they will be comfortable with complexity, successful leaders will also have the capacity to cut through it—to grasp the central tendencies and articulate a clear path forward. An appetite for risk and a commitment to the longer term will also be essential, as some investments will inevitably fail and others will take time to prove themselves.

At the most fundamental level, these companies and their leaders will operate from a mind-set of respect for the larger system that makes their own success and prosperity possible. They will consider it part of their job to ensure that their activities align with the effective functioning of this system and, at a minimum, do not undermine it. Some may call this social responsibility. We see it as enlightened self-interest. But the terminology probably doesn't matter all that much. For anyone who believes as we do that the market system is the most powerful engine yet devised for generating wealth and improving living standards worldwide, what is important is that companies act in ways that ensure the system's ongoing health and sustainability. Given the depth of the challenges to the system discussed here, businesses will need to be inspired and creative in that effort.*

---

*This raises interesting questions for those who teach at business schools: how do we prepare future leaders to operate in high-conflict, low-authority environments *in addition to* operating in traditional low-conflict, high-authority environments? To operate successfully in an ambiguous setting with significant apparent (or real) conflicts among the interests of the relevant players, leaders will need all of the skills they needed before, together with new skills in persuasion, advocacy, legitimacy building, system design, and coalition building. They will need to be effective negotiators—not in the traditional setting, in which a deal to be struck can provide tangible rewards to their counterparts, but in a more general setting, in which the bargaining will be over policies and actions that will play out over a much longer time.

In these more challenging times, leaders will need greater vision of their role in business and society. That is, they must understand the scope, complexity, and importance of the system and their responsibility to act upon the system to preserve and improve it.

What Companies Need to Do

Our research has convinced us that it is imperative for company leaders to examine their strategic priorities in light of the disruptive forces that challenge the market system. We believe that many companies are missing out on opportunities to drive innovation, growth, and profitability by helping address these challenges. What's more, these companies can improve their own functioning and performance by better aligning their operations with the needs of a sustainable market system.

We present these views as hypotheses rather than categorical recommendations, because we have only powerful success stories as evidence for their value. On the other hand, when concrete evidence shows that something previously thought impossible has actually been done, a large sample is unnecessary to establish that it is worth considering in a serious way.

As we reviewed the cases presented earlier and others we have studied, we identified a short list of questions that companies and their leaders—senior managers, executives, boards—ought to ask themselves. These questions suggest a range of activities that companies should consider in formulating a strategic response to the systemic challenges confronting market capitalism.

As discussed, a strategic response is likely to involve a series of actions at various levels of the system. Thus, in presenting these questions, we move upward from individual efforts at the firm level, to collective efforts of firms at the industry level, to cooperative efforts at the national and international levels. We review some of the key

---

Harvard Business School recently introduced a joint degree program with its sister school, the Harvard Kennedy School of Government. This program focuses on the kinds of issues we have raised and represents an important element in a larger redesign of the MBA. There nevertheless remains much more work to be done to equip the rising generations of leaders with the skills necessary to understand, protect, preserve, and advance the system of market capitalism that yet has the potential (but offers no guarantee) to give them—and the rest of us—such enormous benefits. The restructuring of the MBA is in itself a subject worthy of a whole book. Fortunately, a book on this subject, which, like this one, flowed from the HBS Centennial discussions, has recently been published: Srikant Datar, David Garvin, and Patrick Cullen, *Rethinking the MBA: Business Education at a Crossroads* (Boston: Harvard Business Press, 2010).

points from earlier discussions and suggest how the activity relates to the list of disruptors identified in chapter 3.

As individual firms: *What strategic opportunities do these disruptors present for your company?*

Our earlier discussions of GE, China Mobile, Cipla, and Generation Investment Management showed how individual firms could find strategic opportunity in countering one or more of the disruptive forces threatening market capitalism. In the first three of those companies, the critical step came when the firm's top management recognized that it made good business sense to figure out how the firm's core competences could be used to address a truly massive problem. That step when "massive problem" was reframed as "huge opportunity" was fundamental.

The same kind of thinking was involved in IBM's reorganization of its customer-facing activities so that a new unit based in Shanghai focused on the emerging markets.[3] This challenge-as-opportunity thinking was applied by numerous other companies as well: ITC reorganized its distribution system so that the company could bring the poor farmers of rural India into the market system. CEMEX developed new distribution and financing that permitted low-income Mexicans to build homes. Pepsi invested in R&D to grow its portfolio of healthier foods and bring suitable products to undernourished populations in India and other developing countries.

Certain patterns appear in the strategic reformulations that we have examined. In cases dealing with both rural and urban poor, key steps have included the development of widespread, low-cost distribution or financing, or both. For the poor to participate in the market system, they have to have access (distribution) and funds (finance) so that they can invest in tools, fertilizer, or inventory. In all of the cases, but especially with firms like IBM, GE, and Generation Investment Management, which sell to or achieve their impacts through other businesses, a major step has been significant study so that appropriate capabilities can be developed and effective marketing programs devised. Similarly, in all cases, some form of new organizational arrangement has been involved and careful attention has been given to the selection of appropriate measures of performance and incentives.

Finally, top management has maintained a heavy involvement, especially in an articulation of the new strategy that is very visible internally to the people of the organization and in the commitment of appropriate investments.

As associations of firms: *What strategic opportunities do the disruptors present for members of your industry to work together?*

In some instances, the actions needed to address an issue require collaboration among many firms for there to be a successful outcome. Examples of this often involve industry safety. In the United States, a well-known example is industry-supported Underwriters Laboratory, which plays a role in assuring consumer product safety for electric appliances. But the Institute of Nuclear Power Operators (INPO) provides safety inspections for reactors that are relied upon by insurers of nuclear facilities—no insurance without INPO certification. The Chemical Research Council provides funding for the education of chemists and engineers. The Defense Industry Initiative on Business Ethics improved ethics across the industry by prescribing structures and processes that signatory companies could employ to manage business conduct in their own organizations.

In each instance, an important problem facing the industry has been resolved through the creation and funding of an organization that addresses an issue that private firms might find too costly to tackle if their competitors were not also bearing the same cost. Industrywide standard setting provides similar benefits. We are hopeful that some industries will decide that clean air and water are worthy—or, if they want to avoid draconian and inefficient regulation, necessary—objectives and will cooperate on process and product standards that help achieve those goals.

In other cases, industry collaboration can be a first step toward government regulation. For instance, as discussed earlier, the proposed legislation drafted by the U.S. Climate Action Partnership became the starting point for congressional debate on cap-and-trade legislation in the United States. In still other cases, industry groups can mount pilot projects to examine particular problems. For instance, when one of us asked a group of managers from the medical-devices industry to imagine how the industry could collaborate on sustainability issues, they proposed a pilot project to explore what could be done to reduce medical, biological, and chemical waste.

In considering possible collaborative arrangements, business leaders should be clear about the public purpose being served. Competition authorities around the world are rightly wary of arrangements that are designed to suppress competition, but antitrust laws recognize that industry cooperation can sometimes be beneficial for society. A critical step in achieving cooperative arrangements that do not violate the antitrust laws is demonstrating that the arrangements serve the public interest.

To illustrate the range of possibilities that industry groups could consider, we offer some practices that industries might examine and discourage through collective action. For example, the provision of credit to the non-credit-worthy is a pernicious practice that is only attractive if the lender is able to sell the credit to someone who believes the credit is good—that is, only if the sale is associated with an intended act of fraud. Government may well proscribe such practices, but why shouldn't the lending industry set higher standards of its own? To take another example, the de-skilling of jobs often lowers a firm's short-term costs, but, over time, usually reduces the firm's ability to respond quickly to market shifts through innovation. In a similar way, the substitution of part-time workers for full time to lower costs has the effect of depriving a firm of a network of workers who have the capability of innovating. Both practices also lower the incomes of the workers involved. Over time, both practices weaken industry incumbents, but short-term competitiveness may force all firms to follow if one significant member of an industry adopts either of these practices.

As national players: *What strategic opportunities do the disruptors present for your company to work with national governments?*

It is seldom emphasized, but companies often cooperate with national governments either to advance their own aims or to serve larger, public objectives that are not readily amenable to more usual types of government intervention such as regulation or legislation. The simplest examples are in the area of trade, where governments often support the efforts of their nation's exporters with diplomatic and financial assistance. Historically, this tight connection between public and private interests was not unusual. In their earliest forms, corporations were chartered to achieve public goals such as the building and operation of a turnpike or a canal. The relationship of the U.S. government's Defense Advanced Research Projects Agency (DARPA) to the high-tech industry is not thought of as chartering, because it involves a procurement process. But over the years, especially prior to efforts to make the agency's relationships with firms more market-like, DARPA functioned as a rationalizer of research efforts, convening meetings in which tasks on a broad research agenda were allocated among companies. Some firms benefited more than others from the results of DARPA's work, but the pace of progress accelerated. Other public goals, such as energy conservation and environmental protection, might be pursued in similar ways.

The critical idea is that for some objectives, the fastest way to make progress is not necessarily for as many firms as possible to compete for the solution. Sometimes, judicious allocation of tasks among firms and startups is the best approach. A very clear example of the direct application of this line of thought is provided by the case of the Japanese Very Large Scale Integrated Circuit Technology Research Project, in which five large firms and two government bureaus were brought together by Japan's Ministry of International Trade and Industry (MITI) to cooperate in the development of the 64K memory chip. Prior to this project, Japan had seriously lagged the United States in semiconductor memory. After Japan's success in leapfrogging U.S. efforts, the United States responded with the creation of SEMATECH, a consortium of high-tech companies conducting research in semiconductor manufacturing.[4]

Although governments are typically thought of as having more clout than corporations to accomplish a change in industry practice, that is not always the case. To take another example, when the U.S. Department of Agriculture (USDA) wanted to eliminate the practice of pneumatic stunning used on cattle for slaughter—the powerful force sometimes pushed brain matter into the animals' bodies—the department found that it lacked the authority to do so. When USDA officials informed McDonald's of the problem, the fast-food chain quickly rewrote its specifications for suppliers, thus bringing about a change in its supply chain, which then rippled across the industry. The government was later able to secure authority to ban the practice.[5] In another case, the relationship with government worked the other way around: McDonald's mobilized other companies in the restaurant and pharmaceutical industries to encourage and support additional government regulation in Canada to prohibit the incorporation of high-risk material and dead stock into animal feed. The legislation was passed in 2006.[6]

As global players: *What strategic opportunities do the disruptors present for your company to work with international groups and organizations?*

In a similar fashion, companies operating in the international arena often find that unfettered competition is irrelevant or even difficult without rules and an institutional organizing body to supervise the implementation of these rules. Yet, it is not unusual to find that national governments have not cooperated to provide the required institutional arrangements and that international institutions have not focused on the problem. In some areas, the firms of separate nations have collaborated with international bodies to develop regimes of agreements to govern critical or problematic activities.

The shipping industry's arrangements for handling migration issues, for example, offer a model that might be useful in other contexts. In the wake of 9/11, the industry faced onerous new security restrictions in U.S. ports and elsewhere. The restrictions were seriously impeding the flow of international commerce—90 percent of which is carried by sea—and making life difficult for maritime workers, who were often prevented from going ashore after long periods at sea. To address the security concerns raised by the essentially unregulated movement of workers and to speed the flow of maritime commerce again, the shipping industry initiated efforts through the International Maritime Organization (IMO), a specialized UN agency responsible for regulating the industry, to develop a new identity regime for the world's 1.2 million maritime workers. Under the system put in place in 1958 and still in effect in 2001, workers carried paper identity documents that, in participating states, served as substitutes for work or entry visas. Under the new regime devised through the IMO and embodied in a convention adopted by the International Labour Organization (ILO) Conference in 2003 after negotiations between government, worker, and ship owner representatives from the ILO's member states, maritime workers would receive identity documents based on biometric markers derived from their fingerprints. Although the new convention had been ratified by only eighteen member states by 2010, it was widely seen as a promising platform for improving security while recognizing the needs of industry and the rights of workers.

Similar arrangements could be imagined for other kinds of service employment such as agribusiness, hospital, and home help workers. Currently, most illegal aliens work in one of these three job categories. An international identity system that met the approvals of receiving governments would contribute greatly to the resolution of the severe political problems associated with economically driven legal and illegal migration.

The International Chamber of Commerce provides another example in its work facilitating the legal and logistical arrangements for trade and providing for the arbitration of international business disputes between private parties. Its work provides standards for the specifics of contracts in trade—the determination of weights and sizes, the dating of shipments, and the arbitration of disputes between disagreeing parties. The effect is to vastly facilitate the smooth movement of goods.

Chapter 7 provided the example of a single company's taking the lead to organize a coalition that ending up working with one multinational organization and founding another. As discussed, GE was instrumental in mobilizing a coalition of companies to support an OECD convention banning the bribery of foreign officials by companies based in the industrialized world. This group of companies was in turn instrumental in helping launch Transparency International, the Europe-based NGO that tracks perceptions of government and business corruption worldwide.

Imagining Possible Future Roles for Business

The examples in this chapter and elsewhere in the book illustrate ways in which businesses can act on their own to combat negative pressures on the market system and how businesses can cooperate among themselves to help mobilize government action in socially productive ways. While these actions do not all appear yet to be on a scale or of a scope that would address the larger challenges to market capitalism, they may provide platforms upon which larger-scale efforts might be built.

What would be involved if business were to play a more significant role in dealing with the major problems discussed by the business leaders in our forums? For example, the leaders were clearly concerned by growing disparities in income, by problems the mature economies were experiencing with the integration of migrants from developing nations, and by the paralysis of national governments seeking collective action to mitigate climate change. They worried about education, health, and the rising burden of health-care costs. In the aftermath of the *Deepwater Horizon* oil spill, they probably worry anew about industrial accidents on an unprecedented scale and environmental destruction. And they worry about a myriad of other concerns, which, when viewed in the system context outlined in chapter 4, add up to significant threats to the system itself.

To illustrate the lines along which thinking—and action—must evolve, we will describe programs of action that might begin to address some of these issues, drawing on lessons from examples discussed earlier. These are intended only as illustrations of what business leaders might do rather than prescriptions. Indeed, as leaders do begin to address these problems seriously, we are sure that they will devise programs far superior to those we can currently imagine. In any case, effective action will often require effort at several levels: the firm, industry, government, and perhaps multinational institutions.

Health Care

The cost of health care in the United States currently runs at approximately 17 percent of the GDP and is rising. Studies show that this high cost is associated with widely varying cost by region of the United States and that quality is at best not correlated with cost and may in some instances be negatively related.[7] Health-care costs affect the competitiveness of U.S. businesses, but also constitute the leading cause of personal bankruptcy, contributing significantly to the burden of low income. Broad summaries are often dangerous, but many experts believe that problems with cost have their source in the basic organization of health-care delivery and the embedded legacy approaches that characterize the system.[8] And unsustainably high and rising costs in this domain are not inevitable; there are already major subsystems in the United States that deliver far higher-than-average quality care at well-below-average costs.

In other countries, the cost of health care is less and sometimes only half of the U.S. cost as a percent of GDP. Quality is quite variable. Some countries offer their citizens remarkably good care at far lower costs than in the United States. Others are merely lower cost. But in almost all countries, there is dissatisfaction with the quality of care and real concern about rising cost. With the exception of a few advanced industrialized countries with strong national systems, the care provided for those with low income is very poor. And all of this is increasingly a concern for business worldwide.

Given the scale of the problem on the one hand and the existence of very positive models of success on the other, it is surprising that business has on the whole been so little engaged with the question.[9] Companies have been aggressive in developing technology to sell to the various national systems, have organized private delivery systems, and have played an extensive role in providing insurance. The job of reforming health care, however, has been largely left to government. Beyond selling products and services, businesses have confined their efforts to lobbying to affect policy in ways that improve their competitiveness, largely by lowering firm costs. In turn, this has typically meant opposing the taxes that pay for government insurance programs, or the legislation that would mandate broader health programs.

At the level of individual firms, a number of companies have worked aggressively to improve the health of their employees through the elimination of smoking, the reduction of obesity, improved nutrition, and the reduction of the use of alcohol and other recreational drugs. Various experts believe that these four measures are among the most important steps required for improving the overall health of a population; smoking, obesity, and substance abuse alone account for a significant portion—some studies suggest half or more—of current health-care cost in developed nations.[10]

At a minimum, it is not hard to imagine individual companies, industry associations, or international groups joining in some kind of program to drive widespread attention to these three aspects of improved health. There is likely to be opposition from the tobacco, alcohol, and junk-food industries—so it will take aggressive leadership from elsewhere in the business community to make a concerted effort to drive healthier lifestyles.

Broader and deeper efforts might then follow. If it could be achieved, getting better health for less cost would lift an enormous weight currently being carried by the market system worldwide. If business, broadly, comes to see working on this challenge as a way to boost the productivity of the market system as a whole and puts its creative energies into helping societies manage this large and fundamentally important industry more effectively, the results could help to bolster not only health but also support for the market system. Engaging this agenda in a serious way will require, at a minimum, a multisector deliberation involving business, the health-care industry, government, and the public.

Environmental Protection and Industrial Safety

Events such as the *Deepwater Horizon* BP oil spill from the blowout of the Macondo well in the Gulf of Mexico in the spring of 2010 are deeply distressing to the public and to the business community. In the aftermath of the *Deepwater* event, it is difficult to be proud of either government regulation or business self-regulation of oil production safety. But with literally thousands of exploratory and production wells either successfully capped or currently operating without major leaks on the sea floor around the world, their general safety record must be viewed in that light as largely positive. The presently available public accounts of the *Deepwater* event indicate that the standards of performance on the *Deepwater Horizon* rig before the blowout were well below what is recognized as good industry practice. Reports from government investigations of the incident make clear that the kind of knowledge necessary to set standards for performance resides almost exclusively with the companies. Indeed, it is the competitors of BP—ExxonMobil, Shell, and Chevron, among others—that have been most vocal in criticizing its performance. To reduce the risk of future disasters, it would seem that a consortium of businesses would have the best command of the required capabilities to design, test, build, and deploy processes and equipment that would produce the requisite level of safety. Moreover, it is likely to be in both their short- and long-term interests to do so. This is an area where collaboration might well be possible and beneficial. Since the problems faced by different companies are similar, and there are likely to be significant economies of scale in developing the most cost-efficient and effective safety devices and procedures, a collective approach makes sense.

One question posed by this event is whether some industry grouping along the lines of the Institute of Nuclear Power Operators, mentioned above as an example of industry collaboration, might be an effective way of reinforcing the efforts of individual companies. An industry-financed organization—which could be multinational—that sets standards, conducts research, and inspects rigs could prove very useful.[11] Again, the sanction of withdrawal of insurance could prove a powerful mechanism for enforcement against any individual companies that sought to avoid the consortium's reach.

Collaboration within the industry may also contribute more value on the research and technology fronts. With all on notice that one major spill like the Macondo blowout is one too many, there are positive signs that, in its aftermath, business leaders may take more aggressive action to enhance production safety going forward. Two task forces, formed through the American Petroleum Institute, involve a number of energy production companies and other organizations with relevant expertise—one to recommend methods for developing better technologies for maintaining control at the wellhead in emergency situations and the other to recommend methods for developing enhanced containment of oil once it had been released. Preliminary recommendations were released in early September 2010, and work continues. Four major oil companies (ExxonMobil, Chevron, ConocoPhillips, and Shell) are jointly sponsoring the Marine Well Containment Company (and BP has announced plans to join as well) to develop and implement new technologies for containment—and this mandate may expand to include developing better technologies for the prevention of spills as well as for containing them. This effort will probably evolve into a significant effort to pool resources and knowledge and to develop breakthrough safety procedures and equipment, and it might expand its mandate to include a wider range of efforts to prevent emergencies in the first place. In ways like these, business leadership, acting through the development of new institutional structures, can reshape a

significant component of the operating landscape in a way that is positive for business, for the environment, and for the wider society. This
ongoing development could thus be a harbinger of a new and more
aggressive kind of business leadership.

If so, then there is ample room to expand the domain of this form
of innovation. In many areas, industrial accidents continue to pose significant individual, company, and community risks. Chemical manufacturing is famously fraught with potential for disastrous accidents
(and is periodically subject to them). Individual companies and industry groups, such as the chemical industry's international Responsible
Care initiative launched in the aftermath of a Union Carbide plant
explosion in Bhopal, India, in 1984, work on identifying and reducing these hazards. But could new and more aggressive leadership produce a material leap forward in this domain? In part through industry
efforts (since 1974, for example, through the research of the industry-
supported Chemical Industry Institute of Toxicology), a great deal
more has been learned about when we should and should not be concerned about exposure to chemical compounds—but hazardous waste
transport continues to pose potentially significant risks to workers and
to communities. And the need to develop a serious, safe, and sustainable method for the long-term storage of used radioactive materials is abundantly clear. Are these areas where business leaders could
come to more clearly see their collective interest, come together to
develop new institutional structures that could identify significantly
better approaches, and then build the political support necessary to
make them a reality? These seem like relatively low-hanging fruit—a
warm-up, as it were—for larger-scale efforts to organize business leaders to take more significant, intentional, comprehensive, and effective
responsibility for the design, redesign, reform, and management of the
system in which capitalism is embedded so as to better insure its overall social productivity and sustainability.

Income Distribution

As the leaders at our forums were quick to recognize, the problem
of income distribution has multiple dimensions. There is first the
question of absolute poverty. In developing nations, there are billions

who are simply outside the market system. Some nations—China, for example—are addressing this problem by bringing their agricultural poor into the market system in part by relocation to urban centers and in part by modernizing the communication, distribution, financing, and educational services available to the villages. Some companies—China Mobile, for example—have devised strategies that are implementing national policy at a profit. IBM's Smarter Planet strategy is conceived as a way of incorporating this major shift in the approach to poverty into IBM's business model as a defining corporate opportunity.

In these instances, giant enterprises working as leaders have reconceived the "problem" of the rural poor, seeing it now as a massive business opportunity to work with governments, local companies, and village-level enterprise to extend the market system and profit by doing so. We can imagine that the same kind of activity undertaken by many individual enterprises would have a major impact. After all, China Mobile is bringing modern communication and information to literally hundreds of millions of rural Chinese—and that number is by itself already a meaningful fraction of the 3 billion poor in developing nations.

But the problem of inequality also involves the income of the top end of the distribution, and the behavior of that group. Traditionally, this issue has been addressed by governments through progressive tax policy and by society through social norms—not by firm or individual behavior, except to the extent that some firms try to ensure equitable pay within their organization and executives have occasionally limited their own pay. In the domain of philanthropy, the United States has seen the effort by Warren Buffett and Bill Gates to persuade other billionaires to give away at least half of their wealth—an effort that, as of August 2010, had signed up forty families or individuals who had collectively made pledges estimated to be at least $125 billion (and possibly much more).[12] A significant number of other very wealthy people have since followed. So far, this behavior is regarded as bizarre or, at best, idiosyncratic by some observers in other parts of the world—though there are now more and more examples of significant philanthropy from China, India, and elsewhere. Perhaps closer to our concerns are the efforts of business leaders acting as individuals to use their position and their funds on a systematic basis to seek out talented individuals from among the underprivileged in their country to support these individuals' education and development through scholarships. Our forum participants, especially from Latin America, reported this to be an important source of new leadership for the public sector. Widespread use of private wealth to enhance social mobility can only have positive effects.

Concerted efforts of these kinds by business leaders could also lead to progress in related areas. A consortium of business leaders and other individuals might unite first to address aspects of these problems that are most directly within their purview. This might involve the design of jobs associated with their current business operations, the characteristics of the people recruited to work in their systems, and particularly the way their companies use technology to create value. Full-time jobs that permit individual growth and development over a career can make a huge positive difference. Over several decades, the implementation of Lincoln Electric's piece-rate system, for example, has resulted in numerous factory workers regularly earning six-figure incomes that allow them to live in the neighborhoods normally associated with professionals and small-business owners. Taco Bell has made a practice of moving part-time workers into increasingly responsible roles, including regional management. These jobs have also made it possible for immigrants to become integrated into the society with the kind of employment that provides a stable base for a family. Obviously, this is the opposite of firms that have de-skilled work and relied on temporary employees to minimize short-term labor costs.

The availability of good-quality education is directly related to the income distribution problem. Modern business operations—from service work in hotels and hospitals to office work—increasingly benefit from an educated workforce. In nations where education for all is not national policy, groups of firms can have a major impact on the willingness of local communities to pay for education. This almost inevitably will lead to higher taxes to pay for better schools. The question any business leader must face is whether his or her nation can survive in the modern global economy if its workforce is uneducated. If the answer is no, then finding a way to mobilize the entire relevant business community—and others—to help support the needed taxes simply makes sense.

Migration

Even if business does a much better job of including large numbers of today's poor in the market system, the gap between average incomes in the mature nations and those in developing nations is likely to remain large and visible. Eastern Europeans, Middle Easterners, and Africans will migrate to Europe; Latin Americans will migrate north; and South Asians will migrate to the richer countries. Where the migration is solely motivated by the economic gap as opposed to barriers to upward mobility, the migration may be temporary. For example, the large numbers of Philippine workers in the service industries of Asia and the Middle East demonstrate no desire to become permanent citizens. Nonetheless, their presence may be politically destabilizing. In fact, as noted earlier, declining birth rates in the mature nations make immigration a necessity, as does the unwillingness of the local citizens to work in the activities of certain agribusiness and service operations of those nations.

We have already described the arrangement made by the global shipping industry to provide a mechanism for ships' crews to spend time ashore without a normal visa process. A peculiar (and helpful) feature of this challenge, of course, is that seamen are onshore for only a limited time before their ship moves on. Seasonal agriculture, for example, differs materially in involving a longer period. But immigrant farmworkers could be organized on a formal, temporary basis. In turn, visas for health-care workers in hospitals and in individual homes might also be defined by a certain term of work. While efforts at immigration reform have proved that this policy area is a political minefield, it would appear that there is a real opportunity for a consortium of agribusiness companies and a consortium of health-care providers to work out arrangements that might be approved by national governments on an ad hoc basis. These kinds of programs could be organized on a trial basis and among subgroups of nations and might eventually have a significant impact on the global migration problem.

Climate Change

Within a decade, rapid climate shift may come to be recognized by most knowledgeable observers as a reality with costly consequences. This awareness might lead many business leaders worldwide to realize that they were facing major risks that include the severe disruption of international trade and other economic systems and the basic relations between nations and regions. In effect, the kinds of negative developments described in the scenario of chapter 2 might well be coming to pass.

The realization that this was happening will not come suddenly, nor at the same time to all observers. Some business leaders might continue to pay little attention to the issue, effectively assuming that they could wait and see and bank on their capacity to adapt rapidly later. But business leaders from many places around the world might have the dawning realization that the climate-change-related threats to overall future prosperity were significant and rising. At the same time, they may recognize—unless there is unexpected progress in international negotiations in the meantime—that the governments of the major nations were no further along toward an agreement that might mitigate the effects of climate change than they were in 2010.

In this context—building on the (incomplete) work of the USCAP group in the United States—business leaders might begin to self-organize in countries important to resolving the climate-change issues: the United States, China, the United Kingdom, Japan, France, Germany, Russia; and even energy producers like Saudi Arabia, Kuwait, and the Persian Gulf oil states, Norway, Mexico, and others. Perhaps expanding the concept of the USCAP group, these leaders might organize internationally.

Once leaders begin to become seriously engaged in this issue, things might start to change. Interested businesspeople might find one another and begin discussions about what they might do. They could seek ideas about how to shift the balance among opposing forces in their societies so as to favor bargains to reduce greenhouse gas emissions. This might take different forms in different places. In some countries, it could mean a compromise between natural-gas-based and coal-based utilities, while in others, it could involve compensating coal-based utilities for shifts to less carbon-intensive fuels. In still other countries, solutions to the climate-change challenge might involve agreements between energy consumers, energy producers, and other businesses to shift toward the most environmentally friendly fuels. In jurisdiction after jurisdiction, government might then appear on the scene to ratify an agreement worked out in advance—after the heavy lifting had been done by business leaders to develop agreements to reduce overall emissions. Once these agreements had been reached in principle, governments could embody them in rules or laws relatively easily. After this approach had been developed and demonstrated in a few jurisdictions, it might spread of its own accord across other locations.

Again, the long-term effectiveness of these bargains would take time to prove—but realistically, by a decade after the movement started in earnest, five of the six largest carbon-emitting jurisdictions might have significantly reduced the growth rate of their carbon emissions and be on track to produce absolute reductions in emission levels. And in no small measure, this would have resulted from leadership from the business community itself.

Conclusion

The dilemma that we posed at the beginning of this chapter by presenting contrasting views of the role that business can play might be redescribed in the language of public policy. We have argued that there is a series of publicly valued goods and services that the market system requires for it to function properly. But democratic governments around the world seem unable to buy or produce them. The goods in question include the education and public health necessary for inclusion of the better part of the populations of some countries in the market system, migration policies that deal constructively with regional movements, legal systems that effectively and fairly protect and enforce certain rights, and a variety of forms of infrastructure required for competitiveness nationally and for economic efficiency and ecological stability on a global basis.

To the extent that governments are unable to produce or purchase the necessary public goods, then firms will have to find ways to make a profit by providing these goods privately. To do so, they will have to think about how to alter aspects of the system in which their market is embedded so that private action can have its intended consequences. The path of passive acceptance of whatever results from the interaction of firms, Western democratic governments, and state capitalism in the global economy seems likely to undermine the very conditions necessary for sustained economic growth. Calling it "the market" does not change the observation that it is on a collision course with itself.[13]

Our suggestions of how business might tackle some of these challenging and ultimately interrelated problems are one part back to the future and one part call for renewed and greater efforts going forward. We have seen historically some inspired moments of business leadership—in the CED, in the international anticorruption movement, in Cleveland Tomorrow, and in other instances. And we have seen in the present day at least the building blocks of business leadership working to tackle significant challenges—efforts within individual companies, like Cipla, China Mobile, GE, and Generation Investment Management; and efforts across industries, like the USCAP effort and the Marine Well Containment Company. There is every reason to take inspiration from past efforts, but also every reason to look to today's business leaders and those of tomorrow for more. If the disruptive forces that threaten market capitalism are indeed as dangerous as they appear, we will need to see more models of the best business leadership, business engagement, and institutional innovation as exemplified in the past and as imagined for the future.

We hope that the academic profession can contribute to this creative process. As part of that profession, we and our Harvard Business School colleagues see this as an important part of our work at the start of the school's second century. But we also hope—and expect—that the greatest creativity on these matters will come from the business community itself. The free-market system is the most powerful force we know of for producing creative solutions and new opportunities—and we deeply believe that it will prove once again the greatest fountain of original thinking, experimentation, and progress.

It is a hard task that we are setting. Nonetheless, because we are profoundly committed to the benefits that the capitalist market system provides, we believe that it must be undertaken. Our goal in this book has been to argue the necessity—but also the feasibility—of this important work.

Part Three

A Call to Action

9

How Disruptors Interact
and Why It Matters

A DECADE HAS passed since we wrote the first edition of this book. Clearly, the executives who met with us in 2008 were prescient. The problems we read about in today's headlines reflect the force of the disruptors they identified. Parts of the global banking system are still unstable, and new derivative instruments pose problems. Trade war is under way. Inequality has proved to be as disruptive a political force as the executives had imagined. Migration is a crisis both across borders and within countries. The effects of environmental change are regularly in the headlines. The rule of law is breaking down, and corruption is more pervasive. In the richer countries, public health and education are weaker in ways that matter. Pandemics threaten. It is even more obvious that state capitalism and market capitalism are uneasy neighbors. And as noted in the preface to this edition of the book, the explosive growth of digital information and communication has enabled the emergence of powerful new threats to security and political stability.

This chapter begins with a review of the ten disruptors that worried the executives we spoke with in 2007 and 2008. The intervening decade has revealed how these disruptors interact to create problems that are even more complex and intractable than those created by each disruptor alone. Four of these interactions are described later in this chapter. Finally, we describe how the continued inability or unwillingness of governments and multilateral institutions to deal with the disruptors creates ever-increasing risk for business and the market system.

That conclusion in turn leads us to expand on ideas from Part Two, about the role of business. In chapter 10, we examine four companies that have developed strategies for building their long-term success by directly addressing aspects of the disruptors. In chapter 11, we share some practical guidance that emerges from the successful efforts we have observed.

Disruptors Overwhelm Inadequate Institutions

The Financial System

The financial system collapsed between the time we conducted the research for this book's first edition and its publication. The basic causes of the 2008 collapse were found in excessive levels of debt, particularly subprime mortgages in the United States that were used as collateral for a pyramid of new debt instruments. These instruments in turn made their way onto the balance sheets of banks around the world. The underlying mortgages fueled a real estate boom, and when masses of borrowers stopped paying on their mortgages, the pyramid collapsed, bringing down the balance sheets of the lenders—which included some of the world's largest and supposedly most stable financial institutions.

In 2019, the balance sheets of banks had generally been restored, largely because central banks worldwide flooded the system with cash, propping up the asset prices underlying the banks, and partly because bank regulators tightened balance-sheet standards. Unfortunately, new forms of collateralized debt have appeared, and so-called nonbank lenders have emerged to meet the demand for credit by companies with poor credit ratings. Although the financial system today is by some measures more stable than it was a decade ago, new trouble spots have emerged and the ongoing stability of the system is far from assured.

Persistently low and even negative interest rates are evidence of the unusual position taken by central banks. If interest is the time value of money, it is not entirely clear what the implications of a negative interest rate might be. Banks holding cash clearly have an incentive to lend, but the negative interest rate is also a worrisome macroeconomic signal potentially auguring deflation. The very low rates are also a calamity—and a disincentive—for savers.

Ballooning pension obligations present a further problem. In the United States and some other countries, many state, provincial, and local government entities as well as corporations have pension obligations that far exceed their ability to pay. The Hoover Institution estimated the market value of unfunded state pension liabilities in the United States in 2017 at over $4 trillion.[1] This sum surpasses by far the funds in the U.S. Pension Guaranty Corporation. The pensions of millions of those working for state and local governments are at risk. If an attempt is made to pay these retirees in full, a number of jurisdictions may find themselves bankrupt. If the pensions are not paid, then millions of retired people will see an important component of the savings they were relying on for their old age suddenly shrink.

The Trading System

The health of the trading system also receives a mixed assessment. The UN Conference on Trade and Development (UNCTAD) has described international trade patterns over the last few years as being characterized "first by anemic growth (2012–2014), then by a downturn (2015 and 2016) and finally by a strong rebound (2017 and 2018)."[2] The slowing of the global economy in 2019 was expected to result in lower trade numbers. However, the global trading system is functioning reasonably well when judged by (1) its ability to transition from one large global system dominated by China to a more complex set of regional networks and (2) from a trade mix that is primarily focused on materials and manufacturers to one dominated by services and intellectual property.[3] (This evolution is discussed further in the next section.) A major change from 2008 to today is the reemergence of the United States as a net exporter of oil and gas and the rapid growth of renewable energy, although in the aggregate, production of renewable forms of energy is still only 15 percent of total consumption.[4]

The trading system is stressed, however, by uncertainty about international trade rules and by governments' use of economic sanctions and tariffs to achieve political objectives. These governments' high-stakes tit-for-tat "negotiations" threaten to undermine critical processes and relationships that sustain the trading system and that, if destroyed, will be difficult to rebuild. Trade will also be affected as the United Kingdom exits from the European Union.

Economic Inequality and Populism

Having emerged as central challenges in many countries across the world, economic inequality and political populism have moved from a potential disruptor in the past decade to be the center of a global political hurricane today. As discussed at greater length in the next section, the two decades running up to the 2008 financial crisis and the subsequent recovery of the financial system left the middle class far worse off and the top 1 percent in many countries with staggering wealth. China now boasts 285 billionaires.[5] In India in 2000, the share of income of the top 10 percent and the middle 40 percent were the same; by 2014, the top 10 percent had 55 percent and the middle 40 percent held 30 percent. In the United States, the top 1 percent of families control 38 percent of the wealth.[6] Across the world, people in countries whose condition has not improved or has worsened since the 1970s have expressed themselves politically. The concerns of these groups have provided the energy behind a series of populist political movements.

Migration

Migration also developed into a global storm during the post-2008 period. Before 2008, migration had already been steadily increasing. Since that year, political violence in the Middle East, Africa, and Central America and environmental crises around the world have only exacerbated the trend. As of 2000, some 173 million people lived outside the nation of their birth; by 2017, the number had risen to 258 million.[7] The United Nations reported that in 2018, over 70 million people were forcibly living outside their home areas: 26 million were refugees living outside their homeland, and another 41 million had been displaced to a different area of their home country.[8]

Environmental Degradation

Environmental degradation is now widely perceived as a potentially existential threat. The change in perception is due less to the scientific evidence of degradation—which continues to mount—and more to the persistent and pervasive occurrence of fires, typhoons, hurricanes, and floods over the last decade.[9] In late 2019, Australia and California experienced catastrophic fires, and Venice, Italy; Jakarta, Indonesia; and Dhaka, Bangladesh, were flooded.

Failure of the Rule of Law

Primarily because of the failure of several states, the rule of law is increasingly losing ground. As long as kleptocracy was confined to Central Asia, the Balkans, and Central Africa, tribal chiefs or former Soviet bosses were described in the Western press as vestigial disturbances to global progress. But the last decade has seen major problems emerge in South Africa, Malaysia, Brazil, Venezuela, and Russia, countries that, while not thought exactly to be paragons of governance, were generally seen as improving. Some of these are captured states, the economic prize of a family or a clan. Others are simply oligarchic fiefdoms.[10] Recent surveys show that perceived government corruption is a growing problem in the United States as well.[11] In 2018, the United States dropped out of the top twenty in Transparency International's ranking of countries (from least to most corrupt) by perceived levels of corruption.[12]

Public Health and Education

Despite reduced investment in public health and education in developed countries since the 2008 crisis, improvements are evident, especially in the developing world (figure 9-1). According to UNESCO, global literacy moved from 65 percent in 1975 to 86 percent in 2018.[13] Child mortality has declined in most countries, and life expectancy has increased. There are places that, like the United States, have seen declines (and the Centers for Disease Control and Prevention [CDC] reports that "U.S. life expectancy continues to decline"), but

FIGURE 9-1

Two decades of progress in the world's poorest countries

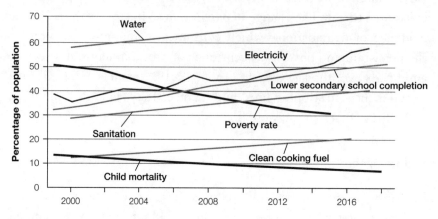

Source: Donna Barne, "Two Decades of Progress in the World's Poorest Countries," World Bank Blogs, December 11, 2019, https://blogs.worldbank.org/opendata/chart-two-decades-progress-worlds-poorest -countries.

Note: Progress among lower-income countries receiving assistance from the World Bank's International Development Association. The graph shows the percentage of the population that has access to at least basic drinking water, basic sanitation, clean cooking fuel, and electricity; percentages of relevant age groups completing lower secondary school and people living in extreme poverty; and mortality rate of children under age five. The declining black lines and rising gray lines both indicate progress.

the aggregate global picture is brighter, largely because of successful efforts of NGOs.[14] As the next section discusses, some new problems in health and education have emerged as growing populations in developing countries move toward unplanned megacities with inferior infrastructure. In addition, fertility is declining in the wealthy nations.

The Rise of State Capitalism

As a source of disruption in the last decade, the rise of state capitalism has primarily resulted from the shift in leadership and policy in China. As long as China appeared to be moving its institutional arrangements for governance toward alignment with the nations of the West, the frictions between countries practicing market capitalism and those practicing state capitalism were accepted as a price of progress. The petrostates, including Russia, were always understood to be managed at the state level, but except when their moves as a cartel had political objectives and especially large impacts, they were usually perceived as manageable actors in the global market.

Because of China's combination of economic size, centralized control, and newfound inclination to assert itself internationally, the country under Xi Jinping has proved to be a very different matter. On the basis of purchasing-power parity, China's GDP passed that of the United States in 2014.[15] This change in status has meant that China's moves to achieve national objectives through the market system by nonprice methods such as state funding have been perceived as threatening to many countries, including the United States.[16]

Radical Movements, Terrorism, and War

The past decade has certainly seen no abatement of radical movements, terrorism, or war. In the Middle East, the withdrawal of the United States from Iraq led to the rise of ISIS and its spread across the Levant and into Africa. In Syria, the response of Assad's government to protesters fleeing drought led to civil war and the emergence of a radical Islamist state in Eastern Syria. The Arab Spring led to several revolts that were crushed. Libya collapsed in civil war. There is ongoing warfare in the Democratic Republic of the Congo. The war in Afghanistan continues. India has moved troops into Kashmir. The Buddhists of Myanmar engaged in ethnic cleansing, ejecting the Muslim Rohingya. China has moved to reeducate its Muslims. Violence as a means to further state (and organized nonstate) ends has been commonplace.

Pandemics

Pandemics have continued and perhaps increased. To some extent, their increased threat is a consequence of other factors such as global travel and weak governance. Medical historians tell us that new diseases have always crossed over from animals or other vectors as the movements of vectors and humans brought people into contact with sources of disease. In recent times, governments have invested in capabilities and cooperated reasonably well to catch these new threats early, isolate them, and sometimes eliminate them. But efforts have not always been so successful. For example, Ebola moved out of the rural areas to which it had generally been confined, invaded several major cities, and even appeared for the first time in Europe and the United States. A review of World Health Organization data suggests that except for malaria, the toll of epidemics is increasing, with opioid abuse in the United States providing a significant new threat.[17] As of early March 2020, a novel coronavirus had claimed over 8,000 lives globally, and infections had been confirmed in 145 countries. It was unclear when and how the pandemic would end.

Inadequate Institutions

In the first edition of this book, in addition to the ten disruptors described, we proposed a possible eleventh. The feckless behavior of governments in many countries as they ignored the ten disruptors leads us to add that possible disruptor to our list. Many executives in our forums said that national governments lacked the economic strength and political will to deal with the disruptors and that our international institutions were not designed with the disruptors in mind. Unfortunately, the past decade has provided more evidence that the executives were prescient. If anything, governments have acted in ways that have aggravated the disruptors, for example, the U.S. tax cut and the strong reaction against migrants in several countries. The U.S. withdrawal from the Paris Agreement on climate change has highlighted the difficulty of forging effective multilateral institutions to address the disruptors at a global level. Similarly, the unilateral abandonment of the Iran nuclear deal by the United States has fueled tensions in the Persian Gulf. These tensions have recently threatened to boil over and have made multilateral international agreements seem more unstable and less likely to be formed in the first place.

Interactions Among the Disruptors

This list of challenges makes for depressing reading. One might have hoped that problems recognized in 2007 would have been dealt with in the years that followed. With partial exceptions like public health and education, that did not happen.

Instead, the decade has produced new threats such as those arising from digital technologies and has seen systematic interactions of many disruptors. Chapter 4 made this point theoretically. There, we described market capitalism as embedded in a context of interrelated forces and arrangements that we called its preconditions, and we discussed how the forces can reinforce or undermine one another. The past decade has revealed the complexity of some of the interactions. We now examine how the disruptors have interacted to create problems that are more complex and that further amplify the threat to market capitalism.

Interrelationships Among Migration, Environmental Changes, Public Health, and Education

Although environmental degradation was not seen as the most immediate threat to market capitalism in our earlier research, business leaders considered it an existential problem. During the past decade, rising temperatures, violent storms, sea surge, and drought have damaged agriculture, flooded cities in both the developed and the developing world, limited the availability of drinking water in major cities, generated unprecedented landscape-scale wildfires, and led to migration and crises in public health in many locales.

Figure 9-2 shows the steady rise in the average temperature all over the planet. The impact of global warming is particularly strong in regions where economic activity, especially agriculture, depends on the availability of water. In the United States, the Colorado River is no longer a completely reliable source of water; the snowpack varies over the years. The U.S. Midwest and Southwest experience more frequent droughts, and the major aquifers in these areas are declining. In Europe, dense populations and warmer climates have led to drought and have stressed aquifers from the Atlantic across into Asia all the way to the Pacific between the northern fortieth and fiftieth latitudes. The Middle East is also stressed. In Africa, the Sahara is expanding southward. India is facing severe challenges as the monsoon season becomes more irregular. Further south, Latin America and Australia have experienced increasing drought.

FIGURE 9-2

Global average temperature anomalies, 1850–2018

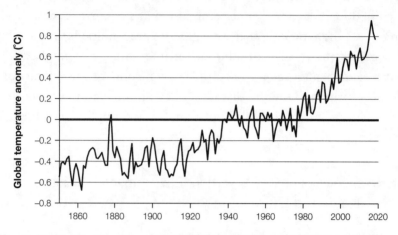

Source: Our World in Data, "Average Temperature Anomaly, Global," Global Change Data Lab, accessed September 17, 2019, https://ourworldindata.org/grapher/temperature-anomaly. Data from C. P. Morice, J. J. Kennedy, N. A. Rayner, and P. D. Jones, "Quantifying Uncertainties in Global and Regional Temperature Change Using an Ensemble of Observational Estimates: The HadCRUT4 Dataset," *Journal of Geophysical Research* 117 (2012), D08101, doi:10.1029/2011JD017187.

Note: Land data prepared by Berkeley Earth and combined with ocean data adapted from the U.K. Hadley Centre. Global temperature anomalies relative to 1951–1980 average.

Over the past decade, the challenge posed by climate change in the form of drought and flooding amplifies problems of migration, generally from agricultural regions toward cities and from lower to higher land. Across the globe, the Middle East, regions north of the equator in Africa, and areas of Central Asia from the Black Sea to Mongolia and Vladivostok are experiencing more frequent and persistent drought.

A drought in northeast Syria can be thought of as the trigger event for the start of the Syrian civil war.[18] People from the region moved south seeking sustenance. Since Syria was a national socialist state, the migrants turned to the government for support. When it was not forthcoming, they protested, and when, instead of receiving help from the government, the protesters were shot at (or worse), some Syrians went to war. More than a decade later, hundreds of thousands have died, and millions have migrated.

This brief summary of the situation in Syria provides a dramatic example of how the disruptors can interact. To begin with, the drought led to internal migration to cities.[19] As often happens, the migrants then faced unemployment and economic stress. When they protested the government's failure to provide assistance, the autocratic Assad government responded violently to the protest. The state's violent response led to civil war, further severe internal displacement, and international migration. In Western Europe, the international flow then exacerbated political problems that arose from the unresolved economic problems triggered by the 2008 financial crisis.

The dynamic of drought-driven migration is not unique to the Middle East. Water scarcity has spurred migration in North Africa, Central Asia, and parts of China. In China, the migration is internal, but the scale of movement is large. On a global basis, observers expect that the exodus from rural areas to urban regions will add two billion city dwellers.[20]

This urban growth in developing countries has led to the phenomenon of poor megacities. Paradoxically, the problem lies partly in the general improvement in public health. Child mortality has dropped dramatically (figure 9-3), and primary education has improved.

FIGURE 9-3

Child mortality by income level of country

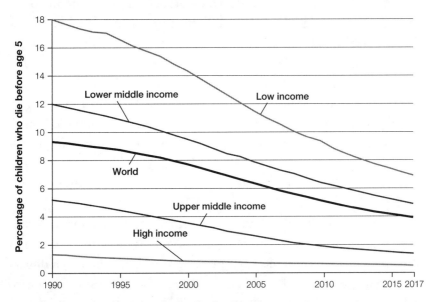

Source: Max Roser, Hannah Ritchie, and Bernadeta Dadonaite, "Child Mortality and Income Level of Country," in *Child & Infant Mortality* (Our World in Data, 2013; updated November 2019), https://ourworldindata.org /child-mortality#child-mortality-and-income-level.

These patterns are not unlike what happened in Europe and the United States during nineteenth-century industrialization. But in those cases, cities such as London and New York, which were dark, crowded, and infested with disease, drew on their new wealth to begin building sewers and water systems and dramatically improving public health. With improved health came falling child mortality and growing populations. Government efforts to clean up the cities were matched by improved public education, producing a healthy and educated population and a strong labor force for the growing industry. The labor force, in turn, fueled the consumption that drove economic growth.

In the developing world, however, the improvement in health is associated with successful efforts by NGOs to eradicate infectious disease, particularly childhood diseases. The megacities of Africa and Southeast Asia thus experience growing populations but lack an improved government or a growing industry.[21] Water, sewers, and employment are all deficient or absent. Moreover, where there is industrial growth in fields such as apparel and light industry, the export markets are crowded with products from competitors, including the Asian Tigers (and domestic firms in developed markets).[22]

Interestingly, well before China's emergence as an economic powerhouse, its so-called barefoot doctors (rural health-care providers with often-minimal formal medical training) brought hygiene to most of its population. Education was also supported. By the 1980s, when industry was unleashed under Deng Xiaoping, a healthy, educated workforce was available to serve its needs. At different times in history, Japan, Taiwan, South Korea, and Vietnam have provided other examples of the same phenomenon—workers with improving health ready to serve industry in a country with stronger governance. It is the absence of such efforts that burdens various nations in Africa, South and Central America, and South Asia.[23]

The exports of China, Taiwan, South Korea, and Thailand, together with protectionism by Western governments responding to postcrisis pressures on their workers, have made it very difficult for producers in emerging markets such as Bangladesh, Pakistan, and Nigeria to drive economic growth with exports. Where governments are weak, the problems are compounded. Consequently, instead of fueling economic growth, the growing urban population drives emigration (figures 9-4 and 9-5).

FIGURE 9-4

Number of international migrants (millions) by region of destination, 2000 and 2017

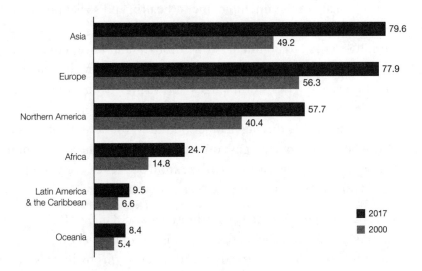

Source: UN Department of Economic and Social Affairs, Population Division, "International Migration Report 2017," United Nations, 2017, www.un.org/en/development/desa/population/migration/publications /migrationreport/docs/MigrationReport2017_Highlights.pdf.

FIGURE 9-5

Immigrants as a percentage of population

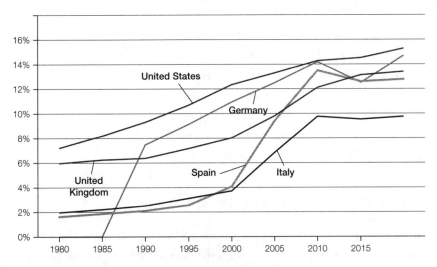

Source: UN Department of Economic and Social Affairs, Population Division, "World Population Prospects: 2017 Revision," United Nations, 2017, https://population.un.org/wpp/.

As noted in chapter 2, the World Bank has estimated that perhaps more than 80 percent of the world's workers in 2030 will be unskilled and live in developing countries. If this projection turns out to be accurate, the scale of the unemployment, health, and social problems outlined above will be enormous.

Returning to the environment, while drought and lower child mortality drive unmanaged growth in the megacities, flooding has created other problems as higher storm surges and rising sea level endanger coastal cities like Dhaka, Bangladesh, and Lagos, Nigeria. Sea-level rise in Dhaka is already driving people south toward the state of Assam in India, where a nationalist government is attacking the non-Hindu Muslim population. The risk of damage from sea-level rise is no less acute in developed nations. Climate Nexus reports that

> climate change has already contributed about 8 inches (0.19 meters) to global sea level rise, and this has dramatically amplified the impact of cyclones and other storms by increasing baseline elevations for waves and storm surge. A small vertical increase in sea level can translate into a very large increase in horizontal reach by storm surge depending upon local topography. For example, sea level rise extended the reach of Hurricane Sandy by 27 square miles, affecting 83,000 additional individuals living in New Jersey and New York City and adding over $2 billion in storm damage.[24]

In sum, environmental and demographic changes have interacted to generate powerful forces, some of which will need a response from the governments of nation-states in the form of infrastructure, education, and public health. At the same time, however, the governance of nations is stressed by economic and political forces generated by the trade and finance systems and their impact on the distribution of the GDP of nations and among their citizens.

Interactions Among Inequality, Trade, and Finance

Of more immediate concern to our executive panels in 2007 and 2008 was income inequality, which they universally linked to the threat of populist, protectionist governments. By 2019, we had witnessed many of the problems that the business leaders had anticipated. The recovery from the financial crisis has been associated with a continuation of the increase in inequality of income and wealth within many countries, but also across regions, while in other countries the gap has narrowed. Speaking generally, OECD countries have done poorly, with some recovering better in recent years.

The picture has a great deal to do with the situation before the crisis and the way its aftermath was managed on a country-by-country basis. In the United States, for example, the economy recovered steadily, but the benefits were captured almost exclusively by the top earners.

The latest numbers from the Congressional Budget Office show the vast gap between income even *after transfers and taxes* in 2013 that were designed to ameliorate the problem (figure 9-6). In the period from 2009 to 2010 in the United States, 93 percent of the recovery in real

FIGURE 9-6

Distribution of income before and after federal transfers and taxes, 2016

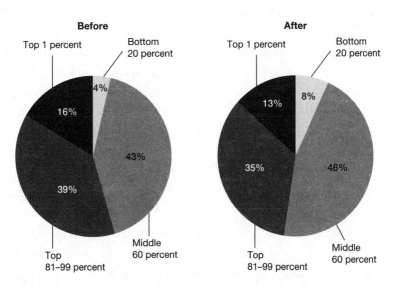

Source: Chad Stone, Danilo Trisi, Arloc Sherman, and Jennifer Beltran, *A Guide to Statistics on Historical Trends in Income Inequality* (Washington, DC: Center on Budget and Policy Priorities, January 13, 2020), https://www.cbpp.org/research/poverty-and-inequality/a-guide-to-statistics-on-historical-trends-in-income-inequality, accessed January 29, 2020.

Note: Figures do not add to 100 due to rounding.

income was captured by the wealthiest 1 percent of households. Similar discrepancies appeared in other parts of the developed world. Why? The answer lies in part with conditions before the crisis and in part with how the crisis was resolved.

Since the oil shock of 1973, earnings of the lower-income part of the U.S. population have increased slowly. Driven by large rises in the price of energy and metals and the hypercompetition in the markets for manufactured goods, the contribution of labor to manufacturing value added declined significantly, while the cost of materials and energy increased. Labor's contribution to nonfarm business income declined from 66 percent in 1972 to 56 percent in 2012.[25] (In effect, the relative value of labor and materials changed—with the terms of trade shifting against the income-earning potential of lower-skilled workers.) Increases in exports of higher-value goods from Japan and, later, Taiwan and South Korea to developed markets in the United States and Europe meant that prices for cars and other consumer durables were under constant pressure. The high quality of these imports also put pressure on U.S. and other Western manufacturers. Their response was often to move sourcing to East Asia. Retailers exacerbated this challenge by moving their sourcing overseas.[26]

For workers in the United States and other Western countries, unemployment and stagnant wages resulted. Later, in the 1990s and early 2000s, the digital revolution put further pressure on wages as some service jobs were replaced with various forms of automated operations.[27] Figure 9-7 shows that real wages for middle- and low-income U.S. workers barely moved between the 1978 oil crisis and 2018.

The global economy also saw a dramatic increase in liquidity as the earnings of the petrostates and the savings from the East Asian tigers (Hong Kong, South Korea, Taiwan, and Singapore) flooded the financial system, driving down interest rates.[28] At the same time, the cost of services such as health care and higher education increased, further squeezing the lower and middle classes of the developed countries, especially those without universal education and health services, and people on fixed incomes.[29] To maintain their consumption spending, workers in the United States turned to the value of their homes. The increased liquidity and low interest rates meant that the value of their houses increased, permitting further borrowing. The early 2000s saw

FIGURE 9-7

Real wage trends in the United States between 1979 and 2018

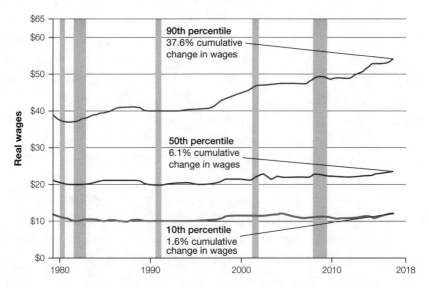

Source: Adapted from Congressional Research Service, "Real Wage Trends, 1979 to 2018," updated July 23, 2019, https://fas.org/sgp/crs/misc/R45090.pdf.

Note: Shaded vertical bars represent periods of recession.

a combination of further financial deregulation and the development of financial derivatives that made it easier for the financial system to securitize and thereby increase the availability of mortgages to low-income borrowers. This borrowing enabled low-income home-owners to maintain their spending—while piling up large amounts of debt.[30]

In much of Europe, the same forces of Asian imports and automation affected the economies, but in those countries, it was governments that borrowed to support the safety net that provided the standard of living of their populations.[31] Outliers to this pattern were Spain and Ireland, where a real estate boom played out much as it did in the United States.

The only exceptions to excessive borrowing by either the government or individuals were Germany and the Nordic countries. There, strong education and business-friendly local policies supported successful export-driven economies. The crisis of 2008 had large impacts on their banks, but their populations were much less affected than those in other European countries.

When the crisis arrived, the economies of Greece, Italy, Spain, and Portugal were hit hard, as their ability to finance their governments' debt was impaired. In turn, that debt sat on the balance sheets of the German and French banks that had helped finance their companies' exports to the Southern European countries. France and Germany used their influence in the European Union to have the European Central Bank buy the debt from their banks, effectively European-izing the debt. But even by late 2019, not all the underlying company debt had been written off, and this debt was weakening the ability of the European banks to finance new growth.[32]

In the United States and other parts of the developed world, governments intervened with regulation after the collapse; the aim was to force banks to strengthen their balance sheets. These governments also used central bank funds to shore up their banks so that these institutions could continue to function.

But the efforts to support the banks provided little in the way of relief to the borrowers. The U.S. government did force banks to recognize and write off their bad debts and supported this effort by buying up bad debt. But the generation of borrowers who funded their expenses with loans on their homes saw their wealth erode as the housing price bubble that had been fueled by subprime mortgage availability collapsed. Many borrowers declared personal bankruptcy or walked away from homes that were underwater (i.e., mortgages higher than the house value). The limited assets that many of these families had managed to build up—largely through homeownership and appreciation in house values—had in effect disappeared. At the same time, companies that had retrenched to solidify their balance sheets laid off workers and froze or cut wages. To the extent that Congress would permit, fiscal policy was also used to support the economy, especially the auto industry and its suppliers. By and large, lower- and middle-income Americans were left out as the macroeconomy began the recovery, which has now continued for ten years (table 9-1).[33]

In Europe, governments imposed various degrees of austerity to restore country balance sheets, but the effect was self-defeating because their economies were slowed by the cuts in spending. The

TABLE 9-1

Real income growth by groups (in percentages)

	Average real income growth	Top 1% real incomes growth	Bottom 99% real incomes growth	Fraction of total real income growth (or loss) captured by top 1%[a]
Full period, 1993–2012	17.9	86.1	6.6	68
Clinton expansion, 1993–2000	31.5	98.7	20.3	45
2001 recession, 2000–2002	−11.7	−30.8	−6.5	57
Bush expansion, 2002–2007	16.1	61.8	6.8	65
Great Recession, 2007–2009	−17.4	−36.3	−11.6	49
Recovery, 2009–2012	6.0	31.4	0.4	95

Source: Emmanuel Saez, "Striking it Richer: The Evolution of Top Incomes in the United States," University of California, Berkeley, Department of Economics, January 25, 2015. This is an updated version of "Striking it Richer: The Evolution of Top Incomes in the United States," *Pathways: A Magazine on Poverty, Inequality, and Social Policy* (Winter 2008): 6–7. Based on previous work with Thomas Piketty. Reprinted by permission.

Note: Computations are based on family market income, including realized capital gains before individual taxes. Incomes exclude government transfers, such as unemployment insurance and Social Security, and nontaxable fringe benefits. Incomes are deflated using the Consumer Price Index.

a. The fraction of total real family income growth (or loss) captured by the top 1 percent. For example, from 2002 to 2007, average real family incomes grew by 16 percent, but 65 percent of that growth accrued to the top 1 percent, while only 35 percent accrued to the bottom 99 percent of U.S. families.

result of such policies in the United Kingdom was particularly strong in the manufacturing and agricultural parts of the country—precisely the areas that would later vote for Brexit.[34] In Germany, the government has run surpluses even while the economy has experienced negligible growth.

By 2020, banks were still funding their lending and investment with short-term capital, and in many countries, they have failed to address the nonperforming loans on their books since 2008. Central bank balance sheets are heavy with debt, and interest rates remain at low—even negative—levels associated with stimulus policies. Income for savers has been limited. Perhaps more worrisome, layered tranches of collateralized loan obligations in the United States are emerging as the new derivatives providing more than $1 trillion dollars of opaque leverage to the system. There is again considerable concern that a new collapse is possible.[35]

The political response to slow growth or no growth in household income has been nationalistic, even nativist. Those hurt by these crises have turned on the immigrants arriving in their countries from the Middle East and Africa. Even immigrants from Eastern Europe have experienced resentment as they used their skills to take decent paying jobs. The "Polish plumber" became an object of derision in the United Kingdom. On the continent, Muslims were attacked in the same way that Donald Trump had condemned Muslims and Mexicans in the United States.

The seeds of populist antipathy to immigration in the United States have deep roots, dating back to its earliest years as a country. After early and mid-20th century limits on immigration were eased off starting in the 1960s, the U.S. government began implementing increased control of immigration under the Clinton administration. Immigration rose steadily under all later administrations, as did deportations, until they peaked in 2013. The global problem has political consequences that reverberate through all administrations.[36]

Undeniably, the problems in developing countries are driving emigration, and the electorates in developed nations are resisting these flows in much the same way that immigration was resisted in the United States at the beginning of the twentieth century. What is new is that the slow growth in the developed nations and the level of economic competition from developing nations has generated a populist and often nationalist response that (among many other problems that it may generate) is disruptive to trade arrangements.

Trade flows have become increasingly complex. What used to be a simple transaction in which goods from one country were moved to another, much as the eighteenth-century economist David Ricardo would have understood, has been transformed into a global network of sourcing decisions.[37] Something as simple as a woman's outfit might be assembled from factories in several countries. A case study of Liz Claiborne, written in 2001, provides an example:

> The Liz Claiborne strategy made sourcing especially demanding. Because the divisions produced coordinated wardrobes,

individual items that were assigned to particular factories—the suit top in China, the bottom in Guatemala, and the blouse in Thailand—had to arrive in the market at the same time matching perfectly—and satisfying US trade legislation in the form of quotas allocated to particular countries. The strategy for managing these demands [was] captured by what Bob Zane described as the "7 C's": Configuration, Consolidation, Certification, Concern, Collaboration, Coalition, and Cost.[38]

Similar complex chains existed in major consumer durables such as cars. In its July 2019 story on trade, the *Economist* reported that "Mexico's car exports to Germany have nearly 40 percent German components by value, while those crossing its northern border have over 70 percent American content."[39] An iPhone made in China would include a chip with U.S. intellectual property, U.S. design, and possibly U.S. hardware, and hence its product value would be substantially from the United States. The fight over 5G (fifth-generation) phones is partially a contest over whether that pattern will continue or whether a Chinese firm, Huawei, will capture global markets with a 100 percent Chinese product.

The observed trends may have multiple sources and might not simply reflect a trade war. The OECD has reported that trade *growth* has fallen from 5.5 percent in 2017 to 2.1 percent in 2019.[40] Some of this decline undoubtedly reflects protectionism as tariffs have cut U.S. exports of soybeans and European exports of steel. But independent of protectionism, multinational companies have been adjusting their supply chains for higher-value goods.

On the one hand, labor costs in China have risen, while new approaches to merchandising that emphasize customization and speed have led multinational corporations to move manufacturing closer to their markets. On the other hand, sellers of labor-intensive goods such as footwear continue to move sourcing to wherever wages are lowest and quality is adequate. For example, in the most recent years, footwear manufacturing has bloomed in Ethiopia. Low-end apparel has moved to Bangladesh, but labor practices—such as those leading to the Rana Plaza collapse in 2013—and poor quality continue to pose problems for manufacturers and retailers based in developed countries.

The complexity of trade and its evolution is described in a major study by the McKinsey Global Institute. The study divides trade into six archetypes of value chains, each type with its own distinct pattern of factor inputs, trade intensity, and country participation: global innovations, labor-intensive goods, regional processing, resource-intensive goods, labor-intensive services, and knowledge-intensive services.[41] The major characteristics of each archetype are different. Global innovations are concentrated in five advanced countries. The portion of labor-intensive goods traded globally is decreasing. Regional processing consisting mainly of heavy intermediate goods is not readily traded, while resource-intensive goods (agriculture, mining, metals, and energy) are geographically concentrated, employ a major portion of the global workforce, and fluctuate dramatically with global output. Labor-intensive services employ large numbers of unskilled workers and have low trade intensity, whereas knowledge-intensive services employ highly paid workers in highly traded outputs. The McKinsey study estimates that trade in knowledge-intensive services is undervalued by more than $4 trillion.

The report also notes that an important driver of many trends in trade is the shift in consumption toward China. Because of the country's extraordinary economic growth, much of what is produced in China now stays in China.

An additional complexity has been created by China's Belt and Road Initiative (BRI). With funding from government sources, Chinese manufacturers are making major investments in Africa, the Near East, and key parts of Europe such as the Greek port of Piraeus to open markets for China that have not already been captured by the West. These investments potentially displace goods and services that might otherwise come from European or even U.S. sources.

Over the last decade, the consequences of these changes in trade have been reflected in the incomes of the nations around the world and their people. But the consequences are specific to geography and economic position. Those who finance the trade or own the successful producers thrive. The booming stock markets have provided historic opportunities for hedge funds to benefit from the growth. The periodic crises—especially the 2008 crash—tend to concentrate wealth. Those displaced or squeezed suffer flat or diminished incomes. These pressures have fueled the political debate about globalization. In retrospect, we could have appreciated the clear signs of the political tension in the Seattle anti–World Trade Organization riot of 1999. In other words, aggregate trade has moved upward with the growth of the global economy, but the changes brought on by trade have had such uneven impacts that the parties injured now constitute a major political force.

A critical question, therefore, is how nations manage those changes. Differences in nations' systems of government have a great influence on the lives of their citizens.

Friction Between State Capitalism and Market Capitalism Aggravates Trade Tensions, Financial Instability, and Inequality

A decade ago, our panel of executives worried about potential collisions between state capitalism and market capitalism. They did not foresee China's BRI—this development initiative was not announced until 2013—but it is a good example of how state capitalism has challenged the global market system.

Russia and China are the two most important examples of state capitalism. Although Russia is possessed of enormous raw material deposits, it is, from the perspective of this discussion, primarily a developer and exporter of oil and gas. Exports represent close to 20 percent of the economy, and these are primarily oil, gas, chemicals, and weapons. Nearly half of Russia's exports, primarily energy, go to Europe. In a $1.6 trillion economy, Russia's 2018 trade surplus of $100 billion, reflecting a significant recovery in oil prices, indicates the critical role that energy production currently plays in Russian economic and political life. The state energy company Gazprom dominates the energy sector. At various times, Russia has used the importance of its exports to Europe as a foreign-policy tool. In other respects, Russia is a relatively closed economy, with limited foreign investments coming into the country.

In the 1990s, with the breakup of the Soviet Union, Russia experienced considerable privatization. But beginning with Vladimir Putin's first presidential term, from 2000 to 2008, the economy has been under the tutelage of the Kremlin. Private ownership remains, but significant companies follow the leadership of the government or risk ceasing to be private. As noted, Gazprom functions as part of the government.

In contrast, beginning in 1979, the Chinese economy experienced a dramatic opening and rapid growth. Foreign investment played a key role as China transformed itself from a supplier of low-cost manufacturers that depended on endless supplies of low-cost labor to a midlevel, developed economy producing globally competitive manufacturers of high-value-added goods such as high-quality garments, pianos, automobiles, locomotives, and electronics. The Chinese economy has two important sectors: private and state owned. The latter has played a critical role in a variety of key industries, such as agriculture, building materials, chemicals, electrical equipment, energy, metals, telecommunications, rail and air transportation, and much of banking. All state-owned enterprises (SOEs) belong to SASAC, the State Authority for Supervision, Administration and Control—a kind of superconglomerate. SASAC approves the strategies, finances, and top personnel appointments of its subsidiary companies. An impressive 119 of the companies in the *Fortune* Global 500 are Chinese (121 are American), and of these, perhaps 80 percent are state owned.[42] The private sector has led the development of automobiles, fast-moving consumer goods (e.g., clothing and shoes), electronics, home appliances, venture finance, and retail—all these products often in partnership with foreign multinational companies.

The preceding description of private enterprises and SOEs is based on market-system distinctions. The line between state control and private control is far less clear in a state-run system like China's. Because all land belongs to the state, many transactions require permits. Finance and foreign exchange are controlled by the government as well, and consequently the Chinese "private" sector is ultimately under government control. Despite this pervasive government presence, China was admitted to the World Trade Organization in 2001. Members believed that China's apparatus of control would gradually be dismantled and that the country would move to resemble something like a market capitalistic country. Under the premiership of Deng Xiaoping and his immediate successors, this supposition seemed to be the case as a vibrant private sector played an increasingly important role in the economy. In the era of Xi Jinping, this direction appears to have changed. The government is constraining freedom of movement by private companies and is providing aggressive support for the SOEs—including the BRI. For example, the boards of directors of private companies above a certain size must include a member of the Communist Party of China. In contrast, financing for the dramatic international growth opportunities provided by BRI is available from government institutions.

To be sure, other countries have managed their growth using significant leadership, coordination, and finance from their government. Both Germany and Japan in the 1960s and 1970s used coordinated industrial, trade, fiscal, and monetary policy to manage export-driven growth. They were followed by South Korea, Taiwan, Thailand, and Singapore. Other countries, such as Brazil, have done the same. We have not described these efforts as examples of state capitalism, because the relationship between private ownership and the state is governed—at least in principle—by more transparent arrangements that keep business and government more separate. Industrial policy rather than state ownership is used to seek government objectives.

The scale and aggressiveness of Russian SOEs in energy and Chinese SOEs in manufacturing have disrupted the smooth progress of market capitalism. The United States and Europe have focused on these challenges for years in their trade discussions. From this perspective, President Trump's use of tariffs can be seen as only a modest shift in a long-standing and increasing tension between state-led systems and other countries' systems. As discussed in chapter 3, state and market capitalism inevitably collide.

These collisions also play out in financial markets, where energy prices, currency exchange, and money flows affect the world's markets. As noted earlier, Russian oil and gas have a profound impact on domestic and global markets, but the high domestic savings rate in China (45 percent of GDP), together with limited tools for private domestic investment, has contributed to the high liquidity in global markets—the savings spilled into the global system—which in turn has driven asset appreciation. The financial instability leading to the 2008 crisis originated in part in Chinese surpluses. But easy, cheap money has fueled the market for corporate control, short-termism, and other negative features of the modern economy. The complex reorganization of trade and the drive for growth among state-capitalist nations have deeply disrupted the functioning of global market capitalism.

The challenge lies in the incompatible premises of market capitalism and state capitalism. Market capitalism is based on the premise that, subject to rules such as national antitrust laws or the trading rules of the WTO, the economic outcomes of free intranational and international trade will yield the best results for all. In contrast, state capitalism holds that economic outcomes should be achieved through active management by the state. Much as a large conglomerate manages its divisions, the state directs its SOEs to act in ways that serve state goals. This conflict of premises makes it hard for the systems to coexist.

A further complexity associated with state capitalism has been the ability of SOEs to make deals with corrupt governments without fear of the legal sanctions that might be applied to private companies. In this way, SOEs have contributed to a decline in the rule of law.[43]

Interactions Between Corruption and Terrorism Strengthen Each Other and Weaken Governance

As noted earlier, our panels of business leaders doubted whether governments and international institutions had the political will and economic strength to address the disruptors they identified. The past decade has not made these problems simpler nor the governments stronger. The stasis the world observed as Britain has struggled with Brexit is an example of this weakness. As we observed in the new preface, the task of government and international institutions has certainly not been made easier by the emergence of digital technology. This new linkage between individuals, groups, companies, and nations—while marvelous at facilitating communication, commerce, education, and medicine—has proved extremely vulnerable to manipulation by corrupt governments, terrorist groups, and autocratic nation-states. At the same time, it has given these groups new weapons of mass disruption.

The scale of corruption is now staggering, but whether it has increased is hard to know.[44] UN secretary-general António Guterres has estimated corruption as at least 5 percent of global GDP. Mark Wolfe, senior U.S. district judge, estimates that captured nation-states (states that are run by, and for the benefit of, a ruling clique or family) represent 10 percent of global GDP.[45] British journalist Misha Glenny has estimated that organized crime (drugs, currency, trafficking, and other smuggling) constitutes 15 to 20 percent of all economic transactions worldwide.[46] Obviously, calculating an accurate estimate of the burden of corruption is difficult, but the problem is enormous and seems to have worsened over the last decade. It poses a heavy tax on affected commerce, diverts revenues from governments into private hands, and provides a motive and funding for violence.

To the extent that corruption is a tax on commerce, it deprives governments of revenue that they might use to improve public health, education, or infrastructure. For example, Gabon is a geographically large nation blessed with oil and minerals. The GDP per capita is $8,300, but most of the population lives with incomes under $2,000 because of massive corruption.[47]

Wherever the state itself has become a corrupt enterprise, the impact on its population is devastating.[48] Corrupt states can also easily become failed states. Afghanistan in the post-Soviet-invasion period is a good example. With government in the hands of warlords, corruption flourished. The Taliban set up home as a reform movement but funded itself through the opium trade. When Osama bin Laden fled Saudi Arabia, he established himself as Afghanistan's guest. Al Qaeda has still not left. Whether Venezuela will become a home for terrorists is not yet clear, but the cabal that runs the state also runs the oil company and the black market and appears to deal extensively in drugs and other contraband. Emigrants from Venezuela to Colombia and Brazil have destabilized some of the remote regions of those countries. More generally, an analysis by corruption watchdog Transparency International shows that countries with higher levels of corruption also have weaker democratic institutions.[49] Over the decade since we first wrote this book, terrorist attacks have continued to escalate (figure 9-8).

Both corruption and terrorism can be thought of as breakdowns in governance. The market system depends on a reliable system for secure ownership and transactions. These in turn require stable currency, reliable banking, honest officials, and safe trade, as well as free and fair courts to settle disputes. While the absence of systematic data makes it hard to assess trends, it is clear that the continued absence of these requisites in a variety of circumstances hinders business's ability

FIGURE 9-8

Number of fatalities from terrorist attacks

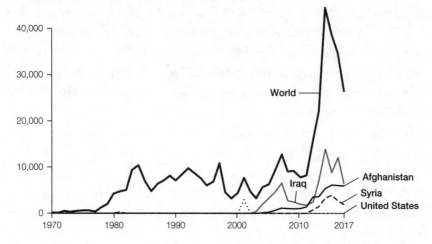

Source: Hannah Ritchie, Joe Hasell, Cameron Appel, and Max Roser, "Number of Fatalities from Terrorist Attacks," in *Terrorism* (Our World in Data, July 2013; revised November 2019), https://ourworldindata.org/terrorism.

Note: Number of fatalities per year from terrorist attacks: total number of confirmed fatalities, including all victims and attackers who died as a direct result of the incident.

to function. More important to the argument of this book, the pervasiveness of corruption implies that business has a high stake in whether countries have effective governance. Business cannot treat countries like hotels that they check into (and out of) at their own convenience. If executives want a favorable environment for doing business, they need to support the institutions necessary to keep corruption and its consequences in check.

Failing governance has also contributed to the problem of pandemics. Pandemics result when deadly disease is allowed to proliferate in the absence of effective intervention by the institutions of public health. Infectious diseases continuously evolve, often in the crossover of pathogens from birds or other nonhuman animals to people, unremittingly confronting human immune systems with new threats. Disease transmission cannot be stopped; it is a feature of our being part of a natural system inhabited by countless other organisms. Since by definition our immune systems have little or no natural defense against recently evolved disease agents such as new viruses and bacteria, these agents can spread rapidly and have devastating effects in a human population. In the past, crossover might wipe out a small rural enclave but cause no larger problem. Today, however, even in remote regions, interactions associated with trade or war enable new diseases to spread more broadly and rapidly. When the diseases reach cities, the threat of contagion becomes much higher, and with air travel, a disease can move across the world quickly. The HIV/AIDS epidemic is an example of such a disaster. By contrast, SARS posed a similar risk but was quickly contained by public health officials when it emerged in 2003. The Zika outbreaks of the last decade have been similarly contained. In both the SARS and the Zika outbreaks, response by reasonably effective governance and national and international health organizations helped contain these emergent threats. The successful responses of these institutions show the importance of investment in, support for, and maintenance of these institutions. In early 2020, the coronavirus began sickening and killing people in China at exponentially rising rates. Reports suggest that the rapid spread is a consequence of government inaction in spite of courageous efforts by doctors and remarkable efforts by scientists.

When government institutions break down or are not allowed to function effectively, the consequences are frightening. The current threat from Ebola, which WHO deemed a public health emergency of international concern in July 2019, is exacerbated because it is taking place in the middle of the civil war in the Congo. The war in turn is fueled by a weak government and the lure of valuable minerals. As people flee the violence, they bring the disease with them. Poor education and limited public health help spread the disease as well. Some villages reject intervention, especially efforts to quarantine their relatives and bury the dead in ways determined by modern science to be safe. Migrants from the violence are reaching cities that lack a structure for tracking them. Again, this situation is an example of the stake that the business community has in effective government.

The point we are making here is not subtle. As argued in chapter 4, effective governance, including the rule of law, is fundamental to the functioning of market capitalism. Conflicts of any kind that undermine the rules by which transactions proceed and disputes are fairly resolved weaken the system. But they also weaken other aspects of society, such as public health. These aspects in turn are required for the successful functioning of the system.

Weak Governments and Outdated International Institutions

In our 2007 and 2008 discussions with global business leaders, many commented on weaknesses in the governmental context. As described in chapter 5, some executives thought that such weaknesses were inevitable because democratic governments would respond to misguided populist sentiment. Others thought the failings arose because the mechanisms of even the best governments were inadequate to the task of moving the world's economies and polities through the difficulties identified in our discussions. None thought that post–World War II institutions such as the United Nations and the World Bank were capable of actions that would ameliorate the disruptors.

Part Two of this book examined these views and laid out our argument for business as a leader. Ten years later, our view can be expressed more emphatically: the problems facing the global market system are severe and appear to be worsening. Indeed, as we have discussed in this chapter, the disruptors appear to feed on and reinforce one another in ways that are creating ever-more-complex problems and putting market capitalism at even greater risk. There is no one comprehensive solution, and governments must be involved. But we stand by our earlier conclusion that business can and must play a role in addressing the disruptors—and can do so in ways that make strategic sense for business.

In earlier chapters, we have offered some examples of companies that were doing just that. In chapter 10, we examine several additional examples from work we have done since the book's publication. These new illustrations again show that if companies bring their considerable capabilities to bear on these problems—often in collaboration with governments and NGOs—they can find creative ways to derive economic value and strengthen their business while also addressing the disruptors and helping build a more sustainable form of capitalism.

The challenge is to mobilize more companies to take on this essential work.

Companies Stepping Up
to the Challenge

THE PICTURE that emerges from the previous chapter is alarming. The income gap continues to widen, and some projections show automation putting millions out of work in coming decades.[1] Carbon emissions are rising, and the world is falling further behind on the Paris Agreement's climate goals. Massive migration looms. Global trade is slowing, and trade tensions between the United States and China promises lasting damage to the world trading system. Meanwhile, right-wing extremist groups are gaining strength in North America and Europe, geopolitical tensions are simmering at flashpoints across the globe, and a cohort of populist leaders in nations around the world openly spurn the rule of law and trumpet their disdain for international institutions, the free press, and scientific inquiry.

The consequences of neglecting problems that ten years ago may have seemed abstract or distant are coming home to roost. They are driving economic, political, and social changes that are affecting companies around the world through supply-chain disruptions, talent shortages, labor unrest, capital-market volatility, consumer distrust, rising security costs, heightened uncertainty, and increased overall risk. For years, business leaders have taken for granted continued globalization, support for free markets, and abundant natural resources. Today, the business community is beginning to recognize that these foundations of the global economy—what we have called the antecedents of capitalism—are actually quite fragile. Their disappearance poses real threats not just to the economy at large but to individual companies' own profitability and potential for growth.

Some companies' very existence may be under threat. Consider California's Pacific Gas & Electric (PG&E), one of the largest natural gas and electric utilities in the United States. Facing an estimated $30 billion in potential liabilities from equipment failures linked to some of the deadliest and most damaging wildfires in California's history, PG&E filed for Chapter 11 protection in January 2019. A *Wall Street Journal* headline called it "the first climate-change bankruptcy."[2] The contributing factors are complex, to be sure, but there is little doubt that the company's operating practices and capital investment program failed to keep pace with the frequency and intensity of wildfires that were increasing because of climate change. In the fall of 2019, hundreds of thousands of PG&E customers suffered temporary losses of power as the company shut down service rather than risk starting more fires.

For other companies, the situation may seem less dire, but the challenges are no less real. In this chapter, we renew the plea for action that we addressed to business leaders in the first edition of this book. We say again, more strongly and with a greater sense of urgency: the time has come for the private sector to mobilize for a major offensive on the problems threatening the global market system. This is not a call for a PR campaign to extol the benefits of markets and globalization. Instead, it is a call to tackle the very real problems that have given rise to the current situation and to work on rebuilding confidence in capitalism by putting it on a more sustainable trajectory. That means showing—not just saying—that capitalism can protect and renew its own foundations (the antecedent conditions) and produce the more equitable and inclusive distribution of wealth and opportunity necessary to preserve its social and political acceptability.

Such an initiative would require business leaders and companies to act both individually and collectively on several fronts to alleviate the disruptors we have identified and to end harmful and corrupt practices that undermine capitalism's foundations. By corrupt practices, we mean, for example, the widespread consumer fraud seen at Wells Fargo; the far-reaching diesel emissions cheat-scheme at Volkswagen; the massive data privacy breaches at Facebook; and the extensive use of illicit payments to win contracts by Airbus, Siemens, Walmart, Odebrecht, and others. Such cases of large-scale corporate malfeasance by once-respected companies powerfully reinforce the perception that capitalism is broken and that business cannot be trusted.

In proposing a private-sector initiative to address these problems, we take inspiration from the success of the Committee for Economic Development. As described in chapter 7, the CED was a private-sector group formed in 1942 with the dual purpose of conducting research and preparing to achieve full employment in the United States when World War II ended. In addition to forming a research group dedicated to conducting research from "the standpoint of the general welfare" rather than from the perspective of any particular political or economic group, the CED also mobilized more than seventy thousand business leaders across the United States to identify business opportunities and plan for their anticipated postwar employment needs. The initiative was strictly about planning—not about substantive directives—and each company was left to decide on its own response, but the initiative focused the business community's attention on a problem that threatened to spawn another great recession or worse. The CED's work, incidentally, earned it widespread praise as a trusted voice of business.

Without a doubt, the effort we envision would be more ambitious even than the CED's. It would be global, involving companies and business leaders from around the world, and its aim would be broader than addressing unemployment. But, like the CED effort, it would be a centrally motivated but distributed endeavor that harnesses the ingenuity of individual companies and business leaders. The effort would use their distinctive capabilities to address problems that make strategic business sense for their organizations. If each of the world's largest companies—say, the *Forbes* Global 2000 or some comparable group—were to make a significant investment in innovations aimed at tackling at least one of the disruptive forces threatening the global market system, the impact could be enormous. In addition to the benefits associated with each company's initiative, such a bottom-up effort would generate a wealth of ideas and innovations that could then be applied more broadly. A serious effort that engaged employees and produced positive results might even increase some of capitalism's appeal among today's young adults.[3]

Earlier in this book, we suggested some innovative activities that more companies could undertake. We considered examples of businesses acting on their own as well as in collaboration with others in their industry or region, and across different sectors. In chapter 6, we examined a series of companies pursuing strategies that sought either to extend the benefits of capitalism more broadly, mitigate its negative effects, strengthen its antecedents, or interrupt negative forces from the outside—the four generic approaches to strengthening capitalism suggested by the framework in chapter 4. The examples included General Electric's ecomagination business; China Mobile's efforts to narrow the digital divide with its rural communications strategy; the approach to sustainable investing developed by the London-based asset-management firm Generation Investment Management; and Cipla Limited's controversial business model for delivering antiretroviral drugs to some of the world's poorest regions. In chapter 7, we looked at examples of business-led efforts to mobilize industry or regional groups to collaborate with one another or with community and government leaders to strengthen the market system.

Since the earlier edition of this book was published in 2011, we have continued to examine companies acting on their own and in collaboration with others to address the disruptors. We have seen exciting examples of what businesses can do when led by imaginative leaders focused on long-term sustainable success. In this chapter, we share a few examples from this more recent work. Like the examples from chapters 6 and 7, these offer further evidence that companies can address these problems without compromising their business objectives and often in ways that advance and complement those objectives.

To be sure, we have found fewer examples than might be expected (or hoped for), given the magnitude and pervasiveness of the problems at hand. Nonetheless, as we detail in chapter 11, momentum is building for more companies to step up to the challenge. In our earlier research, some of the business leaders we spoke with described the problems facing capitalism as "above my pay grade" and best left to government, or beyond their authority as fiduciaries for their shareholders. Since 2011, we have given many presentations and have spoken about these issues with many more business leaders. While we have continued to hear these refrains, we also sense that more business leaders are beginning to view the disruptors as matters requiring their attention and even as business opportunities. A growing number of business leaders are adopting the business-as-innovator and business-as-activist perspectives on these problems (see chapter 5) and are coming to regard concerns about authority and legitimacy as issues to be managed rather than as barriers to action. The following examples will show how some companies are handling these issues.

We have chosen a diverse set of examples to highlight the wide array of possibilities for strategic engagement. One case study examines how JPMorgan Chase & Co. has invested funds and talent in working with community leaders to help bring Detroit back from disaster and bankruptcy, and create economic opportunity for the city and its citizens. In another case study, we show how Cummins has worked with community leaders to strengthen the educational system in its home base of Columbus, Indiana, and to develop Southeast Indiana into a major center of manufacturing. Then we look at how Nike has embedded principles of sustainability into its operations and generated a series of product and process innovations that reduce its environmental impact and reliance on scarce resources. Finally, we examine how Unilever has applied principles of sustainability across its entire value chain and, in doing so, enabled hundreds of thousands of small-scale farmers and distributors to raise their incomes, improved the nutritional quality of Unilever food products, and reduced the company's environmental impact.

As this list suggests, the opportunities for strategic engagement are not restricted to particular industries or sectors, and the forms of engagement are limited only by the imagination and resourcefulness of the executives who lead them. However, a closer look at these examples—their origins, how they evolved, the difficulties they had to overcome, how they were governed and led—is worthwhile. It can reveal patterns that we have observed in successful engagements and offer lessons that may be useful to other companies considering how they might respond to the challenges facing capitalism and the market system today.

Before turning to the cases and the lessons they suggest, a few caveats are worth repeating. By focusing on what business can do, we in no way intend to diminish the importance of government or to imply that business alone can fix all the problems at hand. As we argued at length earlier, collective action will be necessary in many cases, and changes in law and public policy are also needed. Indeed, any business-led initiative to revitalize capitalism should include at least three prongs. One prong—the one we are discussing here—would aim at mobilizing companies for strategic engagement with critical problems in their own sphere of influence. A second, which two of us (Joseph and Lynn) have discussed elsewhere, would focus on strengthening corporate governance to make it more supportive of such engagements and to reduce the incidence of large-scale corporate malfeasance.[4] A third prong, which several commentators have discussed, would aim at developing a set of public policy recommendations and, importantly, building the bipartisan consensus needed to enact them.[5] We envision this third prong as addressing a range of topics, varying by region but also coordinated across the globe.

At the same time, as we have argued earlier in the book, a new and improved form of capitalism is unlikely to emerge without leadership from the private sector. The results of leaving the task to governments are already evident, and the limitations of top-down, government-imposed solutions are well known. Yet public discourse on the state of capitalism has focused very little on the role of the private sector and what it can do, and the level of business engagement to date is modest relative to the seriousness of the situation.

We hope that the examples in this chapter and elsewhere in the book will spark additional ideas and inspire other business leaders to step up to the challenge and perhaps even to join forces in mobilizing an effort of the sort we have suggested. The goal is to multiply the types of initiatives discussed here several thousandfold and for a critical mass of leading companies across the globe to show that they are serious about combatting the threats to market capitalism.

JPMorgan Chase: Investing in Detroit

JPMorgan Chase's investment in Detroit is a good example of how a company collaborated with private and public entities. The investment originated, in part, with a suggestion made by one of the bank's institutional shareholders and involved close collaboration with various agencies of government in Detroit.[6] The example thus brings to the fore the two issues mentioned above—shareholder support and political legitimacy—that are often cited as obstacles to the type of efforts we are proposing.

The company's involvement in Detroit's revitalization began in late 2013 with a phone call to the office of mayor-elect Michael Duggan, former CEO of Detroit Medical Center. The previous year, dismayed by the state of the city, which was sliding toward bankruptcy, Duggan had decided to enter the race for mayor as a write-in candidate, walking the streets of Detroit's African American neighborhoods to get the seventy thousand signatures he needed. Duggan won the Democratic primary, defeating the son of past Detroit mayor Coleman Young and insuring his victory in the general election. When JPMorgan Chase called, Duggan was recruiting staff and formulating a development strategy, starting with a plan to fix some of the city's most basic problems—miles of broken streetlights, buses off schedule, and 911 calls with thirty-minute response times—before tackling its most blighted neighborhoods. Despite several recent redevelopment projects, decades of neglect and mismanagement had left much of the city a shambles.

At the time, JPMorgan Chase was in the early stages of implementing a new approach to philanthropy. Two years earlier, concerned that the bank's $200 million of philanthropic efforts was having limited impact, chairman and CEO Jamie Dimon asked Peter Scher to be head of corporate responsibility. Scher brought deep expertise from his years as a partner at a Washington, D.C., consulting firm with a practice in government relations. He quickly launched a study of the bank's philanthropic efforts, recruiting a high-powered staff from government and the nonprofit sector to help him. By 2013, from numerous commitments that were a mile wide but very modest in depth, and guided by a staff of bank employees near the end of their careers, Scher's group had developed a new strategy that would seek to drive meaningful change in four areas of need. These areas were important to both the bank and the communities in which it operated and matched JPMorgan Chase's organizational strength: jobs and skills, small-business expansion, financial health, and neighborhood revitalization.

Detroit's well-known problems and the bank's long history in the city made Detroit a logical focus for the bank. One of the mergers that led to the creation of JPMorgan Chase involved the purchase of the

National Bank of Detroit by Bank One, where Dimon was CEO before its acquisition. Historically the city's most important bank, JPMorgan Chase had a 65 percent share of the city's consumer banking market and a similar share in other lines of business, but it was unclear how sustainable that business could be if Detroit did not recover. Suffering from decades of decline, the city had declared bankruptcy just a few months earlier and the situation was grave. When the head of the public employees' union, the American Federation of State, County and Municipal Employees, whose pension fund was a JPMorgan Chase shareholder, suggested to Dimon that the bank could do something about the plight of Detroit's municipal retirees, Dimon asked Scher to visit Detroit to see if there was anything the bank could do to help.

The city's challenges reflected its history. Founded in 1701 at the junction of three rivers as a center for fur traders, Detroit later evolved into a center of shipping and, eventually, manufacturing. By the end of the nineteenth century, Detroit had emerged as the home of the burgeoning U.S. auto industry. By the 1930s, the city's needs for labor made Detroit one destination of the great migration of African Americans fleeing violence and poverty in the Depression-era South and of white families leaving Appalachia.

Because of the new Federal Housing Administration's policies on mortgage guarantees, white families could secure loans for homes across the city whereas black families were steered into three increasingly crowded neighborhoods that were considered too risky under the FHA's underwriting guidelines. The FHA deemed these neighborhoods "marginal" and marked them with a red line on its color-coded maps so that banks would know that loan guarantees would not be available for homes in the area, thereby giving rise to the term *redlining*. The resulting segregation was reinforced when World War II brought a second wave of immigration, further increasing the city's population as housing was built to the gates of the factories. Racial tensions increased to the point that in 1943, in the middle of the war, riots erupted.

The surge in auto sales that accompanied the postwar economic boom attracted still more workers to Detroit. With the city too crowded for the giant one-story factories that automakers were then building, production was moved to the suburbs. Thus began the migration of jobs and workers out of the city—except that only white families could get mortgages to move. Detroit grew with the industry, reaching a peak population of 1.8 million in the 1950s and spreading out over 139 square miles (larger than Boston and San Francisco put together).

Over the ensuing decades, several factors contributed to a gradual loss of manufacturing jobs and a shrinking population and tax base. By the late 1950s, automation was already reducing the need for human workers, and with the rise of competition from Germany and Japan in the 1970s, the industry began relocating plants—initially to other states and then outside the United States—to take advantage of looser labor laws and lower labor costs. Even so, poor management left the industry unable to compete with the smaller, more efficient, and more reliable cars produced by Japanese and German automakers in the wake of the 1970s oil shocks. The loss of jobs only exacerbated the city's underlying racial tensions. The city fell victim to race riots that, at times, left extensive property damage in their wake—damage that was often left unrepaired because of a declining tax base, strained budgets, poor management, and corruption in municipal government. Meanwhile, the city's schools were also deteriorating, and in 1999, the Detroit school system was taken over by the state of Michigan.

The global financial crisis of 2008 was the last straw, with both General Motors and Chrysler declaring bankruptcy in 2009 and the Big Three (GM, Chrysler, and Ford Motor Company) seeking financial assistance from the federal government. By 2010, Detroit's population, 80 percent African American, was down to 714,000, its lowest number in a hundred years and below the 750,000 on which the city's finances were premised.[7] Unemployment was at 27 percent, illiteracy was estimated at upwards of 40 percent, and nearly 28 percent of the city's residential properties were vacant.[8] The city's mayor from 2002 until 2008 was under investigation on charges of fraud and corruption, for which he would later be sentenced to twenty-eight years in prison.

Even as Detroit was spiraling toward bankruptcy, enterprising civic leaders were mobilizing for its recovery. Detroit's boom times had left it with several major foundations, including the Ford, Kresge, W. K. Kellogg, and Knight foundations, and the city was home to a number of wealthy individuals determined to see it rise again. In 2000, with the Super Bowl scheduled for Detroit Stadium in 2006, the

Kresge Foundation had partnered with GM and the city to help fund a revitalization project on the waterfront where the stadium was located, saving the waterfront for public recreation. In 2010, in the wake of the financial crisis, Detroit native and founder of Quicken Loans, Dan Gilbert, relocated Quicken's headquarters from the suburbs to downtown and used $2 billion of his own funds to acquire and renovate seventy-eight office buildings. Mike Illich, another native Detroiter and founder of the Little Caesars restaurant chain, acquired and developed at the edge of midtown a large parcel of land that included a new complex with facilities for the city's baseball and hockey teams.

As it became clear that the city needed an overarching plan to guide these well-intentioned and potentially helpful but so far uncoordinated efforts, Detroit's philanthropic leaders convened with the city's government and the leaders of its churches, community organizations, and businesses to draft a strategic plan for the city. The result of the nearly three-year effort was "Detroit Future City," a document that described Detroit's challenges and laid out a growth plan for the future that virtually all the city's civic leaders signed on to in late 2012.[9]

Despite these positive developments, the city's fiscal crisis worsened, and in July 2013 Detroit became the largest municipality in U.S. history to file for Chapter 9 bankruptcy. To raise cash to pay down the city's debt and meet its pension liabilities, city officials considered auctioning off the collection of paintings and sculptures held by the world-famous Detroit Institute of Arts. The proposal provoked an uproar that brought together Detroit's leading foundations, civic organizations, private donors, and state and city officials in the form of a "grand bargain" to save the art *and* protect the workers' pensions. In addition to addressing the immediate crisis at hand, the Grand Bargain strengthened the coalition of city leaders that was in place when JPMorgan Chase reached out to Duggan's office.

The call came at the right time. Duggan's efforts to build his staff and to develop plans to address the city's problems were well under way, but the missing ingredient was funds to support the efforts in the neighborhoods. At Duggan's invitation, Scher, his team, and a group of JPMorgan Chase commercial bankers made their first visit to Detroit in the fall of 2013. The visit kicked off six months of trips by teams from different parts of the bank to listen to what the leaders of Detroit needed and discuss how the banking company could help. The visits were coordinated by a company vice president of global philanthropy. This person was also a Detroit native working in the bank's Detroit office—in other words, she was knowledgeable about local conditions. Scher knew it was not the bank's role to determine what the city's priorities should be, and he believed that trying to do so would never work, anyway. Accordingly, he instructed the bank's executives that they should dedicate themselves strictly to listening to what Detroit's leaders had to say and to understanding the situation in Detroit.[10]

In May 2014, after months of study and discussion, JPMorgan Chase announced a five-year commitment of $100 million to help accelerate Detroit's recovery. Following the bank's four priorities for its philanthropic activities, the team allocated the business and philanthropic capital to five main areas.

The largest portion was invested in housing and neighborhood development through two community development financial institutions (CDFIs) with strong records in Detroit. (CDFIs are private-sector financial institutions certified by the U.S. Treasury's CDFI Fund to receive government funds through a variety of programs and to provide credit and other financial services to underserved markets for purposes of community development.[11]) Both CDFIs were known to the bank, and each institution received $20 million to fund construction and economic development in three neighborhoods the mayor had chosen as the first step in his long-term program for the city. The CDFIs vetted the projects and deployed and administered the loans. Because federal law allowed CDFIs to make loans with more liberal conditions than those the bank could offer, the CDFIs could support projects that did not meet standard market criteria—an important factor at a time when development costs could exceed the expected market value of completed projects. The below-market loans received from JPMorgan Chase enabled the CDFIs to leverage funds from other sources, including the federal government, and in turn to make more low-cost loans to high-risk housing developers and small businesses. The below-market rate, in effect, covered the portion of the borrowing that market-rate lenders would not cover, the so-called non-serviceable gap. Each CDFI also received $5 million in grants to build capacity.

Another large component of JPMorgan Chase's funding—$25 million—went to blight removal and neighborhood revitalization. To address the city's difficulty in locating and prioritizing blighted properties, part of this amount was combined with other funds—from the Kresge Foundation and Quicken Loans—to support the city's development of Motor City Mapping, an app that enabled residents to use their smartphones to photograph a blighted property and send it with a GPS location to city officials who, in turn, could use the resultant map to assess the condition of properties across the city. Another portion of these funds went to a program of home rehab financing for winners in the city's weekly auctions of properties in its land bank. JPMorgan Chase worked with the city and black-owned Liberty Bank, also a CDFI, to develop this program and to enable home buyers to renovate the derelict properties they had purchased even when the cost of renovation exceeded the properties' appraised value, a frequent occurrence, given the depressed residential real estate market. The remainder of the initial $100 million was allocated to projects for workforce development ($12.5 million), small-business growth ($7 million), and infrastructure development ($5.5 million).

In addition to providing funding—and, as it turns out, just as important—the bank established the Detroit Service Corps to supplement the skills and expertise available in its partner organizations. Top JPMorgan Chase talent from around the world competed for the chance to spend three weeks on the ground in Detroit working on projects with the mayor's office, one of the CDFIs, or another of the nonprofits. Although the creators of the service corps initially feared that bosses would not release talented managers for the program, competition to sponsor outstanding people emerged over time and managers began to lobby for their nominees to be selected. Through the corps, the bank brought its employees' expertise to bear on a wide range of strategic projects and exposed the managers to challenges that they probably would not have encountered in the normal course of their careers.

At the outset, Scher and his team put in place a quarterly review process to monitor progress using a variety of metrics linked to the bank's four priorities. The team kept close watch, for example, on funds committed and funds leveraged and the number of loans repaid, affordable housing units created or preserved, participants in workforce training programs, jobs created or maintained, small businesses launched, or individuals getting help to improve their financial health. Scher met regularly with Dimon, and Sher's Detroit team provided quarterly reports to the bank board's public responsibility committee. Dimon and Scher met periodically with Mayor Duggan. Measurable progress was evident in the first year, and after three years, with the development loans being repaid and results exceeding expectations, JPMorgan Chase announced a further commitment of $50 million, for a total of $150 million as of 2017.

The positive results in Detroit prompted the bank team to consider expanding the work to other cities. As the team members examined other candidates, however, they came to realize that Detroit had a number of what they termed *preconditions* that contributed to JPMorgan Chase's success there. They noted, in particular, the progress already under way toward reviving the city, a track record of successful cross-sector collaborations, the existence of an agreed-on plan for Detroit's future, and the presence of skilled political and managerial leadership. All of these factors in combination created an opportunity for the bank to make an impact. It could bring its distinctive resources and capabilities to bear by leveraging the work of others while staying removed from delicate political decisions such as which neighborhoods would get the first investment of resources. With legitimate political leadership in place to set priorities, an agreed-on plan to provide direction, and working coalitions and potential partners ready to join forces, the bank could focus on areas where it could make a contribution.

Although Scher's team concluded that candidates for investment had to satisfy certain preconditions, they also came to regard the model they had developed in Detroit in broader terms as a model for inclusive growth that could potentially be applied elsewhere. After further study, a decision was made to explore the model's applicability in parts of Chicago and in the Anacostia section of Washington, D.C. In 2018, JPMorgan Chase took the further step of announcing that it was taking the model to scale through AdvancingCities, a five-year, $500 million initiative to invest in driving inclusive growth in troubled parts of other cities around the world, including Chicago's south and west sides; Wards 7 and 8 in Washington, D.C.; and the areas of greater Paris with high levels of poverty.

In 2019, the bank committed to increasing its investment in Detroit to $200 million by the end of 2022, aiming to further accelerate the positive trends already in evidence. The city's finances had improved to the point that it no longer needed the oversight structure put in place when it came out of bankruptcy in 2014, and various indicators pointed to an improving overall situation.[12] The city's unemployment rate was down to less than 9 percent, its population decline appeared to have stabilized, companies were moving to Detroit, and the mortgage market was beginning to rebound. Scher said, "For the first time in seventeen years, home values have risen and mortgage lending is up."[13]

Cummins: Building a Global Manufacturing Center

In October 2015, Cummins Inc. celebrated the opening of its new technical center in Seymour, a small town in Southeast Indiana about twenty miles from the company's headquarters in Columbus, Indiana.[14] The nearly 90,000-square-foot facility was built on the same site as the company's recently upgraded and expanded Seymour engine plant, creating a complex that would serve as the global hub for developing, testing, and manufacturing the company's high-horsepower engines, including its largest and most powerful to date, the QSK95. The first in a new line of high-speed, low-emissions engines called the hedgehog line, the QSK95 relied on leading-edge electronics and clean combustion technology and was designed to meet the world's strictest emissions standards. It would be sold to customers worldwide for applications in a range of sectors—locomotive manufacturing, offshore drilling, mining, power generation, larger marine vessels, and others.

The Seymour complex represented a major investment for Cummins, one of the world's leading producers of diesel engines. Its completion marked the culmination of nearly a decade of work that included not only significant technical feats but also major managerial achievements. To develop and build the innovative QSK95, the company had to attract and develop the talent it needed and revitalize a facility that had been targeted for closure at least ten times in the previous fifteen years. The decision to manufacture the hedgehog line at the Seymour plant, rather than in India or the United Kingdom, had not been taken lightly. Finding employees willing to live and work in the depressed town of Seymour had been a challenge over the years, and the local school system was in desperate need of improvement. Cummins executives knew from long experience that managers and employees of the caliber needed for the hedgehog line would be unwilling to move their families to a community that lacked a good school system and rich quality of life.

After debating the pros and cons of alternative sites in 2010, Tom Linebarger, Cummins CEO-designate at the time, and his team decided on Seymour, recognizing that success would depend as much on improving the community and its schools as on refining the engine and production process. Linebarger took comfort in knowing that the Columbus-based Community Education Coalition (CEC), which Cummins had helped form in 1997, was already at work on a multi-pronged effort known as EcO_{15} (Economic Opportunities through Education by 2015) to increase the population, improve educational attainment, and raise household incomes in the Southeast Indiana region, including Seymour. In keeping with the company's tradition of civic engagement, Cummins had been heavily involved with the CEC since its inception. In 2010, five of the CEC's board members were in some way affiliated with Cummins.

The CEC owed its creation to a Hudson Institute report commissioned by the Columbus Economic Development Board in 1996. The report made clear that the city's continued growth and prosperity depended on improvements in its education system. Drawing on a long tradition at Cummins and within the Columbus community, the report catalyzed a coalition of the many and varied stakeholders with an interest in the city's education system. In short order, the group formed an organization with a seasoned human relations professional and former Cummins employee as CEO and a board of directors whose members represented each major stakeholder. These stakeholders included the superintendents of the local school systems, the chancellors of the local colleges, the mayor of Columbus, several business leaders, the president of the local Chamber of Commerce, the president of the Columbus Economic Development Board, and concerned citizens. The board elected Cummins's vice president of community relations as its chair.

Initial funding for the CEC came from Cummins and two other Columbus-based companies, Arvin Industries and Irwin Financial, and the Columbus Economic Development Board. The CEC later secured permanent funding through a grant from the Indianapolis-based Lilly Endowment via the Heritage Foundation, the community foundation for Bartholomew County (where Columbus is located). Of the $5 million grant to the Heritage Foundation, $3 million was used to establish an endowment for the CEC. The CEC defined three high-level goals. First, all students in the county should graduate from high school. Next, all residents should be given the opportunity to attend a two- or four-year college, with the further aim of expanding local college programs leading to well-paying employment sectors. Finally, enough jobs should be available for all graduates to be gainfully employed once they graduated with the required skills.

As noted, Cummins employees were heavily involved in the CEC from the beginning, but they were careful not to dominate or exert undue influence, recognizing that their role was not to dictate the agenda. An earlier effort to bring various stakeholders together led by the Columbus Chamber of Commerce had faltered after it became apparent that chamber members perceived the educators as part of the problem rather than part of the solution.

A first order of business for the CEC was building trust among the participants through open and respectful dialogue informed by research and facts. Through this process, which became a standard operating procedure, the group built consensus around its priorities and could speak with a common voice to the larger community. For example, armed with the fact that the school system was spending 20 percent of its budget on remedial education—information discovered when county school officials invited Cummins accountants to examine the school system budget—the CEC was able to leverage the approval of funds to support at-risk students.

One of the coalition's early priorities was strengthening higher education. Working with local and other allies in the state, the CEC developed a plan for three important Indiana universities— Indiana University-Purdue University Columbus, Purdue University Polytechnic Institute Columbus, and Ivy Tech Community College— to work together in Columbus. The three institutions agreed to offer more degrees directly related to jobs in the community and to build closer connections with the secondary schools in the area. More impressive perhaps, they were persuaded to share a common physical facility—the Columbus Learning Center—whose design and development were orchestrated by the CEC. The coalition got the educators talking to companies about their educational expectations for new recruits and their hiring plans for the years ahead, and set up cross-sector teams to work out elements of the physical design needed to house the various educational programs. The Columbus Learning Center, which was to be managed by the CEC, was completed in 2005. Its classrooms, laboratory spaces, and student services facilities were shared by all three schools. The schools, in turn, expanded their degree offerings to better align with the needs of local employers.

The CEC's second major infrastructure project was designing and building an Advanced Manufacturing Center of Excellence for the high school to use in preparing students for advanced manufacturing, engineering, and technology-related careers. With the new facility located across from the Columbus Learning Center, the manufacturing center's classrooms and labs (including an advanced metrology lab sponsored by Cummins) were easily accessible to students and faculty. The manufacturing center was completed in 2011.

A CEC analysis of the Columbus-area high schools revealed a dropout rate of 15 to 18 percent, a figure that all members of the coalition considered unacceptable and far short of the targeted 100 percent graduation rate. Further analysis found that if students were not on track by third grade, their chances of dropping out before graduation skyrocketed and that many factors contributed to the problem. The study showed, moreover, that 30 percent of the students entering kindergarten were unprepared—a finding that prompted one business executive to comment sympathetically, "If we had a factory with one-third of the raw material flawed, we'd fix it or shut it down."[15]

Armed with its analyses, the CEC devised various programs to address the different aspects of the dropout problem—in each case testing the program through one or more pilots before seeking to introduce it more broadly. Using this model, the coalition developed a number of educational efforts. For example, the Busy Bees Academy was created for early-childhood education. A coaching program identified and supported ninth and tenth graders at risk for dropping out of high school. Another initiative enrolled eligible eighth graders in a state-run program that would give them tuition-free access to any state or community college if they signed up by eighth grade and graduated from high school with an acceptable grade point average.

The coalition typically secured funding for the initial pilot for its programs from local corporations, such as Cummins, and from foundations if successive rounds of pilots were required. Once a successful formula was found, and if the program was thought to be sustainable, the CEC then provided managerial and financial support to secure additional funding and expand the program to its intended audience. In these cases, the coalition might look to the state of Indiana or to local taxpayers for funds. The CEC's thorough analyses usually made a convincing case for its request.

With a track record of early successes, the CEC secured additional funding from the Lilly Endowment to expand the scope and scale of its programs. With part of a major grant from Lilly in 2007, the coalition launched EcO_{15}, bringing together business, education, and civic leaders from ten counties in Southeast Indiana, including Jackson County, where Seymour is located. The initiative aimed to elevate the educational level of the entire region and prepare more residents for higher-level jobs by 2015. The leaders identified advanced manufacturing as the initiative's primary area of focus, with health care, tourism, and hospitality as secondary areas, and set out to raise the educational attainment or professional development of every individual in the ten counties by at least one level. Residents without a high school diploma would be supported in earning a high school equivalency certificate; those without a college degree would be offered the resources to obtain one; and those with a college degree would be encouraged to seek a master's degree or other professional development.

By 2015, various indicators showed that the EcO_{15} initiative was bearing fruit. Between 2008 and 2015, the region's high school graduation rate increased by 12 percent (from 82.2 to 92.2 percent), and enrollments in STEM subjects—science, technology, engineering, and math—increased by 33 percent (from 978 to 1,302). Similarly, between 2009 and 2014, postsecondary educational attainment rose by 10 percent (from 26.7 percent with postsecondary degrees to 29.4 percent). During roughly this same period, employment in the region grew by 5.8 percent (compared with 0.67 percent growth for the state), and average annual wages increased by 9.2 percent (compared with 11.4 percent for the state). The Columbus metropolitan area saw even stronger growth in employment and wages—up 13.7 percent and 15.5 percent, respectively.[16]

In light of these and other achievements, the EcO_{15} initiative's mandate was extended and its name changed to the EcO Network of Southeast Indiana. Under the leadership of a small guiding team and with support from the Lilly Endowment, Cummins, Duke Energy, and others, the EcO Network maintained its mission of creating economic opportunity and moving every resident of the region up at least one level in education or job attainment. The group also continued to focus on advanced manufacturing and health care—the region's largest and best-paying sources of employment—and to encourage students to develop themselves for jobs in these sectors through an expanded array of programs and activities. In 2017, the CEC and its EcO Network were among seventeen U.S. communities to receive the Lumina Foundation's Talent Hub designation for this work.

Cummins's efforts to grow its talent pool, improve local education, and make its surrounding communities more attractive through its involvement with the CEC, EcO, and other cross-sector collaborations appears to have paid off. When Cummins vice president Norbert Nusterer took over as president of the power systems business in 2016, he spoke enthusiastically to the local newspaper about the hedgehog line of engines and the Seymour plant: "It's not just the engine itself that's fantastic; what the Seymour plant has done to manufacture the engine is another total game changer."[17]

Cummins's revered former leader J. Irwin Miller would not have been surprised. In his era, Miller, who was named president of Cummins in 1947 and chairman in 1951, faced a challenge that was not unlike the one Linebarger faced in Seymour: how to make Columbus appealing to the kinds of executives needed to develop the company. Under Miller's leadership in the aftermath of World War II, Cummins management decided to invest heavily in research so that the company would cannibalize its own products rather than wait for competitors to do so. The company also decided to globalize to take part in the rebuilding of Europe and Asia. Cummins built its first overseas plant in Scotland in 1956 and another in India in 1962.

264 I A Call to Action

These decisions meant that the company needed to recruit executives with backgrounds in science, engineering, and international business. In 1950, Columbus was a typical nondescript U.S. city; it had a population of 18,370, a labor force of 7,910, and a median income of $2,676, only about four-fifths of the U.S. median family income of $3,300 at the time.[18] A third of incomes in Columbus were below $2,000.[19] Instead of moving the company to another location, likely to be more appealing to the workforce Cummins needed, Miller decided to invest in making Columbus that location. In 1954, when schools that had been hastily built for the children of returning veterans began to crumble, Cummins responded by offering to pay, through the newly established Cummins Engine Foundation, the architects' fees for the design of the new school if the architect was chosen from a list prepared by the foundation. The program was later expanded to other public buildings, eventually turning Columbus into a nationally recognized showcase for modern architecture. In 2012, the American Institute of Architects ranked Columbus as the sixth-most architecturally important city in the United States.[20]

Through this and countless other initiatives to better the community, Miller and his successors have demonstrated his belief that community health and company health go hand in hand. The philosophy has served Cummins and the Columbus region well. Between 1950 and 2010, Columbus saw population growth of 140 percent (compared with peer cities' 4 percent); labor force growth of 190 percent (peers 17 percent); poverty 11.6 percent (peers 16.3–24.9 percent); and growth in median income by 92 percent (peers 8–44 percent).[21]

In 2019, Cummins celebrated its hundredth anniversary after a year of record revenues and earnings and a record investment of $902 million in R&D the year before. That same year, Cummins ranked number 128 in the *Fortune* 500 list of the largest U.S. companies by revenues, up from 181 in 2009.[22]

Sustainability and Innovation at Nike

Since the late 2000s, Nike has invested in a series of innovations aimed at both reducing its environmental impact and improving the performance of its products and operations.[23] Consider, for instance, its investment in DyeCoo, a small Dutch startup that uses a water-less process for dyeing polyester. The technology has the potential to dramatically reduce the use of water and toxic emissions in apparel manufacturing while also producing a more vibrant and lasting color. Or take Nike's Flyknit, a knitting-inspired technology for making the uppers of performance running shoes virtually waste-free, compared with traditional cut-and-sew methods, and 20 percent lighter than the previously lightest running shoe. Another example is Flyleather, a leatherlike performance material made in part from recycled natural leather fiber through a process that uses less water, produces a lower carbon footprint and less waste, and is lighter and more durable than traditional leather.

The impetus for using social and environmental issues as catalysts for innovation grew out of a series of activities that Nike CEO Mark Parker and the company's sustainability team set in motion just before the financial crisis of 2008. But the approach's roots go back to the mid-1990s, when college students—an important customer segment—mounted a series of protests on college campuses across the United States, challenging labor conditions in factories making Nike products in Asia. The protesters sought to pressure Nike to change what they saw as inhumane practices in these factories and urged university athletic directors to cancel their contracts with Nike for collegiate sports apparel and equipment.

Initially, Nike's management reacted defensively, pointing out that these factories were not Nike-owned at all. Indeed, the facilities were not—they were contract factories to which Nike outsourced the production of its shoes. A core element of Nike's strategy from its 1964 founding by Phil Knight and track coach Bill Bowerman (when the company was known as Blue Ribbon Sports) was product innovation aimed at enhancing athletes' performance. Although the mass customer might not be a competitive athlete, the concept captured in Nike's trademarked swoosh logo was performance. The extraordinarily popular Air Jordan basketball shoe was emblematic. Michael Jordan might wear it because of its features, but millions bought it because of Michael Jordan. Once the shoe was designed, however, production was contracted out to a series of manufacturers across Asia on the basis of quality, price, and ability to meet Nike's demanding supply-chain schedules.

The protests, however, persisted, and Knight turned to Jill Ker Conway, a member of Nike's board and former president of Smith College, for advice. In 1980, Knight had taken the company public with two classes of stock and, through his holdings—all in A shares, which were not publicly traded and which elected the majority of the company's directors—retained effective control over the company. As Nike matured in the mid-1980s, Knight began replacing the family and friends who had constituted the original board with independent directors from a variety of backgrounds in industry, law, finance, academia, and athletics. Among them was Conway, recruited for her expertise in women's issues and her understanding of the student perspective. She was the board's first woman, first academic, and first Australian-born director.

As protests continued, Conway offered to visit some of Nike's contract factories in Southeast Asia on a trip to her native Australia. Thus began an extensive series of visits that eventually led to a major study of conditions in the factories conducted in collaboration with an NGO—one of Nike's first such collaborations—and to a change of direction by Knight. In a speech to the National Press Club in 1998, Knight acknowledged that the Nike name had become synonymous with "slave wages, forced overtime, and arbitrary abuse," and he vowed to do something about it. The company hired its first vice president of corporate responsibility (CR); set up a CR department; created a board-level CR committee, which Conway chaired; and began reporting on CR in its annual report to shareholders. By 2005, the CR department had about 150 members working in the areas of labor, environment, and community investment. The group focused much of its effort on monitoring and remediation, while the board committee similarly spent much of its time, in Conway's words, "putting out fires"—dealing with code violations; labor issues; and environmental, health, and safety problems.

With a shift in the company's leadership in 2006, however, the CR organization and the CR board committee's work evolved. In 2006 Parker succeeded Knight as Nike CEO. Knight stayed on as chairman, but Parker brought to the job a new sensibility and a new leadership team. Parker had started with Nike in the late 1970s at its Exeter, New Hampshire, R&D center and subsequently had held positions in design, research, engineering, marketing, and general management at all levels of the company. At heart, however, he was a designer with a record that included some of Nike's most successful design innovations over the years. He liked nothing better than spending time in the company's "innovation kitchen," where employees worked on secret new ideas.[24] Early in his tenure as CEO, he made clear that he saw it as his job to "make sure that we're innovating in every aspect of our business" and using the company's brand "to create positive change on a larger scale."[25] Before being named CEO, Parker had served as cohead of the Nike brand. In that role, he appointed Hannah Jones, then Nike's CR director for Europe, as vice president of CR for the Nike brand and executive liaison to the board's CR committee.

Jones shared Parker's excitement about the possibilities of innovation and recognized the limits of the department's focus on day-to-day operational compliance. She also thought that Nike's earlier troubles with labor protests reflected insufficient attention to the larger societal and political forces shaping the business environment. In her estimation, Nike's leaders had missed critical signals that could have alerted them to shifting ideas about corporate responsibility and labor standards. In an effort to spark a more forward-thinking outlook in her group and across the management team more broadly, she launched a series of initiatives and accelerated work already under way to integrate environmental considerations into shoe design. She also hired a specialist in scenario planning and trend analysis to help the team better understand the major trends sweeping the world and how they might affect Nike's business in the future.

The multiyear scenario-planning activities that ensued proved seminal in shaping the leadership team's thinking. Detailed models of macrotrends and their effects transformed vague worries about a remote future into concrete business impacts and gave executives from different parts of the organization a more holistic, longer-term view of the business. For example, models could project water shortages and their potential consequences for Nike's business and future growth through such channels as rising costs or labor unrest in water-stressed regions where many of Nike's contractors were located. The exercise had the effect of reducing what academics call the *psychological distance* between the executives and the future effects of the trends examined. Given Nike's culture of performance-focused innovation, it was only natural that executives began to reframe these problems as opportunities—which is precisely what happened.

In the wake of the global financial crisis, the management team radically restructured the Nike organization in an effort to get closer to the customer and to integrate what were by then being called *sustainability factors* into the business. The restructuring encompassed a wide range of changes to rewire the organization: changing the compensation system for sourcing executives, reorganizing and renaming the CR group to reflect the new thinking, and creating dual reporting lines to integrate sustainability and core business functions all the way up to the board CR committee. Eric Sprunk, then president for merchandising and product, joined Jones as coliaison to the committee.[26] As part of the new approach, the company created a sustainable business and innovation lab, bringing in venture-capital and private-equity expertise to help search for innovative technologies and partners, and establishing a sustainable-investment management committee to make investment decisions. Nike's then chief financial officer took on the role of sponsor to ensure that the lab's smaller-scale, early-stage projects would not get squeezed out of the process by Nike's public-company financial model.

The work of the board's CR committee also changed. Rather than focusing only on compliance and risk oversight, the committee began to spend time overseeing innovation, product development, new materials, and sustainability issues more generally. In Nike sports parlance, the committee shifted from just playing defense to playing both defense and offense. Compliance and risk oversight continued to be important, but these were now part of a broader mandate centered on systems optimization and sustainable performance. The committee found itself reviewing investments such as its minority stake in DyeCoo.

Of course, not all of these investments have worked out as anticipated. DyeCoo's waterless dyeing process, for instance, is still not widely used, mainly because of the cost. However, a low-cost, less water-intensive process known as low-liquor-ratio dyeing has in the meantime been widely adopted and uses less water than do traditional methods, though not eliminating water altogether. But Nike has continued to invest in sustainability-driven innovation. At the 2019 FIFA Women's World Cup, fourteen teams wore Nike-designed polyester uniforms made from recycled plastic. Nike's sustainability team today has a dual reporting relationship to the company's chief operating officer and to its president of advanced innovation.[27]

Nike has also continued to press forward on ever-more-demanding targets in areas such as reducing carbon emissions, water usage, and waste; increasing the use of environmentally preferred materials in its products; and improving the sustainability ratings of its contract factories. Through a top-down and bottom-up process comparable to its process for setting financial targets, the sustainability team coordinates working groups for each domain—such as carbon, waste, and water—to help formulate the overall targets and disaggregate them into subtargets for the various functions and business units across the organization.

Over time, industry collaborations have become an increasingly important part of Nike's sustainability efforts, especially for goals that the company cannot achieve on its own. Nike's work with the Zero Discharge of Hazardous Chemicals (ZDHC) program is a good example. In response to a challenge to the industry from Greenpeace in 2012, Nike set for itself the goal of eliminating toxic emissions from its supply chain by 2020. At the time, Nike had over nine hundred suppliers around the globe that were actively engaged in its long-standing Restricted Substance List (RSL) program, but there was limited information about which suppliers were emitting toxins into the air and water and what toxins were being emitted. As work progressed, it became clear that achieving the goal would require industrywide collaboration because many Nike suppliers were also suppliers to its competitors and because different players were taking different approaches to the issue. Nike and other fashion brands eventually came together with their suppliers and other groups to form ZDHC, creating a separate legal entity with its own governance structure to set guidelines, standardize testing methods, and provide a third-party platform for collaboration. Nike's current chief sustainability officer, Noel Kinder, sees these collaborations as crucial, noting that big challenges like global supply chains and climate change are beyond the scope of any one company.[28]

The push to integrate sustainability also continues to evolve internally at Nike. Today, sustainability experts are colocated with line and group functions. Kinder has a mix of direct and indirect reports as well as partners who sit in areas such as product creation, brand, operations and logistics, procurement, retail, and communications. Some of these colleagues and subordinates have a solid-line reporting relationship to their respective function and a dotted line to sustainability. Conversely, the vice president of sustainable innovation sits on the innovation team. According to Kinder, the colocation arrangements have had a multiplier effect and allowed the company to better harness the ideas and energies of employees across the organization.

In 2018, the company launched Nike Valiant Labs, its new in-house business model incubator, naming Jones as its head. Parker, who succeeded Knight as Nike's chairman in 2016, has continued to champion sustainability-driven innovation and is spearheading partnerships with various organizations to rethink footwear manufacturing, transform product creation, and develop new business models that continuously reuse and regenerate materials.[29]

As Nike has pursued its sustainability agenda, it has continued to deliver attractive returns to shareholders and to maintain its position as the world's largest sports apparel and footwear manufacturer.[30] Certainly, management has been somewhat protected from capital-market pressure by the company's dual-class share structure and the controlling stake held by Knight and his family. But it is hard to make the case that Nike's shareholders have suffered because of its commitment to sustainability. Since Parker's appointment as CEO in 2006, Nike's market capitalization has grown from $21.8 billion to over $150 billion, and its stock price has increased by more than 800 percent, compared with 266 percent for the S&P 500 Consumer Discretionary Index.[31] Although it is impossible to know how Nike would have fared in the absence of its investments in sustainability, the evidence suggests that sustainability-driven innovations have been an important contributor to the company's growth and profitability—even as they have helped mitigate harm to people and the environment.

Unilever's Sustainable-Living Plan

When Unilever CEO Paul Polman announced the Unilever Sustainable Living Plan (USLP) in November 2010, commentators took notice. The plan set ambitious goals, to be sure, but more than that, the nature of the goals was highly unusual for a publicly traded, multinational company at the time. Unilever planned not merely to double the size of its business, but to do so while decoupling the company's growth from its environmental footprint and increasing its social impact. In addition to defining a set of environmental goals, the plan outlined three broad societal goals to be achieved by 2020. One was helping a billion people have a healthier diet and better hygiene. A second was raising the incomes of more than half a million small-holder farmers and small-scale distributors by bringing them into Unilever's supply chain. A third was sourcing 100 percent of the company's agricultural inputs from suppliers that met recognized standards of sustainability.[32]

What's more, the plan's environmental goals—for reducing greenhouse gas emissions, water use, and waste—encompassed not only the company's own operations but also the entire life cycle of its products, from the sourcing of raw materials to how the products were used and ultimately disposed of by consumers. Unilever had calculated that consumer use accounted for more than two-thirds of greenhouse gas emissions and half the water used in its products' life cycle, so it was logical to address the whole value chain. Still, as the company acknowledged, the USLP was an unprecedented commitment. Each of the plan's overarching goals was broken out into specific action areas and targets, which totaled more than fifty measurable items.[33]

The plan seemed outlandish to some, and many were skeptical of both the company's ability to meet the goals and the financial benefits of doing so. It didn't help that Unilever had consistently failed to deliver on its promises in recent years.[34] Polman emphasized the novelty of the business model underlying the USLP, but from another angle, he also saw the plan as little more than common sense. "Continuing to increase our environmental impact as we grow our business is not viable. Companies need to take responsibility for the damage they are doing to the planet," he told the *Guardian* when announcing the plan.[35] Later, in an interview with *Harvard Business Review*, he elaborated on the plan's rationale, noting that climate-change effects had cost Unilever $200 million in 2011 and predicting a political crisis if something was not done about inequitable growth. "Total profits of the consumer goods industry will be wiped out in 30 years if no action is taken," he said.[36]

Polman had taken over as Unilever's CEO less than two years earlier, in January 2009, when the company was reeling from the global financial crisis and its stock price was down 35 percent year-over-year. The company's revenue had declined more than 20 percent during the eight years before Polman's appointment, and its stock price had essentially not moved for the previous decade. He recognized that the situation presented a unique opportunity to reshape the business and shake up what he saw as a culture that was too internally focused. Consequently, he acted quickly to reconstitute his top management team and shared the vision that would, over the course of a year, be translated into the specifics of the USLP. During that year, Polman replaced more than a third of Unilever's top one hundred managers.[37]

In his first meeting with analysts, Polman declined to give an earnings forecast, citing the exceptional economic uncertainty of the time and emphasizing the importance of focusing on creating long-term value.[38] The stock immediately lost 8 percent of its value, but Polman saw no other way out of the dilemma between catering to short-term shareholders and making the investments he believed would be needed to create sustainable value over the long term—investments in capital spending, R&D, training and development, branding, IT, and so on. Later, when announcing the USLP, he elaborated on the decision to forgo guidance and invited investors who believed in the business model to invest with the company. Others, he advised, should invest elsewhere.[39] To shareholders who backed his model, he promised to deliver consistent results from year to year even if the returns were not the highest possible every year.[40]

In many respects, Polman's vision meshed well with the company's culture. Unilever had long espoused a "doing well by doing good" philosophy going back to founding figure William Lever. In the late nineteenth century, Lever had built a business by making and selling household soap that he hoped would improve hygiene and reduce illness in the crowded industrial cities of northern England. The company had been at the forefront of the corporate social responsibility (CSR) movement in the 1990s, establishing a CSR group and issuing its first CSR report in 2000. Even before Polman's arrival, a Unilever sustainability team had conducted a comprehensive study to measure the environmental footprint of the company's entire product portfolio, and some company brands, such as Lipton tea and Lifebuoy soap, had taken on significant social and environmental commitments. For over a decade, Unilever had been the top-ranked food and beverage company in the Dow Jones Sustainability Index.[41]

Still, getting executives across the far-flung Unilever organization to buy in to the ambitious USLP presented a challenge. Polman assigned responsibility for developing and implementing the plan to company veteran Keith Weed and named him to a new role that Polman created on the Unilever leadership executive team. The chief marketing and communications officer had responsibility for marketing, communications, and sustainability, and a steering committee made up of category presidents and leaders of key functions was set up.[42] A system of reporting to the board's corporate responsibility committee was also put in place.

Under Weed's leadership, an intensive communications campaign was soon launched for both internal and external audiences, and the real work of implementing the USLP got under way. Putting the sustainable-living plan into practice was far from a mechanistic exercise. In many cases it meant learning, innovating, forming new relationships, and finding a way through uncharted territory—be it setting standards for what would be deemed sustainable, working more closely with suppliers to improve agricultural practices, finding substitutes for saturated fats that would be both healthier and effective in stabilizing food products in tropical climates, and so on. To be sure, there was also plenty of low-hanging fruit. Unilever had experienced a long period of growth with relatively sparse attention devoted to sustainability issues, so when executives turned to these matters, they found many comparatively easy-to-achieve efficiencies in energy, water use, and waste reduction in manufacturing—efficiencies that gave the plan early momentum.

Unilever soon learned that meeting the targets under its direct control was much easier than achieving those that depended on others—targets such as reducing water and greenhouse gas emissions associated with consumers' use of its products. Indeed, over the first three years of the plan, both the per-consumer greenhouse gas footprint and per-consumer water use increased rather than decreased. Unilever doubled down on understanding the contributing factors and finding ways to address them—for example, developing laundry detergents that allowed shorter wash cycles. But it became apparent that the company could not achieve the desired results on its own and would have to collaborate with other organizations to effect the broader changes needed for significant energy and water-use reductions. Unilever accordingly stepped up its involvement with scores of industry, nonprofit, and community groups, such as the Consumer Goods Forum, the World Business Council for Sustainable Development, Oxfam, UNICEF, and the Rain Forest Alliance.

In an effort to address lingering skepticism about the financial benefits of the USLP at a time when global growth was slowing in 2014, the steering committee called for an analysis of all of Unilever's products to determine their growth rates, profitability, and contribution to USLP goals, as well as the brands' association with sustainable living. The analysis identified eleven of Unilever's top brands as "sustainable-living brands"—those that combined a purpose linked to a social or environmental concern with products that contributed to at least one USLP goal. The analysis revealed that, together, the sustainable-living brands accounted for nearly half of the company's growth and were growing significantly faster than the rest of the business.[43] Many executives took the results as evidence that the sustainability plan was indeed enhancing consumer engagement and driving growth.

The findings, in turn, provided the basis for a more explicit effort to link the plan with the company's acquisition strategy. Between 2016 and 2019, Unilever acquired several small, fast-growing, purpose-led companies such as Seventh Generation in the United States, Pukka Herbs in the United Kingdom, and Mãe Terra in Brazil. These acquisitions not only reinforced the USLP and connected the company to millennial consumers seeking healthier, more sustainable products, but also served as a vehicle for learning and innovation within Unilever. The team members in Brazil, for example, saw Mãe Terra's short innovation cycles, dynamic decision making, commitment to purpose, and more personal approach to sales and marketing as sources of valuable learning that they sought to integrate into the larger organization. By late 2018, Unilever had identified twenty-six sustainable-living brands. The company's analysis revealed that in 2017, these brands grew 46 percent faster than the rest of the business and accounted for 70 percent of the company's revenue growth.[44]

Perhaps the most significant challenge to the USLP and to Polman's vision for Unilever came in the form of an unsolicited bid for the company from U.S. food giant Kraft Heinz in February 2017. Jointly controlled by Warren Buffett's holding company Berkshire Hathaway and Brazilian private-equity firm 3G Capital, Kraft Heinz was known for the cost discipline it brought to acquired companies through the use of zero-based budgeting. On making an acquisition, 3G Capital typically removed the company's executives, installed its own people, and set about to reduce costs, cut jobs, raise margins, and increase cash flow for the purpose of increasing earnings and funding further acquisitions. Kraft Heinz's business model could hardly have been more different from Polman's invest-and-grow, long-term-value model. And the two companies had adopted very different stances on environmental and social issues.[45] Although the Kraft Heinz approach has since fallen out of favor, it was cheered by investors at the time.

Unilever's stock price jumped 15 percent on the $143 billion cash-and-stock offer, but the board rejected it, citing "no merit, either financial or strategic, for Unilever's shareholders."[46] The bid was withdrawn, but investors continued to press for improved margins.[47] Two months later, Unilever announced a plan to "accelerate shareholder value creation," committing to improve advertising efficiencies, boost operating margins, increase cash generation, buy back shares, sell its low-growth margarine and spreads business, and consider a range of other structural changes to create value for shareholders, while also reaffirming its long-term model of sustainable value creation.[48] Some commentators saw the bid as evidence that the Unilever model could not survive, but reaction inside the company was more nuanced. Many executives took it as a reminder of the need for vigilance in controlling costs and staying close to the consumer but by no means a rejection of the USLP's basic premises.[49]

When Polman announced in November 2018 that he would be stepping down as Unilever's CEO at the end of the year after ten years at the helm, he was widely credited for his leadership in pioneering a new model of sustainable growth. The press release announcing his departure cited a record of consistent top- and bottom-line growth and a total shareholder return of 290 percent over the ten-year period, well above the median of 165 percent for the other eighteen consumer goods companies in its peer group over the same period.[50] Although the company was lagging on some USLP goals—notably, reductions in water use and greenhouse gas emissions associated with consumers' use of its products—many goals had already been achieved or were on track for achievement by 2020. And Unilever was rated first or second among its peers in leading rankings on sustainability, climate-change readiness, and access to nutrition.[51] Although the verdict on Polman's long-term performance hypothesis was still out in 2019, Unilever's new CEO, Alan Jope, vowed to maintain the company's focus on long-term sustainable growth and, over time, to make every brand in Unilever's portfolio a purpose-led brand.[52]

These cases provide further evidence that business leaders *can* take on the disruptors in ways that strengthen their organizations and advance their companies' commercial interests. Like the examples discussed earlier in the book, the companies highlighted in this chapter illustrate a range of possible approaches to doing so. By helping expand economic opportunity in Detroit and other troubled cities, JPMorgan Chase is strengthening its own prospects in those cities. By helping develop the workforce in Southeast Indiana and working to transform the region into a center of advanced manufacturing, Cummins is enhancing its own ability to compete in the global market for diesel engines. By investing in innovations that reduce the use of scarce resources and cut greenhouse gas emissions, Nike is developing new and improved products and services to support its brand and fuel its own sales. And by sourcing from small-hold farmers, reducing its environmental impact, and improving the nutritional value of its food products, Unilever is strengthening its supply chain and developing new products to drive its future growth.

Notably, each of these initiatives reflects the unique strategy of the company involved. Each is different and deeply aligned with the essential values, skills, and capabilities that arise from the company's own excellence in its core business. This alignment makes these efforts highly effective because they advance the company's strategy and draw on skills already available internally. At the same time, the initiatives can be profitable because they arise out of, and are deeply informed by, the company's own processes and needs.

Although these cases differ along many dimensions, they also share certain commonalities. In the next chapter, we will review some of the patterns running through these and other successful efforts we have observed. These patterns reveal practical lessons that may be useful to other companies in the early stages of developing their own approaches to addressing the forces fueling disruption.

Rebuilding Confidence
in Capitalism

I N THE FIRST edition of this book, we described a set of forces that, if left unchecked, could disrupt the global market system. We called on business leaders to help mitigate these forces by modifying their corporate strategies, investing in innovation, and collaborating to create new institutions. In the past decade, the forces of disruption have gathered strength, and the threat to market capitalism has intensified. The political landscape has shifted to the point that some U.S. contenders for political office are proud to call themselves socialists, and antiglobalism has become a refrain animating political debates across the globe.

As ardent proponents of free enterprise, we find these developments dismaying. To be sure, the problems generated by capitalism as it has been practiced in recent decades are real, as we have described. But the solution is to acknowledge and then fix the problems and improve the system—not to abandon it. Societies can and do strike the balance between individual liberty and centralized authority in different ways (see chapter 1), and all societies rely to some degree on collective effort. But a wholesale embrace of socialism is not likely to address the problems fueling today's discontent with capitalism, and an embrace of socialism will most assuredly create other problems. The settlers who arrived in the New World on the *Mayflower* in 1620 began their plantation at Plymouth Colony in the spirit of a commune, but they soon learned that allocating a plot of land to each family increased the community's production of corn.[1]

Market capitalism powered by private enterprise and appropriately regulated is the most effective system we know of, not only for generating wealth but also for doing so in a way that encourages initiative, resourcefulness, and creativity. One of the system's great virtues is its capacity to spur innovation and evolve organically as the needs of society change. For individuals, market capitalism offers wide berth for expression, entrepreneurship, and personal development. History has shown repeatedly that vesting control over a society's economy in a central authority charged with administering it for the collective good tends to sap individual initiative and breed corruption between the controlling authorities and those subject to their control. Lacking the dynamism spurred by individual initiative, distributed authority, dispersed knowledge, and free-flowing information, these systems tend to become rigid and unable to meet society's most basic needs as they evolve over time.

These are just a few reasons that market capitalism offers the best hope for continuing to improve living standards and human well-being across the world. At the same time, as we have argued, the market system can endure only as long as its foundations are strong, its benefits widely shared, its negative impacts contained, and its resistance to external threats high. Today, capitalism is confronting challenges on every one of these fronts. Every day brings news of political protests, environmental tragedies, resource shortages, corruption, cronyism, and deteriorating institutions around the globe. As recently as late 2019, the *New York Times* was reporting that the world was running out of aircraft and equipment to fight giant fires that are becoming a regular consequence of climate change, with increasingly long and intense fire seasons.[2]

In the past decade, the need for leadership from the private sector has grown more urgent. That's why we are once again calling on business leaders to step up to the problems threatening the global market system and to show that capitalism can sustain itself over time. Besides addressing the problems we have termed *disruptors*, leaders must also run their businesses in a way that provides satisfactory economic outcomes for ordinary people and not just the privileged few, that protects the natural environment and other public goods, and that upholds the institutions that make capitalism and its free markets possible. Call this approach inclusive capitalism, sustainable capitalism, enlightened capitalism, or simply common sense. A system that undermines its own foundations—be they material, social, political, natural, or institutional—will eventually collapse of its own accord or fall prey to hostile forces from without.

For business leaders who see the challenge as too big or as incompatible with their duty to create wealth for their shareholders, we point to the examples discussed in this book. These examples show thoughtful leaders reframing these large-scale problems as opportunities or drivers of innovation and devising approaches to addressing them in ways that ultimately strengthen their companies and make their businesses more sustainable. If readers take only one thing from this book, we hope it is this central point: that it is possible for business leaders to address the disruptors in ways that contribute to their companies' long-term growth and profitability and that respect the bounds of legitimate business activity.

Some strategies will fail, no doubt, and some will be more successful than others. But it can no longer be argued that engaging with these problems is inherently bad for business, incompatible with duties to shareholders, or outside the scope of legitimate business activity. What's needed now is a critical mass of business leaders to take the threats to market capitalism seriously and to adjust their companies' strategies and investment programs accordingly.

In chapter 10, we proposed a business-led effort to mobilize such a group and suggested the broad outlines of what its agenda might look like. Although business leaders themselves are in a better position than we are as academics to develop the outlines further, the effort we have in mind would call on each participating company to develop its own plans for addressing the disruptors, much as the Committee for Economic Development (CED) called on business leaders and companies across the United States to develop their own plans for hiring and employment at the end of World War II (see chapter 7). We envision a steering group to motivate the planning process, but like the CED effort, planning would be fundamentally a bottom-up undertaking. Each company, given its own distinctive capabilities and the needs of its business, would decide which problems to address and how.

The examples we have discussed illustrate the wide range of possibilities on both counts—which problems to address and how to translate them into business opportunities. Some companies, such as JPMorgan Chase and Cummins, have found opportunity in helping revitalize distressed communities and, in so doing, have created new customers and strengthened their workforce, respectively. Others, such as Nike and General Electric (GE), have used the mitigation of environmental problems to drive business-model and product innovation. Still others, such as Unilever and Generation Investment Management, have used a broad set of environmental, social, and economic issues to motivate new business models and new strategies for growth. In some instances, as Cummins did in Columbus, Indiana, and as JPMorgan Chase did in Detroit, the company began by tackling a fairly well-defined problem in a single location and then applied the model developed there to other locations. By contrast, Nike and Unilever both addressed a wider set of issues on a global scale from the start.

Despite the many differences among these examples, they also share some patterns and themes. In the next section, we review some of the most salient patterns we have observed in the hope that they will be useful to other companies as they take on the challenge of developing their own strategies to address the disruptors.

Lessons from the Field

As we have said, the most powerful lesson to be learned from the cases we have studied is that imaginative leaders aiming to build their enterprise for the long term have sought and found strategies that treat threats to the market system as opportunities to strengthen their business. Success in executing on these strategies, however, depends on many factors. Let us examine the most important ones.

Close Attention from Top Management

Top management, especially the CEO, needs to be engaged in developing and implementing the strategy over a significant period. The appointment of a highly competent leader with authority for the initiative is crucial as well, but that does not eliminate the need for CEO involvement. Jamie Dimon appointed Peter Scher to revamp JPMorgan Chase's philanthropic programs, including its efforts in Detroit. But Dimon stayed close to those efforts, receiving regular updates on Detroit from Scher and often taking part in reports to the mayor—sometimes in the living room of a renovated home in Detroit. Although Cummins took great care to avoid conveying the impression that Columbus was a company town, its top management played major roles in city and state affairs, and several Cummins managers and former managers served in leadership roles for the Columbus region's Community Education Coalition (CEC) and EcO Network. Paul Polman gave responsibility for Unilever's sustainable-living plan (USLP) to Keith Weed, a member of the company's executive leadership team, but Polman continued to be the plan's chief spokesperson and leading advocate.

These initiatives are, by definition, out of the ordinary and for that reason alone are unlikely to get the resources and support they need unless they have the visible and ongoing involvement of the CEO. A comment by a JPMorgan Chase executive working on the Detroit project is telling: "When the CEO says that Detroit is important to our firm, there was no question after that. We never had any issue getting support from all other parts of the bank."[3] Similarly, CEO Jeff Immelt's involvement with GE's ecomagination initiative helped counter both internal and external skepticism when it was being developed in 2004, long before climate change was recognized as a critical issue by the business and investment communities.

The CEO's involvement has to be carefully calibrated to avoid undermining the managers in charge of day-to-day operations, but the CEO cannot simply delegate these initiatives and leave them to others. Visible and ongoing commitment from the top is essential.

Strategic Issues for the Company

The list of disruptors laid out in this book is long and includes a multitude of issues that could, at least conceptually, be the focus of an initiative. What we observe, however, is that successful efforts reflect a careful matching of societal need with the organization's strengths and with its business. Successful companies typically devote significant time and resources to identifying and selecting opportunities to bring their capabilities to bear in a way that promises both societal and company benefits. In other words, successful initiatives do not typically appear fully worked out in a flash of insight or inspiration.

Nike, for instance, engaged in extensive scenario planning and analyses of activities across its entire value chain to determine that water scarcity should be a focal point for its efforts. Similarly, JPMorgan Chase's choice of four pillars for its philanthropic activities and its selection of Detroit as a testing ground reflected careful analysis of both the bank's strengths and the needs of the communities where it operated and whose prosperity was key to the bank's own future prospects. At GE, the management team spent nearly a year gathering information, learning about climate science, and analyzing its own capabilities before coming up with its ecomagination initiative. For Cummins, too, its needs as an industrial-equipment producer and its long history of educational engagement going back to the 1950s made the company's efforts to help improve education and support training in advanced manufacturing in Seymour a natural and strategic choice. For another company with a different set of capabilities, that decision would have made no sense at all. In all these cases, the CEO saw the initiative as drawing on existing core capabilities and as integral to the company's long-term strategy—not as a separate add-on CSR program.

In each instance, management also had a clear idea of how the initiative would benefit the company. As we described, Dimon insisted that JPMorgan Chase's work in Detroit was an investment in one of its markets. Cummins invested in Columbus so that it could enjoy the benefits of a supportive headquarters community. (Cummins's success has also made Columbus attractive to other leading manufacturers, including Toyota, which established its first manufacturing plant in the city in 1990 and today is its fourth-largest manufacturing employer.) Nike's investments in DyeCoo, Flyknit, and Flyleather were all aimed at improving the quality and performance of its products while also reducing their environmental impact. And Unilever's sustainable-living programs were the foundation of a strategy for growth. Each of these efforts was socially valuable, but none of them was a charity.

Organizational Design

All these initiatives require some form of organizational change or innovation, whether it is a change in behavior or information flows; the creation of new internal structures and systems; or the creation of entirely new organizations. The maxim that structure should follow strategy is as true for these initiatives as it is for any other management undertaking.

Sometimes, as the founders of Generation Investment Management realized, the structure has to be designed and built from the ground up. Traditional ways of organizing and running an asset management firm would not have worked for the new firm's then-novel investment premise that companies able to navigate the changing macroenvironment, including climate change, would outperform for investors over the long term. Generation Investment Management needed a structure to integrate sustainability research and traditional asset management expertise into a seamless investment process. The company's founding group spent an entire year working to develop such a structure and process before taking any money from third parties.

Similarly, at Nike, the shift from a corporate responsibility focus to a sustainability focus required a change in the organization's structure and reporting relationships all the way up to the board of directors. When the company created its internal sustainable business and innovation lab, the chief financial officer took steps to ensure that its small-scale experimental projects did not get quashed by the large-company financial processes and criteria traditionally used to assess new projects.

More generally, in the cases we've studied, company leaders have paid close attention to the organizational implications of their chosen strategy—whether it is the Detroit initiative at JPMorgan Chase, the sustainable-living plan at Unilever, the community engagement effort at Cummins, the rural communications strategy at China Mobile, the delivery of antiretroviral drugs to the poor at Cipla, or others. For these strategies to succeed, the entire organization has to be engaged and the organizational structure needs to be aligned with the strategy.

Collaboration with Other Organizations

A recurring theme in these efforts is the importance of collaboration—both within and across industries and within and across the private, public, and nonprofit sectors. Because the problems at issue are typically multidimensional, companies often find themselves in need of expertise, resources, or other types of support beyond what is available in-house.

Early in its sustainability journey, for instance, Nike realized that it would need help from academic researchers to carry out a credible study of conditions in its contract factories in Asia. That experience led to many other collaborations, including, most recently, Nike's involvement with Zero Discharge of Hazardous Chemicals (ZDHC), a cross-sector collaboration involving other major brands and industry associations, as part of its effort to eliminate toxic emissions from its supply chain. Similarly, when Unilever ran into trouble meeting its targets for reducing water use and greenhouse gas emissions from consumers' use of its products, company executives realized that Unilever would need to collaborate with other organizations to achieve its goals. The company accordingly stepped up its work with dozens of industry, nonprofit, and community groups around the world.

The case of Cipla, discussed in chapter 6, is worth examining in this regard. The company's success in bringing affordable antiretroviral drugs to millions of people in low- and middle-income countries would not have been possible without extensive collaboration with multiple national governments and numerous nonprofits, foundations, and aid organizations, as well as with the World Health Organization.

Cross-sector collaboration is no less important for local challenges. As seen in the JPMorgan Chase and Cummins examples, geographically focused projects such as helping revitalize Detroit and strengthening southeastern Indiana's education system also required collaboration with a wide range of stakeholders from both private and public sectors. The skills needed for effective cross-sector engagement do not always come naturally to business executives, who tend to be impatient with what they perceive as inefficient decision making in the public sector. But the successful efforts we have observed have been led by individuals who have a deep understanding of, and respect for, the roles played by different sectors.

These executives are also adept at building relationships and working with civic and other community leaders whose outlook may be very different from their own. As described in chapter 10, the precursor to the Community Education Coalition fell apart because the educators felt that some businesspeople were trying to dictate the proceedings and were not listening to what the educators had to say. By contrast, the leaders of the CEC were careful to establish from the beginning that the coalition was a forum for open, inclusive, fact-based discussion among all the coalition's stakeholders. Notably, the processes developed through the CEC's EcO Network have been formalized into a stakeholder engagement process that is being used by CivicLab, an EcO Network spinoff dedicated to advancing civic collaboration.

An Understanding of Political Legitimacy

These examples of effective collaboration point to another, closely related feature of the successful efforts we have studied. They show business leaders who are sensitive to the issues of political legitimacy that can arise whenever companies involve themselves in matters of public concern.

As discussed in earlier chapters, the disruptors involve what economists call *public goods*—goods such as economic opportunity, community well-being, and a healthy environment—that are socially valuable but whose enjoyment cannot be easily restricted only to those who are willing to pay for them. Addressing problems of this type is generally considered the responsibility of governments and duly elected officials authorized to act on behalf of the public, and not the responsibility of private-sector companies, whose interests, abilities, and natural constituencies may lie elsewhere. Companies engaging with these problems can thus find themselves the target of criticism, sometimes unwittingly, for venturing into a domain over which they have neither formal political authority nor accountability to the public.

In the successful cases we have studied, however, the executives in charge have been aware of this potential minefield and have taken care not to overstep their legitimate role. A good illustration is JPMorgan Chase's efforts in Detroit. Although the initiative involved working closely with the city's elected mayor and many other officials, Dimon and Scher were clear from the outset that it was not for the bank to determine Detroit's priorities. Scher set the tone and agenda with his instructions to the executives visiting Detroit during the bank's initial six months of study: they were there to listen to the city's leaders talk about what Detroit needed and to determine how JPMorgan Chase could help. In light of what they had heard, the bankers proposed a list of projects and funding opportunities for approval by the mayor's office, and in implementing those that were approved, the executives took their lead from the mayor and his team. When the JPMorgan Chase team members later sat down to study why the Detroit initiative succeeded, they identified the presence of a highly competent mayor with the political legitimacy to set priorities and the existence of a widely agreed-on plan for the city as two of the most important influences. (A third factor was having a coalition among the city's leaders already in place as a consequence of the planning process and the creation of the Grand Bargain; see chapter 10.) The first two factors, in effect, shielded the bank from charges that it was overstepping its authority or usurping the government's role and allowed JPMorgan Chase to focus on how it could help the city's leaders achieve their objectives for Detroit.

Similarly, the leaders of South African businesses that joined forces in the late 1980s to analyze the future of the country's economy recognized that they could help and support F. W. de Klerk, the head of the dominant Nationalist Party and state president (see chapter 7). They could not, however, take the lead in setting the nation's priorities or dismantling apartheid, given their lack of political authority.

The Cummins case offers another example of leading from behind. Although many Cummins executives or former executives were involved with the CEC, they took care not to dominate, recognizing that it was not their role to set the organization's agenda. They understood that the CEC's success depended on building trust among its participants and achieving consensus around its priorities if the coalition was to speak with a common voice to the larger community.

Ability to Learn by Doing

By definition, efforts to address the threats to market capitalism are risky for the companies that undertake them. Success is by no means guaranteed. Even though companies have resources and capabilities that they can bring to bear, the problems presented typically go beyond businesses' traditional activities and domains of expertise, and the results can take years to manifest themselves. One way for companies to manage this risk is to stage their efforts in a way that allows them to learn and adjust their goals, methods, and commitments as they go. Indeed, learning by doing is a recurring characteristic of all the efforts we've observed.

Consider how the companies discussed in chapter 10 learned as they went. The CEC's use of small pilot tests and, in some instances, successive rounds of pilots, to work out and refine the various programs it introduced to improve the education system in Columbus is one obvious example. Similarly, in Detroit, JPMorgan Chase used trial and error to learn what worked and what didn't. Through this process, the bank developed what is now its model for inclusive prosperity—a model that it created with the Detroit initiative and that is now being used as a blueprint for similar initiatives in other cities.

At both Nike and Unilever, leaders of their respective sustainability initiatives concluded that they needed to go beyond traditional large-company approaches to innovation by opening up space for small-scale experimentation to learn and progress on their larger-scale goals. Nike set up its sustainable business and innovation lab, hired venture-capital and private-equity expertise, and began scanning the world for potential investments in promising technologies to advance its innovation agenda. Unilever developed a plan to acquire a series of small, fast-growing companies committed to defined social purposes as a way to learn and experiment, with the aim of eventually scaling up and integrating successful practices as part of its USLP.

The same pattern can also be seen in the companies examined in chapter 6. As discussed, China Mobile staged an innovation competition among its thirty-one provincial subsidiaries to discover ways to extend its wireless communications network across the country's vast territory to an entirely new customer segment. Through a series of pilot projects, the company also tested different approaches to marketing and distribution, and experimented with using independent sales agents in rural areas. We have already discussed the yearlong project set up at Generation Investment Management that enabled sustainability researchers and traditional asset managers to educate one another about their analytic techniques. The result was a collaboration that created a new investment process to support the company's investment thesis.

Perhaps it is not surprising that the successful efforts we observed all shared a propensity to experiment and learn by doing, given that the problems are large, complex, and outside the traditional scope of most companies' activities. Nonetheless, the prevalence of trial and error and of experimentation is worth noting. Learning by doing and staged commitments may be second nature for entrepreneurs, but are less familiar to large-company executives. These leaders are accustomed to being experts in their domain and to basing big bets on reliable data and extensive experience (a source of comfort they will find unavailable in this new form of initiative). For this reason, leaders of large firms may find it useful to know how their large-company peers have dealt with the uncertainty and risk inherent in these efforts.

Varied Approaches to Funding

As noted earlier, many executives with whom we've spoken cite capital market pressures and shareholder demands for short-term earnings as barriers to investing in solutions to these larger, systemic challenges. These executives point out that such efforts are risky and the results too uncertain and too far off to satisfy shareholders who are seeking shorter-term and more-predictable returns. The stock market's reaction to Polman's announcement of the USLP (an 8 percent drop) and to Kraft Heinz's unsolicited bid for the company (a 15 percent jump) suggests that there is validity to these concerns. We have written elsewhere about the dilemma that boards and executives face when pressed by shareholder activists to take actions to increase the near-term share price at the expense of future prospects.[4]

Despite the problem of short-termism in the capital markets, or perhaps because of it, the successful efforts we've seen have adopted various approaches to funding. Some, like Nike's and Unilever's investments in sustainability, have been funded principally through the company's normal resource allocation and budgeting processes. Unlike Unilever, Nike has been buffered somewhat from capital market pressures by its dual-class share structure and the presence of controlling shareholder Phil Knight on its board. With Knight's support for its strategy, Nike was in no danger of a takeover, although the company is no less answerable to its public shareholders than is Unilever or any other company we have discussed. Nor is Nike immune from the financial pressures coming from its customer, supplier, and labor markets.

Other efforts we've examined have been funded through a mixed model of business and philanthropic capital, combined sometimes with grants from governments, foundations, and other sources as well. Consider JPMorgan Chase's activities in Detroit. As noted earlier, Dimon insisted that the bank's involvement in Detroit was "an investment, not charity."[5] Presumably, he meant that the bank was helping revitalize the city to promote the bank's future growth there—not just to benefit the residents of Detroit. Indeed, that is the crux of the case we have made throughout this book. Nonetheless, when it came to funding its activities in Detroit, the bank put up both business and philanthropic capital and then used those funds to leverage additional support from government programs, foundations, and other organizations.

As described earlier, JPMorgan Chase made a number of direct grants to nonprofits for specific projects, but a significant portion of the capital dedicated to Detroit went into commercial lending to federally certified community development financial institutions (CDFIs) that in turn offered loans to homeowners and small businesses. By lending through the CDFIs, the bank could support projects that did not meet regulatory criteria for standard bank loans, thus filling the gap between what people needed and what conventional lending could provide at a time when property values were distressed. As the loans were repaid, the funds were recycled into other projects. JPMorgan Chase also provided expertise and technical assistance through its Detroit Service Corps.

Cummins similarly used a mixed model, funding some of its community-building activities through its foundation and some through the company's operating budget. Like JPMorgan Chase, Cummins also provided in-kind technical assistance of various types and actively sought to leverage funds from other sources, for example, from foundations such as the Lilly Endowment and through taxpayer support or state funding, for programs that it had piloted and sought to roll out more broadly.

Communication with Investors

As mentioned, executives with whom we've spoken frequently attribute their reluctance to embrace strategies that could help mitigate the disruptors to investor pressure for short-term earnings. Some of the negative sentiment expressed by investors about these efforts probably has more to do with management's failure to communicate their economic benefits than it has to do with differing time horizons. As an increasing number of institutional investors recognize the dangers posed by the disruptors, companies should find it easier to garner shareholder support for their efforts to address these dangers. Indeed, the past few years have seen increasing calls from institutional investors for companies to define their purpose in society, be more transparent about their strategies, consider their environmental and social impacts, and focus more on the long term.

Even if these calls have not yet filtered down to the investment firms' portfolio managers, who continue to be paid for short-term results as measured by standard stock price indices, the shift in rhetoric over the past few years is noteworthy. The increasing number of funds that use social and environmental criteria in their investing decisions suggests that shareholder support for such engagement may be growing, at least among some shareholders. As noted earlier, it was one of JPMorgan Chase's institutional shareholders—the nation's largest public employees' union pension fund—that drew the bank's attention to possibilities in Detroit.

A Defined Governance Structure

The successful efforts we have studied are certainly not casual undertakings and should not be confused with vague commitments to making the world a better place. These are significant investments of corporate time, talent, energy, and resources aimed at addressing serious problems, with appropriate processes and structures put in place to provide direction and oversight. To be sure, the governance processes for these efforts are tailored to the scope and size of the initiative, but they often go all the way to the company's board of directors.

At Nike, for instance, the company's sustainability efforts are overseen by the board's corporate responsibility and sustainability committee, which uses metrics and goals developed through an organization-wide process that involves both top-down and bottom-up elements. In the early days of Nike's efforts, even small investments, such as the one in DyeCoo, were reviewed by the committee after the investment had been approved by management's sustainable-investment group. Similarly, the Unilever board's corporate responsibility committee was charged with overseeing progress on the USLP, and the company publishes a yearly report tracking key metrics for each of the plan's goals.

The same governance discipline can also be seen in other examples. When JPMorgan Chase launched its Detroit initiative, Scher put in place a quarterly review process and tied the metrics for measuring progress to the four pillars of the bank's new approach to philanthropy. Scher met regularly with Dimon and reported quarterly on the initiative to the board's public responsibility committee.

At Cummins, responsibility for community relations rests with all managers, and the company's community-involvement activities are overseen by top management and a designated vice president for community relations. The Cummins team recognized that getting the governance structure right would be crucial to the success of the CEC. As noted earlier, when business and community leaders came together with city officials and educators to form the CEC, they created a board that included members of each stakeholder group and elected Cummins's vice president of community relations as the chair. The CEC's EcO Network has adopted a federation model of governance guided by a small team whose members represent the main groups within the network. The team is responsible for ensuring that the activities of the groups are aligned with one another and with the overarching goals of the collaboration.

As shareholders become more interested in companies' environmental and social initiatives, and as these initiatives play a more prominent role in strategy, transparent governance and board oversight are likely to become even more important. Like Immelt, who was deeply involved with GE's ecomagination initiative when it was under development, business leaders will want to engage their board early on so that the company's directors understand both the financial and social aspects of the strategy and how it will benefit the company.

Personal Conviction

The importance of personal conviction cannot be overstated. The successful efforts we've studied have been launched and led by individuals with high intrinsic motivation. They believe sincerely that these efforts are good for society and their company and will be duly rewarded in the fullness of time. Notably, these leaders are not acting because a large incentive payment is being dangled in front of them.

Consider some of the leaders we have discussed. J. Irwin Miller believed that Cummins could not be a great international company if Columbus was not a great host community. Jamie Dimon saw that JPMorgan Chase could not build on its leading market share in Detroit if the city did not recover. Mark Parker believed that Nike needed a new business model for a world that was becoming more and more resource constrained. Paul Polman was convinced that Unilever and, indeed, the entire consumer goods industry were at risk if companies did not start taking responsibility for the damage they were doing to the planet. Yusuf Hamied, chairman of Cipla, saw the threat posed by HIV/AIDS as devastating to low- and middle-income countries and believed that the price of antiretroviral drugs had to be brought down. Jeff Immelt was convinced that climate change was a "technical fact" and that GE could prosper by helping its customers improve their environmental performance. And so on. In the absence of these leaders' personal convictions, it is unlikely that any of the initiatives described here would have been undertaken, let alone carried out with the commitment and discipline required for success.

Signs of a Changing Outlook

The examples we have gathered in this book illustrate that companies can help mitigate the problems fueling the forces of disruption without sacrificing their business objectives. However, significant progress in alleviating the disruptors and showing that capitalism can function in a self-sustaining way that reinforces its own foundations will require many more business leaders to break out of the business-as-usual mold. Leaders must actively engage with these problems by developing strategies to address them and putting resources behind those strategies. While the level of what we would regard as serious engagement has been modest to date, there is evidence that the momentum for change is building.

One sign is the recent proliferation of initiatives and think tanks focused on better alignment between how the economy functions and the needs of society. Their names suggest their concerns: the Coalition for Inclusive Capitalism, Focusing Capital on the Long Term (FCLTGlobal), the World Economic Forum's Climate Governance Initiative, to mention just a few recent examples. Another sign is the growth in corporate reporting and disclosure frameworks that seek to capture social and environmental aspects of companies' performance. Although a few of these, such as the Global Reporting Initiative, predate the first edition of this book, others—such as the Sustainability Accounting Standards Board, the International Integrated Reporting Council, and the Task Force on Climate-Related Financial Disclosures—have emerged in the last decade.

This same period has also seen striking growth in the amount of capital being managed under some type of environmental or social mandate. According to the Global Sustainable Investment Alliance, the total assets invested or managed using environmental, social, and governance (ESG) criteria in five major markets grew from $22.9 trillion in 2016 to $30.6 trillion at the beginning of 2018. In these five markets, the compound annual growth rate for the 2014–2018 period ranged from respectable to remarkable: Europe 6 percent, the United States 16 percent, Canada 21 percent, Australia and New Zealand 50 percent, and Japan 308 percent.[6] The number of asset owners and managers signing onto the UN's Principles for Responsible Investment has also grown—from 185 in 2007 to 2,300 in 2019.[7]

The striking growth of sustainable investing in Japan partly reflects decisions by the country's Government Pension Investment Fund to sign the Principles for Responsible Investment in 2015 and, subsequently, to incorporate ESG into its investment programs. With about $1.5 trillion in invested assets (nearly five times those of the California Public Employees' Retirement System), the Japanese fund is the world's largest pension fund. It regards itself as both a "universal owner" (a pool of capital so large that it has to be invested in the market as a whole) and a "super long-term investor" (with a hundred-year time horizon).[8]

Investor engagement on climate change, in particular, also appears to be accelerating with the formation of initiatives like Climate Action 100+, launched in 2017 to press the world's largest corporate greenhouse gas emitters to curb their emissions and strengthen their climate-related financial disclosures. As of 2019, the group included some 370 institutional investors, with more than $35 trillion in assets under management.[9]

In parallel with these developments, corporate governance codes and guidelines in key jurisdictions have begun to incorporate social and environmental concerns and to call on boards to take a broader view of their responsibilities. In 2018, for example, the United Kingdom's Financial Reporting Council amended the UK Corporate Governance Code to give boards of directors responsibility for establishing their company's purpose, in response to a series of reports on the importance of purpose to corporate success.[10] In 2019, France enacted a new law providing for companies to write their raison d'être into their articles of association and requiring them to consider the social and environmental effects of their activities.[11] In the United States, leading institutional investors have been calling on boards to engage with shareholders about their long-term strategies and purpose in society. BlackRock CEO Larry Fink's annual letter to CEOs in 2019 underscored the need for business leadership in addressing society's pressing problems. He urged companies to "demonstrate their commitment to the countries, regions, and communities where they operate, particularly on issues central to the world's future prosperity."[12] In his 2020 letter, Fink asked BlackRock's investee companies to disclose their climate-related financial risks and to report on other sustainability issues.[13] He also announced that BlackRock would be "increasingly disposed to vote against directors" for companies that were not making progress on disclosures, plans, and practices related to sustainability.

Another sign is the growing corporate support for the UN's sustainable-development goals. Adopted by UN member states in 2015, the seventeen goals are part the UN's fifteen-year plan to end poverty, protect the environment, and improve lives around the world. At a gathering convened by UN secretary-general António Guterres in the fall of 2019, the CEOs of thirty of the world's largest companies and financial firms pledged to help with funding for these goals. Members of the new group, the Global Investors for Sustainable Development Alliance, also committed to scaling up and speeding up their companies' efforts to embrace the sustainable-development goals.[14]

Perhaps the most surprising development has been the new statement on corporate purpose issued by the Business Roundtable, a U.S. association of CEOs, in August 2019.[15]

Signed by 181 CEOs of leading U.S. companies, including Cummins and JPMorgan Chase, the statement reversed the association's previous view, articulated in a 1997 publication, that the corporation's principal purpose is to generate economic returns for shareholders. The new statement asserted its signers' commitment to all stakeholders: customers, employees, suppliers, communities, and shareholders. Anyone familiar with the history of Business Roundtable statements will recognize that the new declaration is similar to the group's 1981 statement in espousing respect for the claims of multiple stakeholders. Nonetheless, the organization has said that its new statement "outlines a modern standard for corporate responsibility" and is a more accurate reflection of its signers' "commitment to a free market economy that serves all Americans.'"

Within a few months of the Business Roundtable's statement, the World Economic Forum issued a new Davos Manifesto calling for stakeholder capitalism as the best response to today's social and environmental challenges and harking back to the forum's 1973 code of ethics and manifesto. The earlier document spoke to the purpose of management, which it defined as serving "clients, shareholders, workers and employees, as well as societies."[16] The new statement focuses on the purpose of a company, which it defines as "to engage all its stakeholders in shared and sustained value creation."[17] The forum's list of stakeholders is similar to the Business Roundtable's and includes employees, customers, suppliers, local communities, and society at large, as well as shareholders. The new manifesto was on the agenda for the World Economic Forum's 2020 annual meeting.

These and other developments in the last decade or so indicate a growing recognition that business leaders cannot sit on the sidelines as the material, social, political, and legal foundations of the global market system continue to crumble. At the same time, the heated controversy that ensued after the Business Roundtable released its new statement suggests that these ideas are far from universally embraced. And, to our knowledge, the statement has not led to any significant new initiatives or investments by its signers or the companies they lead. So it is hard to say whether the statement will have any practical effect. It is also unclear whether any of the other coalitions, pledges, think-tank recommendations, reporting frameworks, and guidelines that suggest changing attitudes will translate into the more robust form of capitalism that we are calling for.

Conclusion

What is clear is that the threats to the market system that business leaders identified in our research and that we cataloged in the first edition of this book will not fix themselves. As discussed in chapter 9, continuing to leave them unaddressed is a dangerous game. The risk is not just to the abstraction we call the economy or even to the companies that drive it, but to the well-being of billions of human beings around the world who could benefit from the global market system if it were operated more along the lines we are suggesting. The longer this pattern of deterioration is allowed to continue, the more difficult it will be for capitalism to recover from a self-reinforcing downward spiral and the harder it will be to dislodge the antimarket, anticapitalist, and antiglobalization narratives that have gained currency in the past few years. The problems fueling these narratives will only worsen, and the narratives themselves will become more entrenched.

The time has come for business leaders to turn from pronouncements to the demanding work of crafting new strategies to mitigate the disruptors and mobilizing the resources needed to support those strategies. In closing, with an even greater sense of urgency, we renew our earlier plea for business leaders and companies to step up to the challenge of our times. Leaders must demonstrate through their actions that capitalism can deliver broad-based prosperity in a self-sustaining manner—that is, in a way that upholds and reinforces its own economic, social, political, legal, and natural foundations.

We have offered some suggestions on how companies can address the disruptors in ways that make sound business sense. As we have emphasized, business leaders are in a far better position than we are as academics to devise initiatives that will work for their organizations. A coordinated effort by business leaders from companies across the world could have a meaningful impact both on the problems at hand and on the public's attitudes toward capitalism.

What we propose is far from easy. It involves not only putting out the proverbial fire in the engine while flying the plane, but also rewiring the plane's operating system while in flight. But we see no other way to rebuild confidence in capitalism and to ensure its future.

Appendix

Participants in Regional Business Leader Forums

In most cases, participants' titles and affiliations are shown as of the forum dates in 2007–2008; prior affiliations are provided when relevant.

Asia Regional Forum

Dr. Victor K. Fung
Group Chairman
Li & Fung
Honorary Chairman
International Chamber of
    Commerce

Raymond Kwok Ping Luen
*Vice Chairman and
    Managing Director*
Sun Hung Kai Properties

David Murray AO
Chairman
Future Fund, Australia
Former CEO
Commonwealth Bank of
    Australia, 1992–2005

Dato Timothy Ong
Chairman
Asia Inc Forum

Patrick T. Siewert
Managing Director
The Carlyle Group
*Former Group President,
    Asia*
The Coca-Cola Company

Sukanto Tanoto
*Founder, Chairman,
    and CEO*
RGM International
    (now RGE)

Eric Tong-Sheng Wu
Chairman
Shinkong Synthetic
    Fibers Corporation

Jaime A. Zobel de Ayala
Chairman and CEO
Ayala Corporation

Michael Shih-ta Chen
Executive Director
Harvard Business School,
    Asia Pacific Research
    Center

Europe Regional Forum

Bertrand P. Collomb
Director and Honorary
  Chairman
Lafarge

Frank E. Dangeard
CEO
Thomson S.A. (now
  Technicolor)

John Elkann
Chairman
Fiat

Oscar Fanjul
Vice-Chairman
Lafarge and Omega
  Capital
Former Chairman and
  CEO
Repsol

Maurice Lévy
Chairman and CEO
Publicis Group S.A.

Jean Peyrelevade
Chairman
Leonardo & Co., Gruppo
  Banca Leonardo
  (Milano)

Geoffroy Roux de Bézieux
Chairman and CEO
Croissance Plus

Sir David Scholey
Senior Advisor
UBS Investment Bank
Former Executive
  Chairman
S.G. Warburg Group plc

Vincent Dessain
Executive Director
Harvard Business School,
  Europe Research
  Center

Latin America Regional Forum

Carlos F. Cáceres
President
Instituto Libertad y
  Desarrollo, Chile

Jonathan Coles
President, Latin America
The AES Corporation

Ana Maria Diniz
President
Sykue Byoenergia

Jaime Gilinski
Chairman
Gilinski Group

Claudio Haddad
President
Insper Instituto de
  Ensino e Pesquisa

André Roberto Jakurski
Executive Director and
  Founding Partner
JPG Asset Management

Jorge Paulo Lemann
President
Fundação Lemann

Gustavo Roosen
Chairman
Envases Venezolanos S.A.

Manuel Sacerdote
Director
Sapresa

Woods W. Staton
President and CEO
Arcos Dorados, S.A.

Gustavo Herrero
Executive Director
Harvard Business
  School, Latin America
  Research Center

U.S. Regional Forum

Nancy Barry
President
Enterprise Solutions to
Poverty

Hon. Elaine Lan Chao
Secretary of Labor
U.S. Department of
Labor

John Clarkeson
Chairman Emeritus
The Boston Consulting
Group

Ian M. Cumming
Chairman
Leucadia National
Corporation

James Dimon
Chairman and CEO
JPMorgan Chase & Co.

Hon. William H. Donaldson
27th Chairman
U.S. Securities and
Exchange Commission

David N. Farr
Chairman and CEO
Emerson

Paul J. Fribourg
Chairman and CEO
Continental Grain
Company

William W. George
*Professor of Management
Practice*
Harvard Business School
*Former Chairman and
CEO*
Medtronic

Edmund A. Hajim
President
Diker Management, LLC

Jeffrey R. Immelt
Chairman and CEO
General Electric

Hamilton "Tony" E. James
President and COO
The Blackstone Group

Karen Gordon Mills
*Managing Director and
Cofounder*
Solera Capital

Peter M. Nicholas
*Cofounder, Director, and
Chairman of the Board*
Boston Scientific

Henry B. Schacht
*Managing Director and
Senior Advisor*
Warburg Pincus
*Former Chairman and
CEO*
Cummins Engine
Company

C. Dixon Spangler Jr.
President Emeritus
University of North
Carolina
Chairman
Golden Eagle Industries

James S. Tisch
President and CEO
Loews Corporation

Notes

Preface to the Expanded Edition

1. See, for example, various reports by the Intergovernmental Panel on Climate Change (IPCC), especially "Global Warming of 1.5° C," 2018, www.ipcc.ch/sr15. See also Global Carbon Project, "Global Carbon Atlas" (online platform for visualizing the level and impact of carbon emissions), updated to 2019, www.globalcarbonatlas.org/en/content/welcome-carbon-atlas.

2. See, for example, the following four reports that assess the risk to financial system stability today as moderate and that identify current specific risk factors: Financial Stability Oversight Council, *2018 Annual Report* (Washington, DC: Financial Stability Oversight Council, June 20, 2019), https://home.treasury.gov/system/files/261/FSOC2018AnnualReport.pdf; Board of Governors of the Federal Reserve System, *Financial Stability Report* (Washington, DC: Federal Reserve Board, May 2019), www.federalreserve.gov/publications/files/financial-stability-report-201905.pdf; Office of Financial Research, *Annual Report to Congress, 2018*, www.financialresearch.gov/annual-reports/files/office-of-financial-research-annual-report-2018.pdf; and International Monetary Fund, *Global Financial Stability Report: Vulnerabilities in a Maturing Credit Cycle* (Washington, DC: International Monetary Fund Publication Services, April 2019), www.elibrary.imf.org/doc/IMF082/25728-9781498302104/25728-9781498302104/Other_formats/Source_PDF/25728-9781498302173.pdf.

3. Facebook, Inc., September 30, 2019, Form 10-Q filing with the U.S. Securities and Exchange Commission, filed October 30, 2019, www.sec.gov/ix?doc=/Archives/edgar/data/1326801/000132680119000069/fb-09302019x10q.htm.

4. Elizabeth Dwoskin and Karla Adam, "More Than 150 Countries Affected by Massive Cyberattack, Europol Says," *Washington Post*, May 14, 2017, www.washingtonpost.com/business/economy/more-than-150-countries-affected-by-massive-cyberattack-europol-says/2017/05/14/5091465e-3899-11e7-9e48-c4f199710b69_story.html.

5. Verizon, "2019 Verizon Data Breach Investigations Report," https://enterprise.verizon.com/resources/reports/dbir/2019/summary-of-findings, 7.

6. For the U.S. intelligence community's assessment of Russia's efforts to undermine the 2016 U.S. presidential election, see Office of the Director of National Intelligence, Intelligence Community Assessment, "Assessing Russian Activities and Intentions in Recent US Elections," ICA 2017-01D, January 6, 2017, www.dni.gov/files/documents/ICA_2017_01.pdf.

7. Carole Cadwalladr, "Fresh Cambridge Analytica Leak 'Shows Global Manipulation Is Out of Control,'" *Guardian*, January 4, 2020, www.theguardian.com/uk-news/2020/jan/04/cambridge-analytica-data-leak-global-election-manipulation.

8. Financial Stability Oversight Council, *2018 Annual Report*, 7, 107.

9. Aaron Smith and Janna Anderson, "AI, Robotics, and the Future of Jobs," Pew Research Center, Internet and Technology, August 6, 2014, https://pewresearch.org/internet/2014/08/06/future-of-jobs.

10. James Manyika et al., "Jobs Lost, Jobs Gained: Workforce Transitions in a Time of Automation," executive summary, McKinsey & Company, December 2017, 11, exhibit E6, www.mckinsey.com/featured-insights/future-of-work/jobs-lost-jobs-gained-what-the-future-of-work-will-mean-for-jobs-skills-and-wages.

11. McKinsey & Company, "Economic Conditions Snapshot, June 2019: McKinsey Global Survey Results," June 2019, www.mckinsey.com/business-functions/strategy-and-corporate-finance/our-insights/economic-conditions-snapshot-june-2019-mckinsey-global-survey-results.

12. Quentin Fottrell, "Coronavirus Infections Just Surpassed the Total Number of Cases during the 2002–2003 SARS Epidemic," *MarketWatch*, January 31, 2020, www.marketwatch.com/story/in-just-2-months-coronavirus-infections-are-surpassing-total-global-sars-epidemic-2020-01-30.

13. Details of these publications are as follows: Ray Dalio, "Why and How Capitalism Needs to Be Reformed," *Economic Principles*, April 5, 2019, www.economicprinciples.org/Why-and-How-Capitalism-Needs-To-Be-Reformed; Joseph E. Stiglitz, *People, Power, and Profits: Progressive Capitalism for an Age of Discontent* (New York: W. W. Norton & Company, 2019); Paul Collier, *The Future of Capitalism: Facing the New Anxieties* (New York: HarperCollins, 2018); Steven Pearlstein, *Can American Capitalism Survive? Why Greed Is Not Good, Opportunity Is Not Equal, and Fairness Won't Make Us Poor* (New York: St. Martin's Press, 2018); Martin Wolf, "The Crisis of Democratic Capitalism," podcast, *Financial Times*, June 12, 2018, www.ft.com/content/3fbdd2b4-f4d4-4fc4-88eb-4acac31c986a; Peter Georgescu, with David Dorsey, *Capitalists, Arise!: End Economic Inequality, Grow the Middle Class, Heal the Nation* (Oakland, CA: Berrett-Koehler Publishers, 2017); Robert B. Reich, *Saving Capitalism: For the Many, Not the Few* (New York: Alfred A. Knopf, 2015).

Chapter 1

1. Howard Stevenson, "Who Are the Self-Employed?" monograph, Harvard Business School, Boston, January 1983.

2. Robert Kagan, *Dangerous Nation: America's Place in the World, from Its Earliest Days to the Dawn of the 20th Century* (New York: Alfred A. Knopf, 2006).

3. This case is based on Nancy Barry, founder of Enterprise Solutions to Poverty, "Agribusiness and Distribution Systems in China and India," presentation at

HBS-ICC (Harvard Business School and International Chamber of Commerce) Workshop on The Future of the Market System, Harvard Business School, Boston, October 9–10, 2009; and press accounts of ITC and e-Choupal. See also "ITC," a case study prepared under the supervision of Nancy Barry by MBA interns Sandeep Mukherjee, Vikash Patwari, Tarakeshwar Dhurjati, Ed Al-Hussainy, Dhyanesh Shah, and Katie Leonberger, 2008.

Chapter 2

1. As of January 2011, the Organisation for Economic Co-operation and Development (OECD) comprised thirty-four countries, including the United States, Canada, Mexico, and Chile, the countries of Western Europe, Iceland, Israel, Turkey, Japan, Korea, Australia, and New Zealand.

2. For average growth in annual per-capita incomes for developing countries from the 1960s through 2006, see Andrew Burns et al., *Global Economic Prospects 2008: Technology Diffusion in the Developing World* (Washington, DC: The World Bank, 2008), 134, fig. 3.14.

3. Derived from the World Bank, *World Development Indicators*, http://data.worldbank.org/indicator. Calculations based on 123 countries with data on real U.S. dollar GDP for both 1975 and 2002.

4. Richard Newfarmer et al., *Global Economic Prospects 2007: Managing the Next Wave of Globalization* (Washington, DC: The World Bank, 2007), 29.

5. Andrew Burns et al., *Global Economic Prospects 2009: Commodities at the Crossroads* (Washington, DC: The World Bank, 2009), 46.

6. Ibid., ch. 1, esp. pp. 46–47.

7. Newfarmer et al., *Global Economic Prospects 2007*, 57, fig. 2.15.

8. Ibid., 30.

9. Ibid., xiii.

10. Ibid., xiii, fig. 2.

11. Statistics Bureau, Japan, "Population," in *The Statistical Handbook of Japan 2010* (Japan: Statistics Bureau, Ministry of Internal Affairs and Communications, 2001), ch. 2, pp. 10–12, www.stat.go.jp/english/data/handbook/pdf/c02cont.pdf.

12. Newfarmer et al., *Global Economic Prospects 2007*, 45–46.

13. The *Gini coefficient* is a measure of the inequality in a distribution, with a value of zero representing total equality and a value of 1, maximal inequality. Commonly used as a measure of inequality in the distribution of wealth or income in a country, the Gini coefficients for income distributions in countries that have been assessed range from approximately 0.25 (Sweden) to 0.74 (Namibia). For data, see the United Nations Development Programme, *Human Development Report 2010, 20th Anniversary Edition: The Real Wealth of Nations; Pathways to Human Development* (New York: Palgrave Macmillan, 2010), 153–154.

14. Noel Maurer, *The Power and the Money* (Palo Alto, CA: Stanford University Press, 2002), 10–11 and 195–199; Stephen Haber et al., *Mexico Since 1980* (New York: Cambridge University Press, 2008), 8–19; Noel Maurer and Stephen Haber, "Related Lending and Economic Performance: Evidence from Mexico," *Journal of Economic History* 67, no. 3 (September 2007): 551–581.

15. Sari Pekkala Kerr and William R. Kerr, "Economic Impacts of Immigration: A Survey," working paper 09-13, Harvard Business School, Boston, August 15, 2009, abstract available at http://ssrn.com/abstract=1228902.

16. Some of the IPCC's work has been the subject of international controversy. An independent study and report issued in August 2010 called for reforms in the IPCC's governance but did not challenge its main findings. Jeffrey Ball, "Climate Panel Faces Heat," *Wall Street Journal*, August 31, 2010, p. A1. See also InterAcademy Council, Committee to Review the Intergovernmental Panel on Climate Change, *Climate Change Report: Review of the Processes and Procedures of the IPCC* (The Netherlands: 2010).

17. Denver Water, *Solutions: Saving Water for the Future* (Denver: Denver Water, 2010), 32, www.denverwater.org/docs/assets/DCC8BD7A-E2B9-A215-2D2FDDC3D6C736E7/Solutions2010.pdf; Sharlene Garcia, "CFBF Conducts Water Shortage Impact Survey," California Farm Bureau Federation Ag Alert, June 18, 2008, www.cfbf.com/agalert/AgAlertStory.cfm?ID=1080&ck=731C83DB8D2FF01BDC000083FD3C374.

18. Burns et al., *Global Economic Prospects 2009*.

19. Newfarmer et al., *Global Economic Prospects 2007*, 55.

20. National Intelligence Council, *Global Scenarios to 2025* (2008), www.dni.gov/nic/PDF_2025/2025_Global_Scenarios_to_2025.pdf.

Chapter 3

1. "AIG Unit, Goldman Unwind CDS Positions: Source," Reuters, April 12, 2010, www.reuters.com/article/idUSTRE63B0GJ20100412.

2. Henny Sender, "Fed Makes 'a Killing' on AIG Contracts," *Financial Times*, January 20, 2010, www.ft.com/cms/s/0/a70659d4-0543-11df-a85e-00144feabdc0.html#axzz1A1WFPDKP.

3. Burns et al., *Global Economic Prospects 2009*.

4. Ibid.

5. Marshall Goldman, *Petrostate: Putin, Power, and the New Russia* (Oxford: Oxford University Press, 2008).

6. In addition to overfishing and plastic pollution, parts of the Mediterranean Sea and one hundred square miles of gulf waters lying beyond New Orleans so lack oxygen that they are considered dead. The North Pacific Gyre, a known current convergence zone, has been found to have floating marine debris items whose density is reaching a million items per square kilometer.

7. Søren Jensen, "On the Road to Copenhagen: Telling Denmark's Story," presentation given at meeting of the Environmental and Energy Study Institute and the Embassy of Denmark, Washington, DC, November 24, 2009, www.eesi.org/road-copenhagen-telling-denmark%E2%80%99s-story-24-nov-2009.

8. Romano Prodi, interview by author (JLB), Bologna, May 2010; Rachel Donadio, "Young, Smart, and Fearing for the Future," *New York Times*, January 2, 2011.

9. This observation has been variously attributed to people as disparate as Mark Twain, Niels Bohr, Casey Stengel, and Yogi Berra.

10. Nassim Nicholas Taleb, *The Black Swan: The Impact of the Highly Improbable* (New York: Random House, 2007).

Chapter 4

1. The role of the Financial Accounting Standards Board (FASB) may shift somewhat if the United States decides to adopt International Financial Reporting Standards (IFRS). The U.S. Securities and Exchange Commission (SEC) staff has laid out a work plan for considering incorporation of IFRS into the financial reporting system for U.S. companies, and the Commission is expected to make some determination about the U.S. stance in 2011. Since 2002, FASB and the London-based International Accounting Standards Board (IASB) have been engaged in a process aimed at converging U.S. Generally Accepted Accounting Principles (GAAP) with IFRS.

Chapter 5

1. The Center for Responsive Politics, "Lobbying Database," OpenSecrets.org, 2010, www.opensecrets.org/lobby/index.php.

2. The Center for Public Integrity, "State Lobbying Totals, 2004–2006," December 21, 2007, http://projects.publicintegrity.org/hiredguns/chart.aspx_act=lobbyspending.

3. Xavier Sala-i-Martin, Klaus Schwab, ed., *The Global Competitiveness Report, 2010–2011* (Geneva, Switzerland: World Economic Forum, 2010), Executive Opinion Survey, Data Table 1.04, Public Trust of Politicians. (Other editions of this annual publication, back to 2002, also show similar distrust of politicians. The report for 2010– 2011 covered 139 countries.)

4. Gallup, "Confidence in Institutions," July 8–11, 2010, www.gallup.com/poll/1597/Confidence-Institutions.aspx.

5. World Economic Forum, "Trust Will Be the Challenge of 2003," press release, Geneva, Switzerland, November 8, 2002, discusses the Voice of the People Survey results.

6. Edelman, "2010 Edelman Trust Barometer Executive Summary," 2010, 8, figs. 12 and 13, www.edelman.com/trust/2010/docs/2010_Trust_Barometer_Executive_Summary.pdf-www.scribd.com/full/26268655?access_key=key-1ovbgbpawooot3hnsz3u.

Chapter 6

1. Unless otherwise noted, sources for this section include Steve Fludder, "Ecomagination," presentation at the HBS ICC Workshop on The Future of the Market System, Boston, October 9–10, 2009; Herman B. "Dutch" Leonard, "GE's Ecomagination: Interview with Jeffrey Immelt," Harvard Business School, classroom video, April 2, 2006; and various GE publications.

2. Kathryn Kranhold, "Greener Pastures: GE's Environment Push Hits Business Realities," *Wall Street Journal*, September 14, 2007, A1.

3. Ibid.

4. Leonard, "GE's Ecomagination."

5. "Green Is Green at General Electric: Is Jeff Immelt the Man to Pull 'Ecomagination' Off?" *Strategic Direction* 22, no. 9 (2006): 21–23.

6. Unless otherwise indicated, sources for this section include the following: Yong Tao, "Mobile Services and Microfinance at the Base of the Chinese Pyramid,"

presentation at the HBS ICC Workshop on The Future of the Market System, Harvard Business School, Boston, October 9–10, 2009, and subsequent personal communications; William C. Kirby, F. Warren McFarlan, G. A. Donovan, Tracy Yuen Manty, "China Mobile's Rural Communications Strategy," Case 9-309-034 (Boston: Harvard Business School, 2009); "China Mobile," draft case study prepared for Enterprise Solutions to Poverty, Nancy Barry, founder, by MBA interns Thomas Miklavec, Jieun Choi, Rohan Menon, Greg Snyders, Andres Martin Buldu, and Katie Leonberger, 2008, and various China Mobile publications, analyst reports, and press accounts.

7. China Mobile was the successor to China Telecom (Hong Kong) Limited, which had been spun off from the state-owned China Telecom in 1997 and listed on the New York and Hong Kong Stock Exchanges. Through a series of industry restructurings and name changes, China Telecom (Hong Kong) Limited became China Mobile (Hong Kong) Limited and eventually, in 2006, simply China Mobile Limited. See M. L. Cohen, "China Mobile Ltd.," in *International Directory of Company Histories*, ed. Jay P. Pederson (Detroit: St. James Press, 2010), 108, 156–159.

8. Number of rural customers is authors' estimate derived from data published by China Mobile.

9. Quoted in Kirby et al., "China Mobile's Rural Communications Strategy," 11.

10. Unless otherwise noted, this account is drawn from Rohit Deshpandé, "Cipla," Case 9-503-085 (Boston: Harvard Business School, 2006).

11. Yusuf Hamied, interview by Rohit Deshpandé, August 2005, cited in Zoë Chance and Rohit Deshpandé, "Putting Patients First: Social Marketing Strategies for Treating HIV in Developing Nations," *Journal of Macromarketing* 29, no. 3 (September 2009): 227.

12. First Call India Equity Advisors, Cipla Limited, analyst report, April 27, 2009, 4.

13. *Compulsory licensing* in this context refers to the permissible manufacture of patented products without prior approval from the patent holder, upon payment of an appropriate fee. *Parallel imports* refers to the legal importation of goods—here, pharmaceuticals—from countries where they are sold at a lower cost.

14. Espicom Business Intelligence, "Generic Companies Analysis: Cipla, Quarter I, 2009" (Chichester, West Sussex, UK: Espicom), 9.

15. Edelweiss Securities Limited, Cipla, analyst report, August 10, 2009, 5.

16. First Call India Equity Advisors, Cipla Limited, January 29, 2010, 1.

17. Unless otherwise indicated, material in this paragraph is based on Chance and Deshpandé, "Putting Patients First," 222–225 and 227–228.

18. For other companies' approach to the intellectual-property question, see, for example, Lynn S. Paine, "Pfizer: Global Protection of Intellectual Property," Case 9-392-073 (Boston: Harvard Business School, 1995).

19. Chance and Deshpandé, "Putting Patients First," 223.

20. World Health Organization (WHO), Joint United Nations Programme on HIV/AIDS (UNAIDS), and United Nations Children's Fund (UNICEF), *Towards Universal Access: Scaling Up Priority HIV/AIDS Interventions in the Health Sector: Progress Report 2010* (Geneva: World Health Organization, 2010), 53, http://whqlibdoc.who.int/publications/2010/9789241500395_eng.pdf.

21. Simon Dixon, Scott McDonald, and Jennifer Roberts, "AIDS and Economic Growth in Africa: A Panel Data Analysis," *Journal of International Development* 13, no. 4 (May 2001): 411, cited in Chance and Deshpandé, "Putting Patients First," 222.

22. Edelweiss Securities Limited, Cipla, analyst report, May 7, 2010, 3.

23. Estimate from World Health Organization (WHO), Joint United Nations Programme on HIV/AIDS (UNAIDS), and United Nations Children's Fund (UNICEF), *Towards Universal Access*, 5, 54.

24. Unless otherwise indicated, this account is based on Sandra J. Sucher, Daniela Beyersdorfer, and Ane Damgaard Jensen, "Generation Investment Management," Case 9-609-057 (Boston: Harvard Business School, 2009); and on conversations with David Blood.

25. See, for example, Elizabeth Pfeuti, "Blood & Gore Reaps Four-Fold Rise in Profits," *Financial News*, September 22, 2010.

26. See, for example, Forest Reinhardt, *Down to Earth: Applying Business Principles to Environmental Management* (Boston: Harvard Business School Press, 2000); Daniel Esty and Andrew Winston, *Green to Gold: How Smart Companies Use Environmental Strategy to Innovate, Create Value, and Build Competitive Advantage* (New Haven, CT: Yale University Press, 2006); Stuart L. Hart, *Capitalism at the Crossroads: The Unlimited Business Opportunities in Solving the World's Most Difficult Problems* (Upper Saddle River, NJ: Wharton School Publishing, 2005); and C. K. Prahalad, *The Fortune at the Bottom of the Pyramid: Eradicating Poverty Through Profits* (Upper Saddle River, NJ: Wharton School Publishing, 2005).

27. Founded by Nancy Barry, a former World Bank executive and a participant in our U.S. forum in New York.

28. See, for example, Eric Wesoff, "Huge 2010 Finish for Greentech Venture Capital," *Greentech Media*, January 3, 2011, www.greentechmedia.com/articles/read/This-Week-in-Greentech-Finance-VC-MA-IPOs/.

29. Howard H. Stevenson, "A Perspective on Entrepreneurship," ch. 1 in Michael J. Roberts, Howard H. Stevenson, William A. Sahlman, Paul Marshall, and Richard G. Hamermesh, *New Business Ventures and the Entrepreneur*, 6th ed. (New York: McGraw-Hill/Irwin, 2006), 3–15.

30. Chester I. Barnard, *The Functions of the Executive: Thirtieth Anniversary Edition* (Cambridge, MA: Harvard University Press, 1968).

31. Some scholars would call the leaders in these cases *institutional entrepreneurs* because their innovations extend beyond the boundaries of a single company and involve a shift in basic beliefs and assumptions. Change that involves such shifts is also called *divergent change*. On institutional entrepreneurship and divergent change, see, for example, Julie Battilana, Bernard Leca, and Eva Boxenbaum, "How Actors Change Institutions: Towards a Theory of Institutional Entrepreneurship," *Academy of Management Annals* 3, no. 1 (2009): 65–107.

32. Alexis de Tocqueville, *Democracy in America*, ed. J. P. Mayer and Max Lerner, trans. George Lawrence (New York: Harper & Row, 1966), 498. See especially ch. 8, "How the Americans Combat Individualism by the Doctrine of Self-Interest Properly Understood," 497–499.

33. Ibid., 499.

34. See, for example, Edward J. Balleisen, "Policing the Bounds of Commerce: Prospects for a History of Commercial Fraud in America," presentation to Business, Government, and the International Economy Unit, Harvard Business School, Boston, January 2003.

35. Barbara Tuchman, *The March of Folly: From Troy to Vietnam* (New York: Alfred A. Knopf, 1984).

36. Ibid., 126.

Chapter 7

1. An equilibrium, in this sense, consists of an arrangement where workers provide a given amount of labor, owners of capital provide a given amount of equipment and other productive assets, and a set of goods is produced and consumed, where neither individual firms nor consumers can improve their well-being by changing what they supply, purchase, or consume.

2. For example, an argument in this general form was advanced to justify the North American Free Trade Agreement (NAFTA), among many other applications; we will return to this example later.

3. Tyson Slocum, "Blind Faith: How Deregulation and Enron's Influence over Government Looted Billions from Americans," *Public Citizen*, December 2001, www.citizen.org/documents/Blind_Faith.PDF. See also Stephen Labaton, "Enron's Collapse: Regulation," *New York Times*, January 24, 2002; Michael H. Granof and Stephen A. Zeff, "Unaccountable in Washington," *New York Times*, January 23, 2002.

4. David Barstow et al., "Regulators Failed to Address Risks in Oil Rig Fail-Safe Device," *New York Times*, June 20, 2010.

5. Unless otherwise indicated, this section is based on the following sources: Karl Schriftgiesser, *Business Comes of Age: The Story of the Committee for Economic Development and Its Impact on the Economic Policies of the United States, 1942–1960* (New York: Harper & Brothers, 1960); Sidney Hyman, *The Lives of William Benton* (Chicago: University of Chicago Press, 1969); and press accounts provided by CED.

6. Schriftgiesser, *Business Comes of Age*, 14.

7. Ibid., 26; see also Hyman, *The Lives of William Benton*, 265.

8. William Benton to Paul G. Hoffman, November 1943, quoted in Hyman, *The Lives of William Benton*, 290.

9. Hyman, *The Lives of William Benton*, 270.

10. Bylaws as they appear in ibid.

11. "CED Will Continue Economic Studies," *New York Times*, May 24, 1948.

12. "The Economy: The Patient Feels Fine," *Time*, January 21, 1946.

13. See, for example, Schriftgiesser, *Business Comes of Age*, 57. See also Robert M. Collins, "Positive Business Responses to the New Deal: The Roots of the Committee for Economic Development 1933–1942," *Business History Review* 52, no. 3 (autumn 1978).

14. Russell Porter, "Program Outlined by Hoffman Group," *New York Times*, January 13, 1947.

15. See, for example, two recent statements by the Committee for Economic Development, Research and Policy Committee, Washington, DC: "Quality, Affordable Health Care for All: Moving Beyond the Employer-Based Health-Insurance System" (2007) and "Rebuilding Corporate Leadership: How Directors Can Link Long-Term Performance with Public Goals" (2009).

16. For an excellent summary of this decline and the subsequent turnaround, see James E. Austin, "Business Leadership Lessons from the Cleveland Turnaround,"

California Management Review 41, no. 1 (fall 1998): 86–106. The discussion in this section draws heavily from this article and the associated set of teaching cases published by Harvard Business School Publishing.

17. This account is drawn from Benjamin W. Heineman Jr., interview by author (LSP), Boston, June 9, 2010; Benjamin W. Heineman Jr. and Fritz Heimann, "Arrested Development," *National Interest* (November–December 2007); and Benjamin W. Heineman Jr. and Fritz Heimann, "Focus on 'Controlling the Climate' Reducing Corruption Worldwide: Fritz Heimann," *Metropolitan Corporate Counsel* (March 1996).

18. U.S. Climate Action Partnership, "A Call for Action: Consensus Principles and Recommendations from the U.S. Climate Action Partnership, a Business and NGO Partnership," January 2007, http://us-cap.org/USCAPCallForAction.pdf.

19. Angie Drobnic Holan and Lukas Pleva, "Cap and Trade Legislation Stalls in the Senate," PolitiFact.com, July 26, 2010, www.politifact.com/truth-o-meter/article/2010/jul/26/cap-and-trade-legislation-stalls-senate/.

Chapter 8

1. Cited by J. D. Bernal, "The Place of Speculation in Modern Technology and Science," in I. J. Good, *The Scientist Speculates: An Anthology of Partly-Baked Ideas* (New York: Basic Books, 1962), 15.

2. U.S. Senate, *Industrial Relations: Final Report and Testimony Submitted to Congress by the Commission on Industrial Relations Created by the Act of August 23, 1912*, vol. 8 (Washington, DC: Government Printing Office, 1916), 7,660.

3. China Mobile's efforts in rural China, for example, are enabled by IBM products and services.

4. Joseph L. Bower, "Cooperation for Competition: U.S. and Japan," Case 9-386-181 (Boston: Harvard Business School, 1986).

5. Discussed in Ray A. Goldberg and Jessica Droste Yagan, "McDonald's Corporation: Managing a Sustainable Supply Chain," Case 9-907-414 (Boston: Harvard Business School, 2007), 4.

6. Ibid.

7. Elliott Fisher et al., "Health Care Spending, Quality and Outcomes: More Isn't Always Better," Dartmouth Atlas Project Topic Brief, February 2009, www.dartmouthatlas.org/downloads/reports/Spending_Brief_022709.pdf.

8. This is a theme pursued by, among others, Donald L. Berwick, former CEO of the Institute for Healthcare Improvement based in Cambridge, Massachusetts, and since July 2010, the administrator of the U.S. Federal Centers for Medicare and Medicaid Services.

9. An exception is the Committee for Economic Development, which has examined health care most recently in Committee for Economic Development, Research and Policy Committee, "Quality, Affordable Health Care for All: Moving Beyond the Employer-Based Health-Insurance System," statement, Washington, DC, 2007.

10. Donald M. Berwick, Thomas W. Nolan, and John Whittington, "The Triple Aim: Care, Health, and Cost," *Health Affairs* 27, no. 3 (2008): 759–769, abstract at http://content.healthaffairs.org/content/27/3/759.full#R14, citing J. M. McGinnis and W. H. Foege, "Actual Causes of Death in the United States," *Journal of the American*

Medical Association 270, no. 18 (1993): 2207–2212; and A. H. Mokdad et al., "Actual Causes of Death in the United States, 2000," *Journal of the American Medical Association* 291, no. 10 (2004): 1238–1245.

11. The existing industry mutual-insurance organization, Oil Casualty Insurance, Limited (OCIL), based in Bermuda, seems to be headed in the right direction but does not currently have the necessary scale to play this role definitively. It operates as an excess liability reinsurer; the companies it reinsures must self-insure or seek other insurance for the first $25 million of any liability claim, and OCIL then insures them against the part of their loss that falls in the range of $25–$100 million. This mechanism may provide a model for a larger effort, but with a maximum policy limit of $100 million, the scale of the current arrangement is modest compared with what we have in mind. Revealingly, BP is not a shareholder, and OCIL's July 19, 2010, newsletter observes: "OCIL will continue to monitor the impact of the Deepwater Horizon explosion. The Company's exposure to the event is expected to be minimal" (Oil Casualty Insurance, Ltd., "Deepwater Horizon," *OCIL News*, July 19, 2010, www. ocil.bm/ocil/document-center/Media%20Articles/July%202010%20-%20OCIL%20 Communication.pdf).

12. Bradley Blackburn, "The Giving Pledge: Billionaires Promise to Donate at Least Half Their Fortunes to Charity," *ABC News*, August 4, 2010, http:// abcnews.go.com/WN/bill-gates-warren-buffett-organize-billionaire-giving-pledge/ story?id=11325984.

13. This phraseology borrows from Sandra Day O'Connor, who famously made a similar observation about the U.S. Supreme Court's decision in *Roe v. Wade. Akron v. Akron Center for Reproductive Health, Inc.*, 462 U.S. 416, 458 (1983) (O'Connor, J., dissenting).

Chapter 9

1. "Hidden Debt, Hidden Deficits: The 2019 Update," Hoover Institution, Stanford University, June 11, 2019, www.hoover.org/news/hidden-debt-hidden-deficits-2019-update.

2. Quote from UN Conference on Trade and Development (UNCTAD), landing page (https://unctad.org/en/pages/PublicationWebflyer.aspx?publicationid=2446) for UNCTAD, "Key Statistics and Trends in International Trade 2018," report 2019, https://unctad.org/en/PublicationsLibrary/ditctab2019d2_en.pdf.

3. Susan Lund et al., *Globalization in Transition: The Future of Trade and Value Chains* (McKinsey Global Institute, January 2019), 16, www.mckinsey.com/featured-insights/innovation-and-growth/globalization-in-transition-the-future-of-trade-and-value-chains.

4. U.S. Energy Information Administration, "International Energy Outlook 2019," www.eia.gov/outlooks/aeo/data/browser/#/?id=15-IEO2019&region=4-0&cases=Refer ence&start=2010&end=2050&f=A&linechart=Reference-d080819.51-15-IEO2019.4-0~Reference-d080819.52-15-IEO2019.4-0&map=&ctype=linechart&sourcekey=0.

5. Alicia Adamczyk, "The US Is Home to More Billionaires Than China, Germany and Russia Combined," CNBC.com, May 19, 2019, www.cnbc.com/2019/05/09/the-countries-with-the-largest-number-of-billionaires.html.

6. Jesse Bricker et al., "Changes in U.S. Family Finances from 2013 to 2016: Evidence from the Survey of Consumer Finances," *Federal Reserve Bulletin* 103, no. 3 (September 2017): 10, www.federalreserve.gov/publications/files/scf17.pdf.

7. UN Department of Economic and Social Affairs, "International Migrants Numbered 272 Million in 2019, Continuing an Upward Trend in All Major World Regions," *Population Facts* 2019/4 (September 2019), www.un.org/en/development/desa/population/migration/publications/populationfacts/docs/MigrationStock2019_PopFacts_2019-04.pdf.

8. UN Refugee Agency (UNHCR), *Global Trends: Forced Displacement in 2018* (Geneva: UNHCR, 2019), www.unhcr.org/en-us/statistics/unhcrstats/5d08d7ee7/unhcr-global-trends-2018.html.

9. Brian Kennedy and Meg Hefferon, "U.S. Concern about Climate Change Is Rising, but Mainly among Democrats," *Factank*, Pew Research Center, August 28, 2019, www.pewresearch.org/fact-tank/2019/08/28/u-s-concern-about-climate-change-is-rising-but-mainly-among-democrats/; Moira Fagan and Christine Huanga, "A Look at How People around the World View Climate Change," *Factank*, Pew Research Center, April 18, 2019, www.pewresearch.org/fact-tank/2019/04/18/a-look-at-how-people-around-the-world-view-climate-change.

10. Sarah Chayes, *Thieves of State: Why Corruption Threatens Global Security* (New York: W. W. Norton & Company, 2016).

11. Transparency International, "Corruption in the USA: The Difference a Year Makes," December 12, 2017, www.transparency.org/news/feature/corruption_in_the_usa_the_difference_a_year_makes.

12. Daniella Cheslow, "U.S. Slips in Annual Global Corruption Rankings," NPR, January 29, 2019, www.npr.org/2019/01/29/689639808/u-s-slips-in-annual-global-corruption-rankings.

13. The World Bank, "World Development Indicators: Literacy Rate, Adult Total (% of People Ages 15 and Above)," https://data.worldbank.org/indicator/SE.ADT.LITR.ZS.

14. Michael Devitt, "CDC Data Show U.S. Life Expectancy Continues to Decline," *American Academy of Family Physicians News*, December 10, 2018, www.aafp.org/news/health-of-the-public/20181210lifeexpectdrop.html.

15. The World Bank, "World Development Indicators: GDP, PP (Current International $)," https://data.worldbank.org/indicator/NY.GDP.MKTP.PP.CD.

16. See, for example, Graham Allison, *Destined for War: Can America and China Escape Thucydides's Trap?* (Boston: Houghton Mifflin Harcourt, 2017); and William Overholt, *China's Crisis of Success* (Cambridge and New York: Cambridge University Press, 2018).

17. World Health Organization, "Emergencies Preparedness, Response: Epidemic Focus," May 13, 2016, www.who.int/csr/disease/epidemic-focus/global-epidemic-response/en/.

18. Francesca De Châtel, "The Role of Drought and Climate Change in the Syrian Uprising: Untangling the Triggers of the Revolution," *Middle Eastern Studies* 50, no. 4 (July 4, 2014): 521–535, doi:10.1080/00263206.2013.850076.

19. Some accounts cite government policies that encouraged overuse of groundwater reserves. These policies, in turn, increased the vulnerability of the rural population to the effects of drought. See, for example, P. Aguirre, "Drought, Climate Change, and Civil War," *Chicago Policy Review*, summarizing "Climate Change in the Fertile Crescent and Implications of the Recent Syrian Drought," by C. P. Kelley et al., in *Proceedings of the National Academy of Sciences* 112, no. 11 (2015): 3241–3246.

20. Thomas J. Bollyky, *Plagues and the Paradox of Progress* (Cambridge, MA: MIT Press, 2018). In addition to the data, our arguments in this section and other data cited are drawn from this book.

21. Bollyky, *Plagues and the Paradox*.

22. Ibid.

23. Overholt, *China's Crisis of Success*.

24. Climate Signals (a project of Climate Nexus), "Storm Surge Increase," Climate-Signals.org, December 4, 2018. Climate Nexus is a sponsored project of Rockefeller Philanthropy Advisors, www.climatesignals.org/climate-signals/storm-surge-increase.

25. U.S. Bureau of Labor Statistics, "Labor Share of Output Has Declined since 1947," *TED: The Economics Daily*, March 7, 2017, www.bls.gov/opub/ted/2017/labor-share-of-output-has-declined-since-1947.htm.

26. Willy Shih, "Whatever the Outcome of U.S.-China Trade Talks, Global Supply Chains Are Set to Change," *Forbes*, February 19, 2019, www.forbes.com/sites/willyshih/2019/02/19/whatever-the-outcome-of-u-s-china-trade-talks-global-supply-chains-are-set-to-change/#24190d4a2a58.

27. Lund et al., *Globalization in Transition*.

28. Philip R. Lane, "The European Sovereign Debt Crisis," *Journal of Economic Perspectives* 26, no. 3 (summer 2012): 49–68.

29. "Free Exchange / Cost Conscious," *Economist*, June 22, 2019, 65.

30. Peter J. Wallison and Edward J. Pinto, "A Government-Mandated Housing Bubble," *Forbes*, February 16, 2009, www.forbes.com/2009/02/13/housing-bubble-subprime-opinions-contributors_0216_peter_wallison_edward_pinto.html#1aa2dfc4778b.

31. Susan Lund et al., "A Decade after the Global Financial Crisis: What Has (and Hasn't) Changed?," McKinsey Global Institute Briefing Note, September 2018, www.mckinsey.com/~/media/McKinsey/Industries/Financial%20Services/Our%20Insights/A%20decade%20after%20the%20global%20financial%20crisis%20What%20has%20and%20hasnt%20changed/MGI-Briefing-A-decade-after-the-global-financial-crisis-What-has-and-hasnt-changed.ashx.

32. Marcin Szczepanski, "A Decade On from the Crisis: Main Responses and Remaining Challenges," European Parliament Briefing, October 2019, www.europarl.europa.eu/RegData/etudes/BRIE/2019/642253/EPRS_BRI(2019)642253_EN.pdf.

33. John Cassidy, "Ten Years after the Start of the Great Recession, Middle-Class Incomes Are Only Just Catching Up," *New Yorker*, September 13, 2018, www.newyorker.com/news/our-columnists/ten-years-after-the-start-of-the-great-recession-middle-class-incomes-are-only-just-catching-up.

34. Polly Toynbee, "Brexiteers Promised a New Dawn for UK Farming, Not Agricultural Armageddon," *Guardian*, August 15, 2019, www.theguardian.com/commentisfree/2019/aug/15/brexiteers-uk-farming-agriculture-no-deal-brexit.

35. Kenneth Rogoff, "An Economist Explains What Happens if There's Another Financial Crisis," *World Economic Forum*, April 30, 2019, www.weforum.org/agenda/2019/04/an-economist-explains-what-happens-if-there-s-another-financial-crisis/.

36. Philip Bump, "Ted Cruz Gets It Very Wrong on Recent Presidents' Deportation Numbers," *The Washington Post*, December 16, 2015, www.washingtonpost.com/news/the-fix/wp/2015/12/16/the-numbers-ted-cruz-cited-on-past-deportations-during-the-cnn-debate-were-way-off/; Department of Homeland Security, US Immigration and Customs Enforcement, "Fiscal Year 2017 ICE Enforcement and Removal Operations Report," last updated December 13, 3017, www.ice.gov/removal-statistics/2017#wcm-survey-target-id.

37. Ricardo showed how comparative advantage would increase the wealth of both England and Portugal when they traded textiles for port wine.

38. Joseph L. Bower, "Liz Claiborne China," Case 9-301-098 (Boston: Harvard Business School, April 2001).

39. "Supply Chains for Different Industries Are Fragmenting in Different Ways," *Economist*, July 11, 2019, www.economist.com/special-report/2019/07/11/supply-chains-for-different-industries-are-fragmenting-in-different-ways.

40. Angel Gurría, "Opening Remarks," given at the 2019 OECD Forum: Launch of the Economic Outlook, Paris, May 21, 2019, www.oecd.org/forum/2019-oecd-forum-launch-of-the-economic-outlook-paris-may-2019.htm.

41. Lund et al., *Globalization in Transition*, 4.

42. These distinctions are imperfect since many major companies are not state owned but have a provincial development corporation as the major shareholder.

43. Megan O'Sullivan, *Windfall: How the New Energy Abundance Upends Global Politics and Strengthens America's Power* (New York: Simon & Shuster, 2017), 228–229.

44. According to a 2018 Transparency International report, over the past seven years of 180 countries studied, the score of 20 countries improved, 16 worsened, and the remaining 144 made no improvement on corruption. The 2019 Freedom House report, "Freedom in the World 2019," shows declines in aggregate freedom scores in 68 countries between 2018 and 2019. Transparency International, "Corruption Perceptions Index 2018," Transparency International, Berlin, 2018, 6, www.transparency.org/files/content/pages/2018_CPI_Executive_Summary.pdf; Freedom House, "Freedom in the World 2019," Freedom House, Washington, D.C., 6, https://freedomhouse.org/sites/default/files/Feb2019_FH_FITW_2019_Report_ForWeb-compressed.pdf.

45. António Guterres, "Cost of Corruption at Least 5 Per Cent of Global Gross Domestic Product, Secretary-General Says in International Day Message," United Nations press release, December 5, 2018, www.un.org/press/en/2018/sgsm19392.doc.htm.

46. William Grimes, "Wiseguys and Fall Guys, Welcome to Globalization," *New York Times*, April 11, 2008, www.nytimes.com/2008/04/11/books/11book.html.

47. The World Bank, "World Development Indicators," https://databank.worldbank.org/source/world-development-indicators#.

48. See, for example, the extended discussion of corruption and its impacts in Chayes, *Thieves of State*.

49. Transparency International, "Corruption Perceptions Index 2018."

Chapter 10

1. According to Pew Research Center, experts polled in 2014 were about evenly divided on whether automation is likely to displace more jobs than it creates. Aaron Smith and Janna Anderson, "AI, Robotics, and the Future of Jobs," Pew Research Center, August 6, 2014, www.pewresearch.org/internet/2014/08/06/future-of-jobs.

2. Russell Gold, "PG&E: The First Climate-Change Bankruptcy, Probably Not the Last," *Wall Street Journal*, January 18, 2019, www.wsj.com/articles/pg-e-wildfires-and-the-first-climate-change-bankruptcy-11547820006.

3. Several recent polls show that, compared with their seniors, young adults of both parties in the United States have a less favorable view of capitalism and a

more favorable view of socialism. See, for example, Pew Research Center, Survey of U.S. adults conducted April 29 to May 13, 2019, as reported in Hannah Hartig, "Stark Partisan Divisions in Americans' Views of 'Socialism,' 'Capitalism,'" *Factank*, Pew Research Center, June 25, 2019, www.pewresearch.org/fact-tank/2019/06/25/stark-partisan-divisions-in-americans-views-of-socialism-capitalism.

4. For a discussion of changes in corporate governance, see Joseph L. Bower and Lynn S. Paine, "The Error at the Heart of Corporate Leadership," *Harvard Business Review*, May–June 2017.

5. See "Preface to the Expanded Edition" of this book for a review of some changes in law and policy that have been suggested. In Ray Dalio, "Why and How Capitalism Needs to Be Reformed," *Economic Principles* (blog), April 5, 2019, www.conomicprinciples.org/Why-and-How-Capitalism-Needs-To-Be-Reformed, the hedge fund manager and author speak to the importance of building bipartisan support for any proposed changes in policy.

6. Unless otherwise indicated, this section is based on Joseph L. Bower and Michael Norris, "JPMorgan Chase: Invested in Detroit (A)," Case 9-918-406 (Boston: Harvard Business School, March 2018).

7. U.S. Census Bureau, 2010 Census, data for Detroit city, Michigan, Summary File 1, Tables P5, P8, PCT4, PCT5, PCT8, and PCT 11. https://factfinder.census.gov/faces/tableservices/jsf/pages/productview.xhtml?src=CF; Kate Linebaugh, "Detroit's Population Crashes," *Wall Street Journal*, March 23, 2011, www.wsj.com/articles/SB10001424052748704461304576216850733151470.

8. Michigan Department of Technology, Management & Budget, "Employment and Unemployment Statistics for the City of Detroit in July 2010: Local Area Unemployment Statistics (LAUS)," https://milmi.org/DataSearch; Shelly Banjo, "New Yorker's Moves to Boost Michigan's Economy," *Wall Street Journal*, August 6, 2010, www.wsj.com/articles/SB100014240527487037489045754115841566646928; Susan Saulny, "Razing the City to Save the City," *New York Times*, June 20, 2010, www.nytimes.com/2010/06/21/us/21detroit.html.

9. "Detroit Future City, 2012 Detroit Strategic Framework Plan, Executive Summary," https://detroitfuturecity.com/wp-content/uploads/2014/02/DFC_ExecutiveSummary_2ndEd.pdf.

10. Bower and Norris, "JPMorgan Chase (A)," 8.

11. CDFI Coalition, "What Are CDFIs?," http://cdfi.org/what-are-cdfis.

12. Chad Livengood, "State Ends Direct Oversight of Detroit Finances," *Crain's Detroit Business*, April 30, 2018, www.crainsdetroit.com/article/20180430/news/659466/state-ends-direct-oversight-of-detroit-finances.

13. Peter L. Scher, "Return on Community: A Business Imperative," JPMorgan Chase & Co., Corporate Responsibility Report, April 2019, https://reports.jpmorganchase.com/corporate-responsibility/2018/cr-2018-peter-scher.htm.

14. This account is based largely on Joseph L. Bower and Michael Norris, "Cummins, Inc.: Building a Home Community for a Global Company," Case 9-313-024 (Boston: Harvard Business School, March 21, 2014).

15. Cummins executive, interview with author (JLB), June 26, 2012.

16. Data from "Economic Opportunities through Education: Building a Regional Talent and Learning Development System," https://econetworks.org/wp-content/uploads/EcO-Network-2-1.pdf.

17. Kirk Johannesen, "Cummins Veteran Heads New Team," *Republic* (Columbus, IN), September 12, 2016, www.therepublic.com/2016/09/13/cummins_veteran_heads_new_team.

18. For Columbus data, see CivicLab, "Collaboration by Design: The Sixty-Year, Overnight Success Story of Columbus, Indiana," keynote presentation, CivicLab, Columbus, IN, 2017, www.indianalandmarks.org/wp-content/uploads/2018/07/PHP-2018-The-Columbus-Way-Slides-Jack-Hess.pdf. For average U.S. family income, see U.S. Census Bureau, "Income of Families and Persons in the United States: 1950," Report P60-09, March 25, 1952, www.census.gov/library/publications/1952/demo/p60-009.html.

19. CivicLab, "Collaboration by Design."

20. Irina Vinnitskaya, "AIA Ranks Columbus, Indiana as US's 6th Most Architecturally Important City," *ArchDaily*, December 4, 2012. www.archdaily.com/299356/aia-ranks-columbus-indiana-as-uss-6th-most-architecturally-important-city.

21. CivicLab, "Collaboration by Design," 13–15, 18.

22. Blair Claflin, "Cummins Makes Big Jump in Two Key Financial Rankings," press release, Cummins Newsroom, July 19, 2019, www.cummins.com/news/2019/07/19/cummins-makes-big-jump-two-key-financial-rankings.

23. Unless otherwise indicated, this section is based largely on Lynn S. Paine, Nien-hê Hsieh, and Lara Adamsons, "Governance and Sustainability at Nike (A)," Case 9-313-146 (Boston: Harvard Business School, June 2013; revised September 2016).

24. Ellen McGirt, "How Nike's CEO Shook Up the Shoe Industry," *Fast Company*, September 1, 2010, www.fastcompany.com/1676902/how-nikes-ceo-shook-shoe-industry.

25. Mark Parker, quoted in Paine, Hsieh, and Adamsons, "Governance and Sustainability at Nike (A)," 4.

26. These changes are described more fully in Paine, Hsieh, and Adamsons, "Governance and Sustainability at Nike (A)."

27. "A New Challenge for Nike Chief Sustainability Officer Hannah Jones," *brandchannel*, July 3, 2018, www.brandchannel.com/2018/07/03/nike_chief_sustainability_officer_hannah_jones.

28. Information in this paragraph and the next comes from Noel Kinder, interview with author (Lynn S. Paine), August 2, 2019.

29. Walter Loeb, "Retail Person of the Year: Mark Parker, Nike CEO," *Forbes*, January 2, 2018.

30. Andrea Cheng, "Nike, Already World's Largest Sneaker Maker, Proves It's Still a Growth Company," *Forbes*, December 20, 2018, www.forbes.com/sites/andriacheng/2018/12/20/nike-just-proves-its-still-a-growth-company/#5f45300e41f7.

31. Calculations are based on share price and index data for the period January 20, 2006, to December 9, 2019, from Capital IQ, Inc., a division of Standard & Poor's.

32. Unilever, "Unilever Sustainable Living Plan," November 2010, www.unilever.com/Images/unilever-sustainable-living-plan_tcm244-409855_en.pdf.

33. Unilever, "Unilever Sustainable Living Plan Progress Report 2011," www.unilever.com/Images/uslp-unilever_sustainable_living_plan_progress_report_2011_tcm244-409863_en.pdf. See also Christopher A. Bartlett, "Unilever's New Global Strategy: Competing through Sustainability," Case 9-916-414 (Boston: Harvard Business School, August 24, 2016), 3.

34. Andrew Saunders, "The MT Interview: Paul Polman," *Management Today*, March 1, 2011.

35. Julia Finch, "Unilever Unveils Ambitious Long Term Sustainability Programme," *Guardian* (London), November 14, 2010, www.theguardian.com/business/2010/nov/15/unilever-sustainable-living-plan.

36. Adi Ignatius, "Captain Planet: An Interview with Unilever CEO Paul Polman," *Harvard Business Review*, June 2012.

37. Bartlett, "Unilever's New Global Strategy."

38. Thomson Reuters StreetEvents, "Final Transcript, UL-Q4 & Full Year 2008 Unilever PLC Earnings Conference Call," February 5, 2009, 11.

39. Michelle Russell, "Unilever 'Green' Plan Needs to Attract the 'Right' Investors," *Just-Food*, November 15, 2010.

40. Jennifer Reil and Roger Martin, "How Unilever Won Over Shareholders with Its Long-Term Approach," *Globe and Mail*, October 13, 2017, www.theglobeandmail.com/report-on-business/careers/management/how-unilever-won-over-shareholders-with-its-long-term-approach/article36538572.

41. Material in this paragraph is based on Bartlett, "Unilever's New Global Strategy."

42. Unilever, "Sustainable Living Plan Progress Report," 2011, 40.

43. Unilever, "Mobilising Collective Action, Unilever Sustainable Living Plan, Summary of Progress 2015," 8–9, www.unilever.com/Images/uslp-mobilising-collective-action-summary-of-progress-2015_tcm244-424809_en.pdf.

44. "Unilever's Sustainable Living Plan Continues to Fuel Growth," press release, Unilever, October 10, 2018, www.unilever.com/news/press-releases/2018/unilevers-sustainable-living-plan-continues-to-fuel-growth.html.

45. CDP (formerly Carbon Disclosure Project) categorized Kraft Heinz as a laggard in climate-change readiness: "Top FMCGs in Race to Keep Up with Conscious Consumers," February 25, 2019, www.cdp.net/en/articles/media/top-fmcgs-in-race-to-keep-up-with-conscious-consumers.

46. Nicholas Megaw, "Unilever 'Sees No Merit' in Kraft Heinz Offer," *Financial Times*, February 17, 2017, www.ft.com/content/d73cb5fa-c326-3733-a13a-a5bc7e8a18da.

47. "The Parable of St. Paul," *Economist*, August 31, 2017, www.economist.com/news/business/21727908-unilever-worlds-biggest-experiment-corporate-do-gooding-parable-st-paul.

48. "Accelerating Sustainable Shareholder Value Creation," press release, Unilever, April 6, 2017, www.unilever.com/news/press-releases/2017/Accelerating-sustainable-shareholder-value-creation.html.

49. In chapter 11, we discuss the importance of engaging with shareholders about initiatives like Unilever's and others discussed in this chapter.

50. "Unilever CEO Announcement: Paul Polman to Retire; Alan Jope Appointed as Successor," press release, Unilever, London/Rotterdam, November 11, 2018, www.unilever.com/news/press-releases/2018/unilever-ceo-announcement.html. Total shareholder return calculation for Unilever's peer group is based on financial and share price data as converted to U.S. dollars at spot price as of August 20, 2019, where applicable, from Capital IQ, Inc., a division of Standard & Poor's.

51. According to an Oxfam study covering the period 2013 to 2016, Unilever moved into first place among its peers on Oxfam's sustainability metrics in 2016: Oxfam, "The Journey to Sustainable Food," Oxfam briefing paper, April 19, 2016, https://oi-files-d8-prod.s3.eu-west-2.amazonaws.com/s3fs-public/file_attachments/bp-journey-to-sustainable-food-btb-190416-en.pdf. CDP (formerly Carbon Disclosure Project) puts Unilever among the leaders in climate-change readiness: "Top FMCGs in Race to Keep Up with Conscious Consumers," *CDP*, February 25, 2019, www.cdp.net/en/articles/media/top-fmcgs-in-race-to-keep-up-with-conscious-consumers. Unilever ranked second in Access to Nutrition Foundation, *Global Access to Nutrition Index 2018* (October 31, 2018), www.accesstonutrition.org/sites/us18.atnindex.org/files/resources/atni_report_global_index_2018_0.pdf. Even skeptics acknowledged that Unilever's record, though far from perfect, compared favorably with that of its peers. See Daphné Dupont-Nivet, "Inside Unilever's Sustainability Myth," *New Internationalist*, April 13, 2017, https://newint.org/features/web-exclusive/2017/04/13/inside-unilever-sustainability-myth.

52. Lucy Tesseras, "Unilever CEO says Keith Weed's Replacement Will Be a 'CMO++,'" *MarketingWeek*, June 19, 2019, www.marketingweek.com/unilever-keith-weeds-replacement-cmo.

Chapter 11

1. William Bradford, *History of Plymouth Plantation, 1620–1647* (Boston: Massachusetts Historical Society, 1912), 1:299–303, manuscript pages 96–97.

2. Damien Cave, "The World Burns All Year: Are There Enough Planes to Douse the Flames?" *New York Times*, November 23, 2019 (print edition), A4, www.nytimes.com/2019/11/21/world/australia/fires-water-tankers-climate-change.html.

3. Quoted in Joseph L. Bower and Michael Norris, "JPMorgan Chase: Invested in Detroit (A)," Case 9-918-406 (Boston: Harvard Business School, March 15, 2018), 8.

4. Joseph L. Bower and Lynn S. Paine, "The Error at the Heart of Corporate Leadership," *Harvard Business Review*, May–June 2017.

5. Bower and Norris, "JPMorgan Chase," 1.

6. Global Sustainable Investment Alliance, "2018 Global Sustainable Investment Review," 2018, 8, figure 2, www.gsi-alliance.org/wp-content/uploads/2019/06/GSIR_Review2018F.pdf. (In Japan, assets managed under a sustainability mandate grew from JPY 840 billion in 2014 to JPY 231,952 billion in 2018.)

7. UN Principles for Responsible Investment Association, "About the PRI," Signatory Growth chart, www.unpri.org/pri/about-the-pri.

8. See Government Pension Investment Fund, "Policy to Fulfill Stewardship Responsibilities," revised November 18, 2019, www.gpif.go.jp/en/investment/Policy_to_Fullfill_Stewardship_Responsibilities_201911.pdf; see also Siobhan Riding, "World's Biggest Pension Fund Steps Up Passive Stewardship Efforts," *Financial Times*, September 15, 2019, www.ft.com/content/8e5e0476-f046-3316-b01b-e5b4eac983f1.

9. Climate Action 100+, "Global Investors Driving Business Transition," www.climateaction100.org. See also Climate Action 100+, "2019 Progress Report," September 2019, https://climateaction100.files.wordpress.com/2019/10/progressreport2019.pdf.

10. Financial Reporting Council, *UK Corporate Governance Code*, July 2018, www.frc
.org.uk/getattachment/88bd8c45-50ea-4841-95b0-d2f4f48069a2/2018-UK-Corporate
-Governance-Code-FINAL.PDF, 4. See also Big Innovation Centre, *The Purposeful Company Policy Report* (London: Big Innovation Centre, February 2017), www.
biginnovationcentre-purposeful-company.com/wp-content/uploads/2017/11/feb-24
_tpc_policy-report_final_printed.pdf; and Big Innovation Centre, *The Purposeful Company
Interim Report* (London: Big Innovation Centre, May 2016), www.biginnovationcentre
-purposeful-company.com/wp-content/uploads/2017/11/thepurposefulcompany_
interimreport.pdf; David Kershaw and Edmund Schuster, "The Purposive Transformation of Company Law," working paper 4/2019, London School of Economics, Law,
Society, and Economy, available for download at the Social Sciences Research Network library, http://ssrn.com/abstract=3363267.

11. The Pacte Law is described in English at "PACTE: The Action Plan for
Business Growth and Transformation," French government website, www.gouverne
ment.fr/en/pacte-the-action-plan-for-business-growth-and-transformation. See also
Margaux Renard, "The French 'PACTE' Law: Growing Space for Social and Environmental Topics in Corporate Management of French Companies," *Hogan Lovells
Focus on Regulation*, June 6, 2019, www.hlregulation.com/2019/06/06/the-french-pacte-
law-growing-space-for-social-and-environmental-topics-in-corporate-management-
of-french-companies.

12. Larry Fink, "Purpose and Profit," 2019 letter to CEOs, January 2019, www.
blackrock.com/corporate/investor-relations/larry-fink-ceo-letter.

13. Larry Fink, "A Fundamental Reshaping of Finance," 2020 letter to CEOs,
January 2020, https://www.blackrock.com/corporate/investor-relations/larry-fink-ceo-letter.

14. UN Department of Economic and Social Affairs, "Global Investors for
Sustainable Development Alliance," un.org/esa/ffd/ffd-follow-up/global-investors-
for-sustainable-development-alliance.html. See also Andrew Edgecliffe-Johnson,
"Global Business Chiefs Pledge to Boost Sustainable Development," *Financial Times*,
October 16, 2019.

15. Business Roundtable, "Statement on the Purpose of a Corporation," https://oppor
tunity.businessroundtable.org/ourcommitment/. A pdf of the statement, last updated
September 6, 2019, is available at https://opportunity.businessroundtable.org/wp-content/
uploads/2019/09/BRT-Statement-on-the-Purpose-of-a-Corporation-with-Signatures-1.pdf.
See also Business Roundtable, "Business Roundtable Redefines the Purpose of a Corporation to Promote 'An Economy That Serves All Americans,'" press release,
August 19, 2019, www.businessroundtable.org/business-roundtable-redefines-the-purpose-
of-a-corporation-to-promote-an-economy-that-serves-all-americans.

16. For the 1973 Manifesto, see Klaus Schwab, "Davos Manifesto 1973: A Code
of Ethics for Business Leaders," World Economic Forum, December 2, 2019, www.
weforum.org/agenda/2019/12/davos-manifesto-1973-a-code-of-ethics-for-business-
leaders.

17. For the 2020 Manifesto, see Klaus Schwab, "Davos Manifesto 2020: The Universal Purpose of a Company in the Fourth Industrial Revolution," World Economic
Forum, December 2, 2019, www.weforum.org/agenda/2019/12/davos-manifesto-2020-the-
universal-purpose-of-a-company-in-the-fourth-industrial-revolution.

Index

Note: Page numbers followed by *f* refer to figures; page numbers followed by *t* refer to tables; page numbers followed by *n* refer to notes.

About the Authors

Joseph L. Bower is the Donald K. David Professor of Business Administration, Emeritus, at Harvard Business School, where he has been a leader in general management for over five decades. His research has focused on the challenges involved in leading companies as they deal with important changes in the economic, social, and political environment. His books have examined government efforts to shape the restructuring of industries (*When Markets Quake*), the crafting of strategy through resource allocation and CEO succession (*From Resource Allocation to Strategy* and *The CEO Within*), and the interaction of business and government in the United States (*Two Faces of Management*). With Lynn Paine he cowrote the 2017 *Harvard Business Review* article, "The Error at the Heart of Corporate Leadership," which examines the strategic costs of short-term focus on maximizing stock price. Previously, Bower served as Senior Associate Dean of Harvard Business School, founding Chairman of the school's General Management Program, cofounder of the Harvard Kennedy School's Senior Managers in Government program, and codeveloper of the Kennedy School's course in public management. In addition, he recently developed a new course on strategic management in the public sector. Bower currently serves on a number of company and nonprofit boards.

Herman B. "Dutch" Leonard is the Eliot I. Snider and Family Professor of Business Administration at Harvard Business School and Cochair of the school's Social Enterprise Initiative. He is also the

George F. Baker, Jr., Professor of Public Sector Management and Cochair of the Program on Crisis Leadership at the Harvard Kennedy School. His work at Harvard Business School has focused on corporate social responsibility and the leadership of socially oriented components of business organizations. His work at the Kennedy School focuses on the management of large-scale risk. Leonard is the author of *Checks Unbalanced*, a book about off-budget spending and commitments by government. In addition, he is a coauthor of *Entrepreneurship in the Social Sector*, a casebook that focuses on major change in socially mission-driven organizations, and a coeditor of *Managing Crises* and *Public Health Preparedness*, two casebooks about the management of large-scale risk events. He holds a PhD in economics.

Lynn S. Paine is the John G. McLean Professor of Business Administration and Senior Associate Dean for International Development at Harvard Business School. She has written widely on leadership and corporate governance, with a focus on achieving both ethical and financial excellence. Her most recent articles for *Harvard Business Review* include "A Guide to the Big Ideas and Debates in Corporate Governance," "Sustainability in the Boardroom," and (with Joseph Bower) "The Error at the Heart of Corporate Leadership." Her books include *Value Shift* and *Cases in Leadership, Ethics, and Organizational Integrity*. Cofounder of the required MBA course, Leadership and Corporate Accountability, she currently cochairs the school's programs on corporate governance and boards of directors. She has served on numerous boards and advisory panels, including the Conference Board's blue-ribbon Commission on Public Trust and Private Enterprise following the collapse of Enron and the Conference Board's Task Force on Executive Compensation following the financial crisis of 2008.